CW00588252

First Steps in Shares

FINANCIAL TIMES

In an increasingly competitive world, we believe it's quality of
thinking that will give you the edge – an idea that opens new
doors, a technique that solves a problem, or an insight that
simply makes sense of it all. The more you know, the smarter
and faster you can go.

That's why we work with the best minds in business and finance
to bring cutting-edge thinking and best learning practice to a
global market.

Under a range of leading imprints, including Financial Times
Prentice Hall, we create world-class print publications and
electronic products bringing our readers knowledge, skills and
understanding which can be applied whether studying or at work.

To find out more about our business publications, or tell us
about the books you'd like to find, you can visit us at
www.business-minds.com

For other Pearson Education publications, visit
www.pearsoned-ema.com

First Steps in Shares

Peter Temple

FT Prentice Hall
FINANCIAL TIMES

An imprint of Pearson Education

London ■ New York ■ San Francisco ■ Toronto ■ Sydney ■ Tokyo ■ Singapore
Hong Kong ■ Cape Town ■ Madrid ■ Amsterdam ■ Munich ■ Paris ■ Milan

PEARSON EDUCATION LIMITED

Edinburgh Gate
Harlow CM20 2JE
Tel: +44 (0)1279 623623
Fax: +44 (0)1279 431059

Website: www.pearsoned.co.uk

_____

First published in Great Britain in 2001

© Pearson Education Limited 2001

The right of Peter Temple to be identified as Author of this work has been asserted
by him in accordance with the Copyright, Designs and Patents Act 1988.

ISBN 0 273 65289 3

British Library Cataloguing in Publication Data
A CIP catalogue record for this book can be obtained from the British Library.

All rights reserved; no part of this publication may be reproduced, stored in a
retrieval system, or transmitted in any form or by any means, electronic, mechanical,
photocopying, recording, or otherwise without either the prior written permission
of the Publishers or a licence permitting restricted copying in the United Kingdom
issued by the Copyright Licensing Agency Ltd, 90 Tottenham Court Road, London
W1T 4LP. This book may not be lent, resold, hired out or otherwise disposed of by
way of trade in any form of binding or cover other than that in which it is published,
without the prior consent of the Publishers.

10 9 8 7

Typeset by Northern Phototypesetting Co. Ltd, Bolton
Printed and bound in Great Britain by Bell & Bain Ltd, Glasgow

The Publishers' policy is to use paper manufactured from sustainable forests.

Contents

About the author viii
Acknowledgements ix
List of figures xi
List of tables xii

Introduction – Learning the rules of the game 1

57 varieties 1
The game of investment 2
The objective 4

1 Investing your money – fact, fiction, fear and greed 7

Shares and bonds – what they are and how they work 8
Shares and bonds – the history 12
Animals in the market jungle … 15
… and what they don't have in common 18
Investment choices 19
Why the stock market matters 24

2 Temperament and tools 27

Avoiding the traps 28
No pain, no gain 31
Is investment the right thing for you? 33
An investor's checklist 34
The tools 36
Basic costs 41

3 Checking out the numbers 45

Fundamental analysis vs technical analysis 45
Basic accounting concepts 47
Annual reports and accounts 47
Understanding the profit and loss account 48
Key profit and loss ratios 51
Price-earnings ratios, EV/EBIT, and dividend yields 52

Understanding cash flow statements 56
Understanding the balance sheet 59
Key balance sheet ratios 61
How is the company performing? 64
Universal Widgets – buy or sell? 65
Analyzing bond fundamentals 66

4 Analyzing price movements – timing your trading 69

First principles – understanding market psychology 70
How simple technical analysis works in practice 71
Trends 72
Different chart types 74
Moving averages and variations on the theme 79
Momentum and how to gauge it 83
Charts v fundamentals 88

5 The mechanics of dealing 91

An honest broker … 92
… but which service to choose? 94
The 'job spec' for your broker 97
Working out what you need 100
How to choose 103
How to deal … and what happens afterwards 105

6 Portfolio building blocks 109

Your personal balance sheet 109
Risk 112
Overall portfolio strategy 113
The building blocks 119
What next? 125

7 Designing your portfolio 127

Simple strategies for maximum return and minimum risk 127
Portfolio structure 140
Measuring gains and losses 142

8 Computer-aided investment 145

Monitoring your money 146
Investment software basics 149
Downloading data 152

Charting software 155
Software with fundamentals 157
Options software 158
Cost comparisons and functionality 160

9 The online investor – shares and the internet 163

Getting connected 163
Using the web 165
Resources for investors 167
To connect or not? 181

10 More advanced stuff – ratios and charts 183

More financial ratios 183
Additional charting and share price analysis techniques 193
Postscript – interpreting 'creative' accounting 199

11 More advanced stuff – valuing shares 203

Discounted cash flow 203
Using EVA 207
Reinvested return on equity 208
Sum of the parts analysis 212
Valuing internet businesses 214
Assessing incubators 219

12 Investing my money 221

Phase One: July 1986 to January 1988 222
Phase Two: January 1988 to September 1992 227
Phase Three: September 1992 to December 1995 229
Phase Four: December 1995 to June 1998 232
Phase Five: June 1998 to date 233
Performance measurement 236
Lessons for first-time investors 237
Spending your gains 238

Index 241

About the author

Peter Temple is a Yorkshireman who has lived in London all his working life. An economics graduate, he worked in fund management and investment banking for 18 years before becoming a full-time journalist and author in 1988. He is a Fellow of the Securities Institute and a former member of the London Stock Exchange.

He contributes regularly to the *Financial Times*, *Investors' Chronicle*, *FT Export*, *Shares*, and a number of other publications and financial websites. He is author of several books, covering subjects as diverse as traded options, online investing, venture capital and hedge funds.

Away from writing, his interests include keeping fit (walking and swimming), travel and crosswords. He and his wife Lynn live in Woodford Green and have two grown-up children.

Acknowledgements

Although this book is based on my 30 years of experience working in or writing about the investment scene, pulling all the material together involves a lot of people.

Nick Wallwork, who now works for John Wiley & Sons in Singapore, originally commissioned much of the material in this book and he has my thanks for getting the show on the road, as it were.

Over the years, my investment education has been broadened by contact with many different individuals and I would particularly like to thank Jeremy Utton at Analyst plc for the part he has played in that process. Early chapters on fundamental analysis and the later chapter on share valuation have been partly influenced by some of his ideas.

The sections on charting and share price analysis owe a considerable amount to the various friends and contacts I have made over the years in the investment software and technical analysis community. They are probably too numerous to mention, but particular thanks should go to Phil Blacker and Mitchell Brooks at Synergy, Jeremy duPlessis at Indexia, and David Linton at Updata.

The charts used in Chapters 4 and 10 were obtained using, respectively, Winstock's 'The Analyst' software, and Ionic Information's Sharescope package. Thanks are due here to John Ingram at Winstock and Martin Stamp at Ionic. Early drafts of the material on investment software appeared as articles in the *FT*'s 'Weekend Money' section, and I acknowledge the generosity of the *FT*'s Simon London in allowing me to use his readers as guinea pigs in this way. The section on valuing internet companies in Chapter 11 is a condensed version of an article first published in the Insinger Townsley Internet Quarterly.

In its present form, the idea for this book came out of discussions I had with Jonathan Agbenyega at Pearson Education, who has been a cheerful and enthusiastic supporter of the project and my quest to bring it a wider readership, as well as suggesting a number of improvements and additions in both content and design. He has my grateful thanks for that. Thanks also to my project manager, Penelope Allport, for the book's smooth running.

Screengrabs feature in a number of chapters and have been reproduced by kind permission of (in order of appearance): Winstock Software; Intuit; Ultra Financial Systems; Comdirect; Download.com; and Ionic Information. The cartoon in Chapter 1 is by Martin Talks.

ACKNOWLEDGEMENTS

Finally, this book would have taken appreciably longer to produce but for the efforts of Lynn Temple, my wife and business partner. These ranged from transcribing a large number of tables and accounts data from the original manuscript and my notes; collating data on software companies and financial websites; and reading, correcting and printing the final manuscript immediately prior to its submission to the publisher. As usual, her help has been indispensable.

Any errors that remain are my own.

Peter Temple
February 2001

Figures

4.1   Nikkei – support and resistance levels

4.2   FTSE – uptrend

4.3   £/$ – downtrend

4.4   ICI – daily bar chart

4.5   ICI – candlestick chart

4.6   GUS – 'head and shoulders top'

4.7   GUS – moving averages

4.8   GUS – a simple MACD

4.9   GUD – OBOS based on 50-day moving average

4.10 GUS – 21-day momentum indicator

4.11 GUS – RSI pattern

4.12 GUS – stochastic indicators

7.1   UK gilts yield curve

8.1   Quicken screengrab

8.2   ULTRA screengrab

9.1   Comdirect screengrab

9.2   Download.com screengrab

10.1 Coppock indicator for the FTSE-100

10.2 Confidence limits

10.3 Volatility

Tables

1.1   What shares and bonds offer
1.2   What different investments offer
2.1   Investor information – basic costs
3.1   Universal Widgets: Profit and Loss Account (£m)
3.2   Universal Widgets: Cash Flow Statement
3.3   Universal Widgets: Consolidated Balance Sheet
5.1   Broker services – what they offer
5.2   Online brokers and their charges
5.3   Placing an order – a step-by-step summary
6.1   Impact of bid-offer spread and dealing costs on stop-loss position
6.2   Best buys in different circumstances
7.1   Impact of different returns on gilts vs equities
7.2   Impact of index-tracking investment on volatility portfolio
7.3   Double-whammy effect of variations in investment trust discounts
7.4   Impact of options on a conservative portfolio
7.5   Illustrative percentage portfolio weightings for different circumstances
8.1   Finance summary
8.2   Main software suppliers
8.3   Data sources summary
9.1   UK-based internet service providers
9.2   Search engines
9.3   Software download sites
9.4   Selected newspaper sites
9.5   Selected exchange websites
9.6   Best corporate websites
10.1 Pubco – Profit and Loss Account items and related ratios
10.2 Pubco – Cash Flow Statement and ratios
10.3 Pubco – Summary of Balance Sheet items and ratios (£000)
11.1 Typical discounted cash flow model – figures for British Telecom
11.2 Reinvested return on equity – how it works
11.3 Universal Widgets reinvested return on equity – different assumptions
11.4 Universal Widgets – sum of the parts analysis
11.5 Example of an internet stock valuation model
12.1 Phase One – 30 June 1986 to 31 December 1988
12.2 Phase Two – 1 January 1988 to 31 July 1992
12.3 Phase Three – September 1992 to December 1995
12.4 Phase Five – 1 June 1998 to date

Introduction – learning the rules of the game

This book is designed to help you become familiar with the process of investing your money.

The purpose of investing differs from individual to individual. You might just want more cash for a holiday or a new car, you might want your investments to produce extra income, or you might want them as a long-term investment to provide for an affluent retirement. You might simply relish the challenge of pitting your wits against the market.

In this book we will look mainly at shares, how to investigate and assess their relative merits, and how to go about trading them in the market. But we'll also look at other forms of investment, such as bonds, options and unit trusts, how they differ from shares, their relative riskiness, and how they can be blended with shares coherently in a portfolio to give you the right mixture of risk and reward.

But make no mistake about it; the stock market – the collective name for the market where all types of shares and securities are traded – is a battle of wits. And you need to keep your wits about you to survive and do well.

One reason for the battle of wits is the market's sheer diversity. There are buyers and sellers, short-term speculators and patient long-term investors. There are those who invest for income, and those who look to maximize their capital gains. There are professionals and amateurs of varying degrees of skill. There are domestic investors and those with an international perspective. All these individuals have different personalities, different goals, and a different view of risk.

57 varieties

If the stock market were simply about trading a single uniform commodity – apples or oranges, wheat or Deutschmarks, say – there would be plenty of excitement from the interplay of these different facets and objectives alone. But what makes the stock market fascinating is the rich variety of companies whose shares are listed. The Heinz slogan, '57 Varieties', applies in a big way in the stock market. If we add in bonds, unit trusts, and other forms of investment, the variety increases even more.

There are nearly 3,000 listed companies in the UK and many more in other markets overseas. All these markets contain many different shares. There are shares in large companies, small companies, exciting high-tech companies, boring utilities running gas, electricity and transport, companies run by consummate professionals and others run by incompetents, rogues and charlatans, companies run by teams and companies run by a 'one-man band'.

There are shares in companies with lots of cash and companies with high borrowings. There are shares in companies that generate cash and companies that consume it. There are shares in companies that are sensitive to interest rates and those that aren't, and in companies whose fortunes are guided by the price of a single commodity, like gold, coal, oil or bananas.

Then there is the outside world of economics and politics and the cycles that shape it: of recession and boom; of high interest rates and low interest rates; and of devaluations, currency crises, elections, wars and all types of uncertainty.

In the bond market you can opt for government bonds (known as 'gilts' in the UK), but even these have widely different characteristics. Some are much more volatile than others. Some offer high rates of interest: some very low or even zero rates. Some have just a few years to run before they are repaid: others have a maturity date far into the future. Then there is an infinite variety of investment decisions that can be made using options, and thousands of unit trusts to buy.

Finally there is the psychology of how the crowd of individual investors that the market represents reacts to these various stimuli.

This array of investment choices and market influences can be bewildering. My aim is to take you through it logically and explain how all the pieces fit together.

The game of investment

If you find all this talk of money boring, then investing in shares, bonds or unit trusts directly is probably not for you. Hand over the money you want to invest to an independent financial adviser or stockbroker and they will invest it on your behalf, but one way or another you'll pay a fat fee for the privilege.

I think investment is fun. From time to time it can be painful. But there are few other human activities that combine the disciplines of sound analysis and diligent detective work, of astute timing with the delicious thrill of making money through backing the right horse or guessing right in a poker game.

The word 'game' is important. The best definition of what makes stock market investment tick is actually contained in a dry economics textbook.

John Maynard Keynes wrote *The General Theory of Employment Interest and Money* in the early 1930s but Chapter 12, entitled 'Long-Term Expectation', is as relevant today as it was then.

Here is a flavour of it:

The actual, private object of the most skilled investment today is 'to beat the gun' ... to outwit the crowd, and to pass on the bad, or depreciating, half-crown to the other fellow ... It is, so to speak, a game of Snap, of Old Maid, of Musical Chairs – a pastime in which he is victor who says 'Snap' neither too soon nor too late, who passes the Old Maid to his neighbour before the game is over, who secures a chair for himself before the music stops.

These games can be played with zest and enjoyment, though all the players know that it is the Old Maid which is circulating, or that when the music stops some of the players may find themselves unseated ...

To change the metaphor slightly, professional investment may be likened to those newspaper competitions in which the competitors have to pick out the six prettiest faces from a hundred photographs, the prize being awarded to the competitor whose choice most nearly corresponds to the average preferences of the competitors as a whole; so that each competitor has to pick, not those faces which he himself finds prettiest, but those which he thinks likeliest to catch the fancy of the other competitors, all of whom are looking at the problem from the same point of view.

In the paragraph above substitute the words 'most attractive' for prettiest, 'share' for face and 'investor' for competitor, and you begin to get the idea.

Keynes also says: 'The game of professional investment is intolerably boring and overexacting to anyone who is entirely exempt from the gambling instinct; whilst he who has it must pay to this propensity the appropriate toll.'

What gives these quotations some piquancy is the fact that not only was Keynes an outstanding economist but he was also the Bursar of Kings College, Cambridge and managed its investment portfolio with considerable skill for many years.

So he was not just a theoretician. He played the game too. His example also shows that, provided the right techniques are practised, successful investment need not be unduly time-consuming. The Bursar of Kings managed the college portfolio with just a few minutes' attention at the beginning or end of each day.

Keynes was also famous for his distaste of long-term investment. To him is attributed the most famous of phrases on the subject: 'in the long run, we are all dead'. But *The General Theory* also exhorts the reader to remember that long-term investment is inevitably more laborious and more risky than devoting one's study to 'guessing better than the crowd how the crowd will behave'.

This is interesting, not least because although well-known investors like Warren Buffett make a point of advocating that shares be held for the very long term, Keynes was an example of a hugely successful investor whose time horizons were much shorter. Although I would not advocate day-trading, it's OK in my view to hold shares for a comparatively short period, if you have a good reason for selling when you do so.

Investors are often castigated for short-termism, but not usually by companies whose shares are doing well, and invariably by people who have little active interest in investing themselves.

For the past 30 years I have made my living either working in or writing about the stock market. For much of that time I have been an investor myself. I am, of course, no Keynes. And even with 30 years' experience I am only too well aware that it is still possible to be careless, to make silly mistakes, to buy the wrong share, or to sell the right one too early.

But nothing equals the feeling of having selected a share, seeing it rise steadily, doubling or trebling one's money, and then selling it at the right price, neither too early nor too late, and pocketing the gain and beginning the process all over again.

The objective

What I want to do in these pages is to give the average person with some money available to invest the practical tools needed to begin investing successfully and some guidance on where and how to learn more about the market.

The aim, in short, is to cut through the jargon that many professional investors and stock market writers use, and express these ideas in a simple, accessible and understandable form.

To understand markets we have to look at their history, the characters that people the market, and at the reasoning and emotions that in equal measure drive them. We need to investigate different types of investment and their characteristics, and to look at why it is important for everyone to appreciate what the stock market is and why it behaves as it does.

Later on in this book we will look also at the mental characteristics required to be a good investor, and how an individual's financial circum-stances dictate the type of investment activity he or she should pursue. Then there is the importance of setting realistic targets and having down-to-earth expectations. And there is the question of what the would-be investor might need to spend on the basic equipment required to begin investing.

The objective of most investment is to buy low and sell high, or to generate income. In short, to maximize the total return (whether it's a capital gain, or income, or a combination of the two). While bearing in mind what Keynes said about the activities of long-term professional investors, it is worth examining some of the techniques that experienced investors use to assess the worth of individual shares.

This will take us into basic accounting concepts, and the importance of cash flow and balance sheet strength. It will also take us into learning how to calculate basic investment ratios and the importance to attach to them. It takes us into valuing bonds and examining options.

These concepts are not that complicated and they are described in words that the average reader of the stock market pages of the daily or Sunday newspapers might meet on a regular basis: yield, price-earnings ratio, gearing, return on capital, redemption and maturity, call and put.

Not having dealt in the stock market before, the first-timer will need the services of a stockbroker. How to go about choosing the right one is a subject in itself and we will look at this in some detail, as well as how to place an order with a broker to buy or sell a share, bond or option and what happens, or should happen, afterwards.

As well as what the professionals term 'fundamentals', we also need to look at how studying the history of a share price can betray little details that might be important in timing purchases and sales. And there are also other investment techniques that help decision making, including assessing the volatility of the investments you hold, and their relative risk.

Spreading risk is an important aspect of investment, and it is worth looking at all types of investment and how these can fit into a coherent strategy designed to improve both income and capital gains. Different types of investment may be more appropriate at particular times in the market cycle, and we will look at how to assess this. Keeping score is important too. Measuring one's performance relative to the riskiness of your investments is an aspect that is sometimes neglected by the private investor.

Most of the donkey work that successful investing has always involved – keeping track of how much your shares are worth, and producing returns for the taxman – can now safely be computerized, and a huge amount of information is now available online over the world wide web, including online dealing services. We'll look at this aspect of investing your money in some detail too.

We'll also look at some of the more advanced share assessment techniques that the professionals use, and how the big developments in electronics and subsequent changes in the way markets are organized will affect investors.

Finally, I will share with you some of my own experiences – both good and bad – as an active private investor over the past 15 years.

Above all, my aim is to get you started as an investor and dealing confidently with brokers and the other professional people with whom all investors have to interact, to get you assessing and investigating shares and other investments in the right way, timing purchases and sales correctly and building up good trading disciplines.

It is an easier process than it once was. The market is more accessible to the independent private investor, dealing costs have come down and information about investing is more readily available.

All will be well, provided that you learn to take the rough with the smooth and above all remember that there is an indissoluble link between risk and reward. The investments that seem to offer high returns are the ones on which you can lose your shirt.

Genuine undervalued situations are rare, but they can be found, more often than not in places where few have chosen to look. Recognizing those opportunities for what they are is part of the art of successful investing.

I hope that, having read this book, you will be able to find the occasional one.

Investing your money – fact, fiction, fear and greed

All of us have been to a market. It might have been a local street market, a car boot sale, a Mediterranean fish market, a Middle Eastern souk or some other location where buyers and sellers got together.

The market for shares or other investments like bonds and options is not that different from any of these. At any Sunday morning car boot sale or antiques fair you can find run-of-the-mill items, overpriced rubbish and, just occasionally, an item whose true value has not been recognized.

Similarly the stock market contains investments that are worthy, but correctly priced, those that are of poor quality and overpriced, and those that are a bargain. Spotting the bargains is the objective of most investors.

What complicates matters is that there is a large number of different investments to choose from, and over time each will move in and out of favour. One type of market background will favour shares in big companies rather than those of smaller ones, another might mean that bonds or cash are better investments than shares, and so on.

An investment that appears cheap now may look less attractive in a year's time. Either its price will have moved up, or else circumstances will have moved against it. Another that looked unexciting a year ago might suddenly see its prospects transformed.

Ultimately what governs the price of anything, and shares and other types of investment are no exception, is the interaction of supply and demand. But a point to bear in mind is that markets do not necessarily, or even often, act logically.

The history of the world's stock markets shows great waves of pessimism and optimism. Sharp turning points have not been uncommon, often marked by some dramatic event. The Wall Street Crash of 1929, the October 1987 Crash, the surge in the UK stock market that followed Britain's exit from the European Exchange Rate Mechanism in September 1992, and the collapse of the dot com bubble in 2000 are all examples of this phenomenon.

On a smaller scale too, individual shares and different sections of the share market move in and out of favour. It happens for reasons which may have an element of logic but where the reasoning is often exaggerated, as the technology share boom of late 1999 bore out. Bonds too move in and out of favour, and other forms of investment have their proverbial 15 minutes of fame.

The recent fashion for dot com stocks was just one example of the herd mentality that markets display. At different times in the past there have been others: privatized utilities, drug companies, biotechnology groups, public house operators, Italian government bonds, renewable energy companies, forestry, and so on.

So, as Keynes pointed out, the art of investment is not only to judge which shares look undervalued at any point in time, but also to anticipate and profit from the moods of the market and the dictates of fashion.

> Selecting which competitors in the beauty contest are likely to catch the eye of the judges is the name of the game. Not only does one need a smattering of economics and accountancy to get to grips with the stock market, but also an understanding of crowd psychology.

Selecting which competitors in the beauty contest are likely to catch the eye of the judges is the name of the game. Not only does one need a smattering of economics and accountancy to get to grips with the stock market, but also an understanding of crowd psychology.

Examining exactly what shares are and looking back at the history of 'the market' can help us understand all this better.

Shares and bonds – what they are and how they work

We all think we know what stocks and shares are. You would not be reading this book if you did not have a view on that. But it is worth dwelling on these with a bit more precision.

Shares

At its simplest a share is a stake in a company. But it is its precise entitlements and legal status that make it interesting.

The typical company might have creditors to pay and bonds and bank loans outstanding, as well as having shareholders. The point of shares is that they stand last in line for any payout if the company is wound up. But while creditors only get what they are owed and bankers and bond-holders only get their loans or bonds repaid, shareholders own what remains, in exact proportion to their individual shareholdings.

Let's look at an example to make this clear. Imagine a company called Universal Widgets. Universal Widgets has total assets of £100,000 and has issued 30,000 shares. It has unpaid bills (creditors) of £20,000 and owes its bank £50,000. What is left over, £30,000, is owned by the shareholders. In the jargon this is known as shareholders' funds, or net assets.

Because Universal Widgets has 30,000 shares outstanding, this means that each share has an underlying value of £1. A holder of 100 shares would be entitled to £100 if the company were wound up. But a holder of 200 shares would be entitled to £200, and so on. Each share represents an equal (or equity) stake in the business. For this reason shares are often known as equities.

Now let's take the example a stage further.

Suppose in the course of the year Universal Widgets makes a profit, after paying off interest and taxes, of £20,000. It can do one of two things with this profit. It can distribute some of it to shareholders in the form of dividends, and keep the rest, or it can retain all of it. Either way, the money belongs to the shareholders.

Say the company pays out a dividend of £6,000 and keeps £14,000 as retained profits. What happens? The shareholders receive a dividend of 20p per share (£6,000 divided by 30,000 shares).

Assuming there has been no change in bank borrowings or the amount owed to creditors the retained profit of £14,000 increases shareholders' funds from £30,000 to £44,000. So the shareholders have done well. Not only have they received a 20p dividend for each share they hold, but the retained profits have increased the underlying value of their stake in the company from 100p per share to 147p (£44,000 divided by 30,000 shares).

The crucial point to understand, however, is that if the shares are freely traded in the market their price need have no precise relationship to the underlying value of the shareholders' net assets of the company. It is this fact that makes shares so interesting. In some cases shares do stand close to their net asset value, but many do not.

The precise relationship is governed by other factors: the company's prospects and the likelihood or otherwise of further profit increases in the future; the level of dividend payments; whether or not the company has a high level of borrowings; whether its assets are an important factor in determining its profitability; and many other factors.

A good reason for this is that the company's most important assets – its brand names, perhaps, or simply its staff and their relationships with customers – are often not included as assets in the balance sheet. 'People businesses', like advertising agencies or fund management companies, often generate profits disproportionately bigger than their conventional balance sheet assets might suggest was likely.

In addition, at any time the market may well be looking not at the most recent figures for a company's profits and underlying assets, but at how it expects them to change in the future. In other words it is expectations that govern how share prices move.

Bonds

A bond is normally a listed investment that pays a fixed rate of interest and is repaid at a specific point of time in the future. Its interest rate, or coupon, is known in advance and is based on a specific face value, which may well be different from the price you pay.

Let's say a company has issued a bond that pays 8 per cent interest and was issued at 100. This means that for every nominal £100 of the bond you hold you will get £8 a year interest. Simply because of supply and demand, you might be able to buy the £100 bond in the market for less than its face value, say £90. If so, you will still get the £8, but your percentage return (known in the jargon as the yield) will be 8/90 (or 8.9 per cent) rather than 8/100.

The point to remember about bonds though, is that as we said earlier, they generally rank pretty high up the pecking order when it comes to getting repaid if the company goes bust. In that sense they are less risky than shares, where you could in theory lose your entire investment. This could happen with a bond, too, but it's less likely, because bond holders are entitled to a piece of the assets left. Indeed the bond may be secured against a specific asset, rather like your mortgage is secured against your home. (See Table 1.1.)

So, bonds can be less risky, especially gilts – which are bonds issued by the British government. Most UK investors who buy bonds directly usually buy gilts. With gilts there is no risk you won't get repaid, but that doesn't mean you can't lose money in them. The price of bonds tends to fluctuate in line with views about interest rates and inflation. Because they have a fixed rate of interest, bonds are unattractive if inflation is on the up, so their prices tend to fall (and hence their yields rise) to compensate.

With both shares and bonds, perceptions rather than logic are what govern their prices. With shares it is expectations about the future level of company profits: with bonds the price reflects perceptions about trends in interest rates and inflation, as well as the creditworthiness of the company or government issuing the bond.

Table 1.1 What shares and bonds offer

Type	Income	Capital growth potential	Risk of loss
Shares	Dividend (variable)	Should grow with profits	Some or all
Bonds	Fixed interest	Limited or negative	Limited

If you buy shares today, one reason may be based on the expectation that the company's profits will continue to rise and that therefore your shares will be worth more. But you may also be doing so for other reasons.

It could be that you believe that the profits are not going to grow particularly rapidly but that the share price stands at a substantial discount to what a predator might think the company is worth. A friend may have told you they are a takeover candidate.

Or you might buy because you believe the market is going to rise and, if it does, then the shares will automatically go up in sympathy.

If you buy a bond today, you might do so just because it offers an attractive income, or you could be speculating that interest rates are likely to fall and hence the yield on the bond will look more attractive, pulling in buyers and causing its price to rise.

Because there is often little logic to the way the price of an investment moves, investors need to have strong nerves to withstand the psychological pressures fluctuations in price produce. Investment is all about controlling the emotions of fear and greed we all possess.

To illustrate the psychology of investment, let's look at the following stages of an investment.

Stage One.   Let's assume you invest £2,000 in Universal Widgets and sit with the shares for a month or two. The price doesn't move much and you lose interest.

Stage Two.   Then one day you discover the shares have dropped 10 per cent in a single day. The company has issued a warning to investors that its recent trading has been disappointing.

Your £2,000 investment is now worth £1,800. Do you sell and take the loss, or wait in the hope that the share price will eventually shrug off the bad news?

You decide to sit tight.

Stage Three.   The next day the shares drop another 10 per cent. In two days, your loss has grown to nearly £400!

Fear now replaces the original motive of greed that you felt when you bought the shares. You have lost nearly £400, but if you wait another day or two to sell the shares could be worth even less. Better to get out now while you can.

Stage Four.   If you sell now you have crystallized the loss. What if the shares then recover ...?

All investors from time to time have to face the pain of losing money. But one of the points this example highlights, apart from perhaps explaining why markets swing around the way they do, is another very important aspect to equity investment: the concept of limited liability.

Limited liability means that an investor in a company's shares can lose no more than his or her original investment. An individual shareholder's liability, if the company is wound up, is limited to the size of the original investment – irrespective of how much its bankers and creditors might be owed.

On the plus side too, once you have bought your shares, there is theoretically no limit to how much they can rise: you will participate for as long as you hold the shares.

Shares and bonds – the history

The concepts of equity investment and limited liability go hand in hand and were originally designed to encourage investors to risk money in speculative ventures that might produce a big return, but equally could see a total loss. Bonds have a long history, and were once by far the most common form of investment by individuals.

The first public limited liability company to which investors subscribed for shares was the East India Company, formed in 1553. The oldest company still trading is thought to be the Hudson's Bay Company, formed to trade with Canada and now domiciled there but still listed in London.

Investors in other early companies, such as the South Sea Company, set up in the early eighteenth century, fared less well. The so-called South Sea Bubble, the product of widespread and rampant speculation, resulted in many fortunes being made and lost and in the idea of equity investment being set back for many decades thereafter.

Bonds have been issued by governments for centuries for the purposes of public finance, not least of which was financing wars, when bond buying was considered a patriotic duty. One of the oldest British government securities is War Loan, reflecting its original purpose. In the UK, 'gilts' (bonds issued by the Treasury and guaranteed by the government) have been firm favourites of cautious investors and a staple of investment by pension funds for many years.

At times in the recent past, however, the supply of these bonds has shrunk as government borrowings have been repaid and one current topic is whether or not pension funds should be permitted to invest in other types of bond (foreign government debt, for example, or bonds issued by companies) in order to give them a wider choice of fixed interest securities to choose from. This is important for some investors, because short supply of suitable investments has affected the yields available on pensioners' annuities.

Back in the share market, it was in the seventeenth and eighteenth centuries that the idea of a market for trading in the shares of these limited liability companies first took root.

Initially brokers met in coffee houses in the City of London and traded shares face to face on the basis of the principle of 'my word is my bond'. One of these venues, Jonathans, became a subscription club and in 1773 changed its name to The Stock Exchange and subsequently developed a system of trading on a market floor, which lasted until the mid-1980s.

This system coalesced into a method of trading that relied on a dual structure. Stock*brokers* dealt with the public that wished to buy and sell shares and bonds and acted as their agents in the market. Stock*jobbers* acted as wholesalers, keeping a 'book' of shares in which they specialized and which they bought from and sold to the brokers, adjusting the price to reflect supply and demand. Bonds were dealt in the same way, with specific firms often tending to specialize in making markets in 'gilts', while the Bank of England in the past also sought to influence interest rates by periodic intervention in the market.

The attraction of this market-making system was that the jobbers were obligated to quote a price and buy and sell on demand, and therefore had to ensure that they had an adequate supply of stock, but not too much, to satisfy the demands of buyers and sellers.

In October 1986 this system was changed, in response to government pressure on the Stock Exchange to make itself more competitive. For the first time firms operating on the Stock Exchange could combine both jobbing (now officially known as market-making) and traditional, so-called 'agency', broking. Many large securities firms now also trade actively on their own account.

At the same time the market for both shares and bonds went from being centralized on a single trading floor to a system whereby market prices were posted on a central electronic bulletin board and, rather than taking place face to face, dealing was done over the telephone.

In effect the market migrated to large purpose-built dealing rooms and the cables that connected them, rather than being contained in a single physical space. The benefit of these changes was that London cemented its position as an international centre for share trading. In short, the market abandoned many of its club-like practices and opened its doors to all and sundry. Many old-established brokers were taken over by foreign banks and others wishing to gain a presence in London.

Current developments

As time has gone by many other stock exchanges have abandoned the trading floor, and migrated to electronic dealing. Aided by electronic systems, it is now possible to run a market based on the electronic matching of buying and selling orders at a particular price in what amounts to a continuous auction.

These electronic order-driven markets now predominate both for shares and for other types of investment. Among other technological developments has been the development of software used by market-makers to deal automatically for private (or 'retail') investors at the prevailing market price. Many online dealing services now link their clients directly to these systems – allowing investors to trade immediately at a guaranteed price without any human intervention.

Share markets are now heavily electronics based, with computerized trading, more open access to the market for private investors, and many other features unheard of a few years ago. Bonds have participated in this revolution to some degree, though they have tended to be less automated. This is changing now, and in future it is likely that dealing in shares and bonds will be all-electronic.

There are those who bemoan the passing of the market floor. But unlike a market for produce or, say, antiques, for shares and indeed for other products like foreign currency there is no pressing need for a physical market.

This is because everyone can have confidence that the rights attached to buying a share or a bond are identical. Each share or bond in a particular company has the same rights as every other one. In other words the market is homogeneous. Although each company may be different, unlike an antiques market there is no need physically to see or inspect its securities (shares or bonds) to establish that they have the particular attributes which the market says they have.

One of the interesting side effects of the new market for the private investor has been the development of low cost, so-called 'execution-only' stockbrokers. Because there is no longer any need for a broker to be physi-cally based in the City of London to trade shares, a number of brokers have set up in out-of-town locations to offer cut-price dealing services to private investors.

By offering no advisory services and because of high throughput and sophisticated electronic trading systems, these brokers can offer independent investors a cheap yet worthwhile service that would not have been economic ten years ago. This has big implications for the way an individual investor can operate.

Another aspect of this is that linkages between stock exchanges in different countries, and their administrative counterparts, mean that for the first time brokers are able to offer clients in, say, the UK a hassle-free means of dealing in shares in, for example, the UK, France, Germany, or the USA from a single point. Investigating shares in different countries is no different to doing it in, say, the UK. The same techniques can be applied and the internet has made information on individual companies much easier to come by.

In the end, though, what makes a market function the way it does are the individual buyers and sellers who participate in it. Whether they deal frequently or only occasionally, what their attitudes and motives are, their financial requirements and their time horizons, all have an impact on the way shares move, and on what types of share they choose.

So let's now have a look at some of the characters typically involved in the market.

Animals in the market jungle ...

© Martin Talks 2001

Fred the Fund Manager

Fred is a fund manager. He works for a leading fund management group looking after the investments of a group of different pension funds. He is a 45-year-old grammar school boy who used to work for a stockbroker but got bored with this and thought he would try life on the other side of the fence. But life for Fred is almost as cut-throat as the broking business.

The performance of his funds is measured on a quarter-by-quarter basis, and any dip in performance has to be explained to sceptical trustees who are very conscious of their responsibilities and tend to be suspicious of any new forms of investing.

There are any number of competing fund managers who could do the job if Fred's performance falls away, so there is little point pursuing investment strategies that take a long time to come to fruition. The result is that Fred and his ilk are often accused of short-termism.

Mickey the Market-Maker

Mickey used to sell fruit and veg in Walthamstow market, but got into the City in the 1980s when all the big securities firms were recruiting traders. First he worked on the floor of the market, but now he spends his days in front of a bank of computer screens buying and selling shares from other market players and betting on their price movements to make his firm some money.

Mickey's actions used to be able to make the price of a single share move up and down several per cent in the course of a single day, but now electronics are taking over. Mickey is paid a big salary, with bonuses on top, but the job doesn't have a lot of security. As he gets older, or starts losing his touch, or begins drinking too much, his duties will be taken over by someone younger and fresher.

The pressure's increased lately too, because as more investors are using the internet to deal and there is more computerized trading, fewer market-makers are needed. Driving a minicab or becoming a day-trader looks the best option now. If only he'd saved those bonuses ...

Hugh Sloane-Portfolio

Hugh is a salesman for a blue-blooded firm of stockbrokers. His job is to talk to Fred and people like him and get him to buy shares that his firm has acquired or to match a selling order from another of the firm's clients.

Not much up top, but at least Hugh went to a good school and knows how to behave at the lunch table. Although Hugh and Fred have to talk to each other, or at least exchange e-mails now and again, their backgrounds are very different and they don't like each other.

But Fred knows that Hugh's firm now and again can put some attractive new issues his way, so he doesn't complain too much and gives the broker an occasional order. Hugh meanwhile dreams of when his wife will inherit Daddy's money and they can retire from Wandsworth to life in the country.

Marvin the Quant

Marvin is, of course, an American. He works for a firm of quantitative fund managers (known in the trade as 'quants'). Quants invest scientifically using the statistical properties of individual groups of shares and different markets to tune their investment strategy. Their deals are often large-scale and managed by computers. Marvin looks forward to the day when computers can do all the work and he can go back to Harvard to finish his PhD in mathematics.

Last year, though, some of his more geeky friends set up an internet company and he might just have joined them.

Now he's glad he didn't!

Aunt Agatha

Everyone knows Aunt Agatha. Widowed and of advancing years, shares are her little hobby. The modest capital she inherited when Bertie died is mainly invested to give her a steady income, but she keeps a little on one side to invest in interesting situations her broker finds out about for her.

She swaps tips with her cronies at the bridge club and then phones one of those nice young men at Killik to check them out. So far her little nest egg has not dwindled by too much, but she's still waiting to make a big killing.

Joe Soap

Joe works at the local detergent factory, but when his premium bond came up in the early 1980s he put some of the money into those new-fangled privatization shares – and did rather well. He sold some of them straight away but kept a few and now has a modest little portfolio of water and electricity company shares, and some BT shares he forgot he owned.

If he knew more about the market he might invest more actively but there never seems to be the time – and anyway he can't stand those toffee-nosed brokers. He's wondering if there might be something in this internet thing and whether he can use that to buy and sell shares.

Still, the management have just bought the soap factory from its old owners and reckon that they can float it on the stock market in a few years time, in which case he might get some shares in that too.

Graham Average

Graham Average and his wife Deirdre live in a nice detached house in Surbiton. Graham works in Whitehall and Deirdre teaches at the local primary school. They have a comfortable lifestyle, their children have left home and a year or two back they inherited some money when Graham's father died. Some of the money has been put into a unit trust and some went to buy a new car, but Graham has always been interested in dabbling in the stock market and now wants to become more active to increase the size of his retirement nest egg.

He has seen the sort of money some people seem to have made in the stock market, and wonders how he can go about doing the same.

Dave Day

Dave's a day-trader. Every day he sits at home and tries to make money buying and selling shares dozens of times a day. Despite some scepticism from his wife, he chucked in his job as an estate agent, remortgaged the house and had about £100,000 to invest.

Unfortunately despite spending out on all the latest computer kit, he just got started when the market in the technology shares took a tumble and his £100,000 is now worth £50,000. He can't take a holiday, and divorce proceedings look likely if his luck doesn't improve.

Meanwhile there's that nasty pain in his shoulder from tapping away at the keyboard too long each day. As a way of life, he had thought it would be easier.

... and what they don't have in common

All these people are connected to the stock market in some way, either professionally or because they have savings they wish to invest, or an existing portfolio of shares. But, as these simple examples show, they all have different motives.

Fred is assessed on a quarter-by-quarter basis, and on the basis of his performance against the market as a whole and those of his competitors. It doesn't matter to him if the funds he is managing go down in value, provided that the market has gone down by more than that and his competitors haven't performed any better than he has.

Mickey is dealing on a very short-term basis, trying to make sufficient profit for his firm to justify his salary and bonus and trying above all to avoid a big losing deal, which would mean instant dismissal.

Hugh Sloane-Portfolio may not get the sack (after all he did go to the same school as his boss) but he does need to make sure that his clients keep dealing and he keeps booking commission for his firm. And while he might think all this talk of money is vulgar, what he really needs is to avoid putting his clients into duff shares.

Marvin is looking for the package of shares that exactly matches the risk and return criteria he has fed into his computer model.

The amateur investors are more sensitive than the fund manager, broker, or market-maker to an actual monetary loss. That an investment has gone down by less than the market is no cause for celebration; if they sell after a drop in price they have lost real money.

Aunt Agatha relies on her investments to produce income.

Joe Soap is vaguely suspicious about the market, but it has treated him well and he wants to find out more. But he is more likely to sell the shares he has than buy new ones.

Graham Average has money to invest and is looking for longer-term capital growth.

Dave is interested in making a quick killing to recoup his losses.

It is probably obvious from these descriptions that the stock market has horses for courses. Different investors will invest in different ways over any given period of time.

Some will buy shares or bonds and hold them for long periods; others will trade shares more actively. Some will look more favourably on shares and other securities that return a decent income in the form of dividends or interest payments; others will be more interested in capital growth. Some will want to invest in big solid companies; others will want something with a little more spice.

The actions of the professionals, for whatever reason, can either work for or against the interests of the private investor.

So what types of investment are available?

Investment choices

For the purposes of this book we are assuming that the investor mainly wants to buy plain, straightforward ordinary shares, and perhaps a gilt now and again. But it is not quite as simple as that. It's worth remembering that there are many types of shares and bonds that can be considered. All of them may have attractions in certain circumstances.

From the shares standpoint, the following main categories stand out:

■ blue chips
■ growth shares
■ income shares
■ cyclical shares
■ smaller companies
■ penny shares
■ utilities
■ commodity shares
■ investment trusts.

Of other types of investment, there are:

■ gilts (government bonds)
■ preference shares
■ convertibles
■ options
■ unit trusts
■ tracker funds and exchange traded funds.

Let's just consider each of these categories separately for a moment and look at their characteristics (see Table 1.2).

Blue chips

So called because blue chips are supposed to be the most valuable in the casino, these are large, financially solid companies that have been around for years and their shares are widely held by both professional and private investors. They may be household names like Tesco or Bass, or more obscure industrial companies like Invensys or Hanson. No investor is going to go radically wrong buying them for the long term, but equally their performance is unlikely to be racy and, as the example of M&S shows, there can be surprises. Typical examples: Sainsbury; Diageo.

Growth shares

Often more highly prized by investors, these are companies that have managed to produce consistent above-average growth in revenue and profits for several years, and look likely to continue to do so. The reason is usually good management methods or else a strong presence in a growing market. Ultimately companies like this can end up being blue chips. The most recent examples have been in the high technology arena. Typical examples: Sage; Psion.

Table 1.2 What different investments offer

Type	Safer or riskier	Income	Uses
Blue chips	Safer	Average	General investing
Growth	Mixture	Low but growing	General investing
Income shares	Riskier	High but stable	Income generation
Cyclical shares	Mixture	Average	With the cycle
Smaller companies	Riskier	Low but growing	General investing
Penny shares	High risk	Low or nil	Speculation
Utilities	Safer	High but stable	Income generation
Commodity shares	Riskier	Average or low	Against cycle
Investment trusts	Safer	Average	Diversification
Gilts	Safer	High but fixed	Income
Preference shares	Safer	Fixed	Income
Convertibles	Safer	Fixed	General investing
Options	Riskier	None	Gearing/hedging
Unit trusts	Safer	Varies with fund	General/access
Trackers/ETFs	Mixture	None	Diversification

Income shares

Income shares are those whose price action may be unexciting but which continue to pay out generous dividends and as a result yield very good returns to investors. Provided that companies like this have sound finances, the high dividend stream can continue for years. Companies of this type are usually conservatively managed, operating in mature industries that generate cash. Typical example: British-American Tobacco.

Cyclical shares

These are shares in companies whose fortunes are tied closely to the economic cycle. These companies normally show large swings in profitability and are valued accordingly by the market. Typical examples: ICI; Corus.

Smaller company shares

Smaller companies can be the most exciting part of the market, since there is always the possibility of investing early on in a company that may become a growth stock or blue chip of tomorrow. Investment in smaller companies needs to pay particularly close attention to the quality of the company's management, and whether or not the company really has a unique selling point or a novel new product. In addition, smaller company shares often need to be given time to mature for their full share price potential to be realized. Though smaller company shares tend to perform better than their larger brethren in the long term, in down phases of the market they can sometimes be poor investments. Typical examples: Inter Link Foods; HACAS.

Penny shares

Penny shares are those priced at fractions of a pound, say 20p or less. They may be shares whose price reflects concern about their financial position, or simply companies that have gone out of favour with investors, or where profits are currently at a low level. Although there are big gains sometimes to be had in penny stocks, they require very careful investigation and can be risky. Typical examples: e-xentric; Pacific Media.

Utilities

Utilities are a comparatively new investment category in the UK, dating from the wave of privatizations in the 1980s and early 1990s. They supply basic services like gas, water and electricity under an environment that is often heavily regulated. Many utilities are also income stocks but, as the events of the past year have shown, they can have takeover spice too. The drawback, as also demonstrated in the past year, is that their regulated nature makes them subject to political pressure. Typical examples: BG (formerly British Gas); Severn-Trent; Railtrack.

Commodity shares

These are investments in companies whose profits and therefore share price is dependent on the value of a particular commodity, such as gold or oil. Often in extractive industries like mining or oil exploration, or else in primary produce like wheat or other agricultural crops, the prices of commodity shares move at variance with the rest of the stock market and tend to do best in the later stages of a stock market cycle when economic activity is strong. Typical examples: BP; Rio Tinto.

Investment trusts

These are collective investments, set up with a fixed pool of money, in which investors can buy shares. There are many different types of investment trust, from those investing in a broad range of companies and markets around the world to those specializing in a particular sector or country. Their share prices tend to track the value of the underlying investment portfolio, sometimes with a discount, and they can be a useful investment for those with only a limited amount of money to invest, or as a means of investing in areas which might otherwise be too difficult or risky for an individual to contemplate, such as venture capital or emerging markets. Typical examples: 3i; Foreign & Colonial Emerging Markets.

Shares are not the only game in town, as we'll explore in more detail later. A big investor like a pension fund will typically have a mixture of investments: bonds to provide predictable income, shares to add some extra return, and even property and other alternative investments such as venture capital and hedge funds.

For private investors, the practical alternatives are slightly more limited, but risk and return on a basic share portfolio can be modified by using some of the examples outlined briefly below:

Gilts

Most investors buying bonds end up buying gilts (or, if outside the UK, their particular government's bond issues). As we mentioned earlier, bonds are not risk-free, in the sense that they move up and down as interest rates respectively fall and rise. It is their regular income that is often the attraction for investors, plus the certain knowledge that they will be redeemed at their face value at some point in the future.

Preference shares

Preference shares are half way between bonds and shares. They offer a fixed return, but rank ahead of ordinary shares in any winding-up of the company concerned. There is extra security, but only limited prospect for capital gain. Because of this, they have had few attractions for most investors.

Convertible bonds

These are more popular. Effectively they are corporate bonds which also contain an option to convert the holding into ordinary shares at a known time and on the basis of a pre-set formula. The result is that while offering a fixed return for the time being, if the share price rises they will also be seen as more valuable, because of the option to convert. They can therefore be a relatively low-risk way of getting a decent return but still having some potential for capital growth.

Options

In stock market terms an option is a right (but not an obligation) to buy or sell a parcel of shares at a predetermined price for a given length of time. Options are also available on popular stock market indices. An option to buy is a call option. An option to sell is a put option. Options are traded in the market independently of their underlying shares. They can be used either as a geared up way of participating in a rising or falling share price, or as an insurance policy against such a move. They are therefore quite useful for adjusting the level of risk in a portfolio, without buying or selling the underlying shares. Chapter 7 will cover how this is done in more depth.

Unit trusts

These are collective investments but are open-ended pools of money, with the value of the units rising and falling with the value of the underlying investments. The great strength of unit trusts is their variety, and the fact that they allow investors to gain access to a spread of investments in sometimes obscure areas.

There are, for example, unit trusts investing in corporate bonds, in venture capital, in hedge funds, and in emerging markets, all of which are difficult or risky for the private investor to access on their own. The only drawback with some of them is management fees and commissions, which sometimes can limit the size of return you make.

Tracker funds/exchange traded funds

Some unit trusts are constructed to exactly mimic the performance of an index, allowing investors to participate in the movement in the share market in a totally passive way. Exchange traded funds have recently been introduced and do more or less the same thing, but can be bought and sold in the market, avoiding the paperwork involved in buying unit trusts. ETFs are also likely, eventually, to be available to track individual sectors.

By mixing different types of shares, you can tailor your investing to the underlying economic background. By picking different industries, you tend to reduce your risk as well, and a blend of large and small companies will provide spice combined with solidity. Also, by using other investment media such as gilts, options, convertibles, and trackers, you can refine the way your portfolio behaves.

The art of investing is to do this so that you produce a good steady return commensurate with the level of risk you are comfortable running. Be aware that generating a very high return is usually only possible at the expense of incurring extra risk. The risk is that eventually the market or the shares you hold will turn sharply down, depleting your capital.

There are other ways of controlling the risks you run, but a sensible spread of investments is one of the easiest ways of sleeping well at nights.

Why the stock market matters

It is possible that, having read thus far, you may have concluded that the investment scene is far too complicated to be of interest to you. The stock market, you might think, is too remote and complicated, and investment in shares – let alone other types of investment – can only ever be for the rich.

For most people this is a mistaken view. Whether they realize it or not they have a stake in the market.

Any individual with a life assurance policy or a pension entitlement has an indirect interest in the stock market and how it performs. Life assurance companies and pension fund managers take the savings of ordinary individuals and invest them on their behalf, in the stock market and other investment classes.

Direct stock market investment by individuals is all about taking any surplus savings you may have and doing the same thing yourself.

Another thought-provoking aspect of this is the willingness of successive generations in Britain to invest in property. Buying a house using borrowed money (a mortgage) is an investment decision.

It may be complicated by the fact that everyone needs somewhere to live, and therefore this geared-up investment in property can be justified on other grounds. But it is interesting to muse what might have happened if, instead of investing in property, the post-war generation had rented its housing and invested its income in the stock market instead. Property investment has its drawbacks, as people who have in the past been caught in a negative equity trap can attest.

Compare investing £100,000 in a broadly spread portfolio of shares, even at the very top of the market in 1987, with putting an equivalent amount into acquiring a semi in Surbiton at the peak of the property market in 1989. The share portfolio would be way ahead. And remember too that property is harder, more costly, and more stressful to buy and sell than a portfolio of blue chip shares.

It is also the case that, partly as a result of the Thatcher era of privatizations, and partly because of changes to the structure of the City itself, the market has become more accessible to the man (and woman) in the street. Tax-efficient savings choices which take in direct equity investment are increasingly the norm. Information on shares and markets that was once solely the preserve of a privileged few is becoming more readily available at an economic price to those prepared to seek it out.

The next chapter looks at whether direct investment in shares and other types of investment is the right thing for you, what you can expect shares to do for you, what basic skills are needed to assess the relative merits of different companies, and how much the information that you need actually costs.

IN BRIEF

- The market in shares and bonds is little different from any other place where buyers and sellers get together.
- The stock market (and this includes bonds as well as shares) rarely behaves logically. It is subject to many whims and fashions.
- The value of shares derives from what is left over after bankers' and other creditors' bills have been paid. But shares offer the investor limited liability. No investor can lose more than his or her original investment.
- Bonds offer a fixed return and relative safety.
- Trading in shares demands a disciplined approach.
- Different individuals buy shares for different motives and have different time horizons.

■ There are many different types of shares, not all of which will be suitable for or acceptable to different individual investors.

■ Risk and return are linked, but there are many ways investors can reduce the risks they run, and still get good returns.

■ Investment in any type of security (such as shares or bonds) should always be viewed in the light of an investor's other assets and financial commitments.

■ The stock market is much more accessible than it once was to ordinary investors.

Temperament and tools

The stock market is not a place for the faint-hearted. The reason, as we found in the previous chapter, is its tendency only to see life in stark terms.

Share prices often react sharply, either upwards or downwards, to the announcement of company results. This happens not because the figures are good or bad in an absolute sense but because they are better or worse than the outcome the market expected, however illogical or inaccurate that expectation may have been.

Shares can also move materially because of broking analysts' interpretation of the nuances of post-results meetings. The requirement is now placed on UK companies to disclose potentially price-sensitive information as soon as possible. Consequently all but banning one-on-one analyst briefings, through which news might in the past have been informally leaked into the market, has tended to highlight surprises when they occur.

When one-on-one briefings began to be discouraged some years ago, it was thought that this rule would mean that violent gyrations in share prices would be lessened. In fact in some cases share prices have, arguably, become more volatile. Warnings about poor trading tend to come out of the blue.

One of the other frustrations the average private investor may experience is that he or she may often feel they are the last to receive a particular piece of information. By the time they do hear about it, the share price concerned may have moved. New technologies hold the key to solving this problem. The advent of the world wide web and the phenomenon of financial portals and corporate websites mean that information is much more readily available than it once was. More of that in later chapters. But although the playing field has been levelled to a degree, it is unwise for private investors to imagine that they can beat the professionals in their speed of reaction to a surprise announcement.

About seven ago, the *Investors' Chronicle* ran an article outlining the various emotions to which investors can be prone, and how to guard against them. Some of the lessons it draws out bear reiteration (see 'Avoiding the traps' below).

One of the most important aspects of successful investing is that it often involves making decisions that run contrary to 'normal' human behaviour. The investor must learn to be dispassionate about the process of investing and the risks involved.

Thinking calmly and logically about the investment process can be difficult when significant sums of money are involved.

It is not unusual, for example, for large gains or losses to appear virtually overnight, or equally for an investment to sit neither gaining nor losing value for a long period before suddenly exploding into life.

Just as maddening, the market's reaction to long-awaited events can be subdued. There are any number of market maxims that detail how to react in such situations. 'Buy on the rumour: sell on the strike' is one often used about the oil exploration industry, for instance.

To put it more generally: in the stock market, as sometimes in life, it is 'better to travel hopefully than to arrive'. In other words the market is all about anticipated events, and the reality – when it arrives – is often viewed as something of an anticlimax.

With this in mind the important point is to have clear and logical goals, a plan of action, patience, a willingness to take the rough with the smooth, and the flexibility to change your plans if circumstances dictate.

Avoiding the traps

A look at some of the common traps that investors can fall into illustrates the kind of approach needed when dealing in the market.

Trap 1. Averaging down.   The scenario runs something like this. You invest a substantial amount of cash, perhaps a fifth of your portfolio, in a share. It falls 15 per cent almost immediately. The temptation is to compound the error by buying more shares at the lower price. In fact the correct course of action is to examine why the price has fallen and whether or not you made a mistake in buying the shares in the first place.

Either way the optimum course of action is to cut your loss immediately. Doubling up in the hope that the shares will recover increases your exposure to a share that is already acting in a suspect manner.

The normal human emotion of pride, tinged with a little hope, in this instance suggests the wrong course of action. At the very least, you need to have a very good reason for doing it. In my own dealing, I can think of only four occasions in 15 years when I have done this, two of which resulted in heavy losses.

Trap 2. Not running profits.   As well as cutting your losses quickly, the next most basic lesson of stock market investment is to learn to 'run' your profits. In other words, don't sell purely because you have accumulated a good gain if there is no pressing reason to do so. The result could well be missing out on a much larger one. Like fine wine or malt whisky, investments need time to mature and selling too early can mean missing out on a vintage performance.

Keep your nerve and don't give way to the fear of losing an already handsome profit. But remember …

Trap 3. Not selling deteriorating performers. If a share has a good gain but the share price shows signs of flagging it is prudent to sell before the paper profit already built up disappears entirely. An alternative strategy, if the share has done very well, is to sell sufficient of your holding to recoup your original outlay, effectively meaning the remaining shares are 'in for nothing'. You then have the option of continuing to participate in the shares if their rise resumes, or you can sell the remaining holding if their performance deteriorates further.

On occasion investors feel that they should show loyalty to a particular investment that has served them well. This is absurd. In the book *The Money Game* (Vintage Books, 1976) – one of the best texts on investing ever written – the writer 'Adam Smith' (in reality a US fund manager masquerading under the pseudonym of the famous economist) coined an apt phrase to guard against this misplaced sentimentality. He said, to paraphrase slightly, 'always remember that a share doesn't know you own it'.

Loyalty or affection for a stock in the face of deteriorating performance has no place in successful investment.

Trap 4. Not cultivating contrary thinking. There are times in investment when it is right to follow the crowd, but often it is those who buy when things looks blackest and sell when there is unbounded optimism who prove to be the really successful investors.

One of the best times to buy ordinary shares in recent years, for example, was in the turmoil that surrounded Britain's decision to leave the ERM in September 1992, or around the time of the collapse of the Long Term Capital Management (LTCM) hedge fund in September 1998. On the other tack, in July 1987, a listed British company chartered Concorde for a week to fly a party of 90 analysts and journalists around its operations in the UK, Europe and North America. In hindsight this proved to be a good signal of the top of that particular market cycle. Herd mentality was also much in evidence in the early 2000 dot com 'bubble'.

Don't follow the herd: better to follow your own instincts and researches. Remember that rampant corporate excess or a frenzied atmosphere can be a good indicator that the market is overvalued.

Trap 5. Not diversifying risk.   Later in this book we will look at the best way to build a sensible portfolio of shares and other investments. It is sometimes tempting, if a particular type of investment has worked well, to buy similar ones in the hope of repeating the trick. Comfort with the familiar is a basic human trait, but does not sit well with a rational investment strategy designed to minimize undue levels of risk.

To give an example, you may have made a good profit buying the shares of a small brewery, but the reasons for the gain may be specific to that company: perhaps the impact of a change of management or some other factor. Buying the shares of other small breweries at the same time risks skewing your investment too much towards one industry. Then, if an adverse change does occur, all your investments will deteriorate.

A bit of thought and investigation is sometimes required. Recently many investors have sought to diversify away from growth stocks in the telecoms and media area by buying high yield corporate bond funds, unaware perhaps that many of the bonds held by these funds are ones issued by … telecoms and media companies. The result is an investment portfolio with greater risk rather than less.

Employ some lateral thinking when choosing investments.

Trap 6. Clinging to the familiar.   Few individuals like change or the unfamiliar. We might be more comfortable buying shares in Tesco or Sainsbury than we would buying the shares of an obscure small Midlands engineering company. But the chances of the price of a small little-known company rising (under the right conditions) are far better than those in a well-known company that is more intensively researched by City analysts.

One of the most successful US fund managers, Fidelity's Peter Lynch (now retired), positively revels in obscure companies. He describes his ideal investment as one that has not had a visit from an analyst for years, has an uninspiring name, has a business that is either obscure or downright disgusting, and is located in a nondescript town. He reasons that the more obscure and little-known a company's shares are, then the greater the share price potential when it is finally discovered.

Be brave and independent, but do your homework.

Positive qualities needed by investors

To sum up, the examples above highlight the following positive qualities needed by investors:

- absence of pride or any tendency to rely on forlorn hope
- patience and strong nerves
- absence of misplaced loyalty to inanimate objects (i.e. shares)

- ability to go against the crowd and a mistrust of conventional wisdom
- independence of mind and thoroughness.

It is a rare investor that possesses all these qualities. In my own case, as the examples in Chapter 12 will demonstrate, I am unemotional about the stocks I own, and a good, independent contrary thinker. I cut losses quickly – sometimes not quickly enough, as it turns out. But the basic flaw in my investment strategy is a lack of patience and a tendency sometimes to lock away profits too early. I am trying to cure myself of this. Recognizing one's own failings is the first step to correcting them, or at least trying to.

No pain, no gain

I suspect a tendency to take profits too early is a fault to which many private investors are prone. In the past it may have reflected, in the case of those who come from relatively modest backgrounds, the fact that making money from investing in shares has not generally been the norm. There can be a temptation to nail profits before they get too big.

Newer investors in the market for the past year or so have had the reverse lesson, especially if they were heavily into technology shares. They may have had no problem letting their profits run, although the publicity given to so-called day-trading tends to encourage the reverse, but they will also have had a very sharp lesson that shares can go down as well as up.

Among older investors perhaps, or those with a highly developed social conscience, there is the perception that profit made on share trading is unearned – consequently, feelings of guilt can cloud rational decision making.

In fact most money made through investing in shares is hard-earned, not least because the investor is putting his or her own capital at risk, and more often than not using up considerable mental energy researching investment opportunities and monitoring the performance of the shares chosen.

The important point about any investment strategy is to be realistic about what it can do for you: you must have clear and realistic goals and expectations.

> Most money made through investing in shares is hard-earned, not least because the investor is putting his or her own capital at risk, and more often than not using up considerable mental energy researching investment opportunities and monitoring the performance of the shares chosen.

To a degree this becomes easier with experience, but it is a vital aspect to think about before investing. Many investors are paralyzed by indecision precisely at the time decisive action is required, and a lost opportunity, or an actual cash loss, can be the result.

One important starting point is to set what might be called the 'pain barrier', often called a 'stop-loss'. This is an amount beyond which a share will automatically be sold. In the case of my own investments, where I might normally deal in units of £4,000–£5,000, I have set this barrier, not as a percentage, but at an absolute amount of £750. My only really significant losses have occurred when I have ignored this rule in the hope that a share would recover – only to have to sell at a much bigger loss later.

On the other side of the coin, I am reluctant to set a specific limit on when profits should be taken since this varies considerably with circumstances. A very rapid rise in a share for no apparent reason giving a substantial profit may be justification enough, especially if the share then begins to lose its momentum. Only experience can tell here.

The important point is to try and come to a realistic assessment of where you believe the share price could go over a specific period and what action you would take if this point is reached much sooner than you anticipate. While I think day-trading is a 'mug's game' for most private investors, there is no doubt that certain shares from time to time move between relatively predictable limits over periods of weeks and months, and the astute investor can take advantage of this.

Another crucial point is that although it is desirable to set some broad parameters for your trading, they should not be adhered to willy-nilly if circumstances change. If the outlook for a particular share suddenly improves (results prove better than expected; a takeover bid is in the offing; management changes have been announced), it may be wise to revisit your views about the likely share price potential. It pays to be flexible.

Finally, there is much to be gained – as your trading progresses – from studying both successes and failures to try and improve things next time round. If the mistakes of the past are studied, then it should be possible to avoid making them a second or maybe a third time.

As a postscript, dealing in bonds is generally less fraught, and different rules apply. There is little need to worry about the security of your capital in a government bond like a gilt, but the price will move up and down according to market views on interest rates. You need also to be aware when interest payments are due. Gilts are dealt in on the basis of a price plus 'accrued interest', which reflects the number of days since the last interest payment.

With all this in mind, let's have a look at a basic mental checklist that needs to be completed before we go on to the mechanics of picking and administering investments.

Is investment the right thing for you?

It is an old truism of stock market investment that the money you use, especially for investing in shares, should be money you can lose. In practice, of course, only an occasional investment may have to be totally written off, but most investors go through periods when they feel the pain of real losses as well as sometimes (we all hope) the euphoria of significant gains.

The real point here, though, is that investments often take time to bear fruit and it is not helpful to be forced into selling prematurely because the cash is needed for other purposes.

The other sense in which this term is used is that cash earmarked for investment in shares should not be pre-empting funds which could more efficiently be employed elsewhere.

You should be satisfied that, for instance, you have sufficient cash to pay any outstanding debts, to take care of regular financial commitments, including a mortgage, insurance requirements, school fees for children, if appropriate, as well as general living expenses.

The requirement or desirability of investing in a pension scheme should also be assessed and priority given to making an investment that way too. Most pension schemes represent a collective investment in the broad stock market and since the investment can be accomplished in an attractive tax-efficient way, this avenue should be thoroughly explored before money is allocated elsewhere.

It is not unknown, for instance, for individuals to invest money themselves that could usefully be invested in the market indirectly through tax-deductible contributions to a pension scheme.

The last thing I want to do is dissuade an investor who wants to have the 'fun' of pitting his or her wits against the stock market from doing so. But the process of getting started as a share investor involves considering all the available financial options and making a rational decision about the correct course of action to pursue. You might decide that improving your house, or investing more in your pension is a more effective way of accumulating capital. That is a legitimate choice.

Let's say, however, you do decide that you want to invest in shares. It is not really my job here to specify a particular minimum level of available capital below which investment in shares should not be considered feasible.

The advent of no-frills stockbroking has meant that dealing in shares can be accomplished by the man in the street with the minimum of fuss and formality, and it is perfectly possible to start in a small way through investing a few thousand pounds, gradually build up a portfolio of shares, and have some fun – perhaps investing in smaller companies, penny stocks, and new issues.

Low-cost dealing, and particularly the advent of flat-fee internet broking services priced at less than £10 a trade, has substantially lowered the threshhold at which it becomes economic to be a do-it-yourself investor. With five or six shares to achieve sufficient diversification, it is possible to have a reasonable portfolio with less than £5,000 invested.

But this is only a guide. I am emphatically not here to advise the person with, say, a couple of thousand pounds to spare, against investing in the market. Sadly, though, it is true that the bigger the amount you have to invest, the cheaper the process becomes and the more choices you have.

An investor's checklist

With all this in mind, the following is a checklist of 20 questions you need to answer before proceeding further.

1. *Am I secure in my job or business and sure that I will not have any sudden requirements for cash to supplement my normal earnings?* If you can't answer 'yes' to this one, it may be necessary to set aside some cash to cover this eventuality.

2. *If in employment, do I have redundancy insurance to cover mortgage payments?* If no, see the answer above.

3. *Do I depend on my spouse/partner having a regular income and how secure is he/she in his/her job. Could I weather the loss of this income without worrying unduly?* If no, make sure that there is some income-producing reserve set aside to cover this eventuality.

4. *Do I have sizeable outstanding credit card bills or other debts that should take priority?* If so, as an expensive mode of borrowing, they should be paid off before any cash is earmarked for investment.

5. *Have I sufficient capital/income to take care of regular items such as school fees over an extended period (and allowing for inflation)?* If no, cash should be earmarked for a savings vehicle to take care of this.

6. *Could I cover any unexpected private medical bills if necessary?* If no, consider private medical/permanent health insurance.

7. *Have I invested fully in a personal pension that is up to the limits of my tax-free percentage of income?* If not, arguably this should have the first call on available income or capital.

8. *Am I likely to have the opportunity to invest in shares in the company I work for?* If so, you should consider whether you need to retain cash for this specific purpose.

9. *Am I expecting any major capital sums to come my way in the near*

future i.e. from inheritances, maturing insurance policies etc? If so, tailor your investment strategy accordingly.

10. *Do I have a lump sum to invest now?* If yes, do not earmark all of it for shares. Consider investing some in fixed income investments and a proportion in other assets.

11. *Is my partner/spouse in agreement that it is desirable to invest money in shares?* If no, reconsider your decision.

12. *Is he/she aware of the risks involved in investing in the stock market?* If no, they should be acquainted with a realistic assessment of the risks.

13. *Having decided that a specific sum can be invested in the stock market, is it sufficiently large and is my tax position such for it to be worthwhile sheltering investment income or capital gains in some way?* If so, you may need to consider ISAs or other tax-efficient investments.

14. *Assuming a specific sum is earmarked to invest in shares, am I primarily aiming to invest for income or capital growth?* Your choice of investment will be dictated by the answer. Income seekers will need to look at bonds, bond funds and higher-yielding shares and unit trusts.

15. *What tolerance of risk do I have?* It is important to determine this in advance and to recognize that higher than normal returns are only possible by investing in higher-risk shares where the possibility of some loss is greater. Your tolerance of risk may well depend on the size of the funds you are proposing to invest relative to any other assets you may have.

16. *Am I cool, calm and collected, or of a nervous, jumpy disposition?* If the latter, then the stock market is not the place for you.

17. *Do I have a broker through which I can deal in ordinary shares?* If not, think carefully and investigate a number before choosing one. If possible, and if you want to be a 'do-it-yourself' investor, choose one that offers a low cost 'no-frills' service.

18. *If I already have an existing relationship with a broker, how do the firm's charges compare with others in the market, and is the service I am getting the one I require?* The answers to these questions will determine whether or not you might need to look elsewhere.

19. *Am I happy to have my investment held through the broking firm's nominee arrangements?* Settlement is simpler and dealing cheaper if you agree to this. Individual membership of CREST is also an alternative.

20. *Am I computer literate?* Computers are increasingly used by private clients to monitor their portfolios, access information over the internet and to deal online. This greatly simplifies the administration of an investment portfolio.

The 'identikit' investor

From the answers to the above we can draw the 'identikit' investor profile of the person most likely to be a successful investor in shares:

■ retired, in a secure job, or self-employed in a successful business

■ has sufficient capital to cover contingencies such as sickness, redundancy, etc.

■ has fully provided for pension arrangements and other liabilities such as school fees

■ is computer literate

■ does not have an unduly onerous tax position

■ is a calm and collected individual with a reasonable tolerance of risk

■ has a spouse or partner who is happy with the decision to begin investing

■ is happy to trust a broker to handle investment administration.

It is unlikely that every potential investor or reader will fit this identifit picture exactly. The most important aspect is, as we stated at the beginning of this chapter, that investment should only be conducted from a secure financial background. Investing in shares, bonds and other types of securities is not a way of getting rich overnight, and should not be undertaken with cash that might soon be needed for other purposes.

The tools

As well as not being for the faint-hearted, investing in shares is not for the lazy either. The potential for success in any investment increases in proportion to the amount of time spent researching it. Keeping score, monitoring investments once they have been bought, is also an important part of making investment decisions.

At any point in time you may need to know when a particular share or bond investment was acquired, what it cost, and what its current value and therefore your profit or loss is. Rather than wait for the evening or morning paper to arrive to find out how your shares are doing, you may wish to monitor them in the course of the trading day.

To evaluate shares and bonds properly, you will need to undertake research and be prepared to do 'number crunching', and you may wish to see how the price of a particular investment has performed in the recent past. You might want to obtain or subscribe to various publications in order to gain additional information and new ideas.

It is obvious just from this simple list that doing the job properly entails some costs. These costs can be broken down into a number of areas and we look at these in some detail below.

Newspapers and other regular publications

There are few successful investors who are not avid readers. To keep abreast of the market you need to read the *Financial Times* on a daily basis, and perhaps one other quality broadsheet. The *Daily Mail* is also particularly noted for its City coverage. The *Wall Street Journal Europe* is also a good information source, and has a cheap annual 'delivered-to-your-door' subscription deal.

Sunday papers are often used as channels to leak information about corporate developments, new issues and the like into the market, and can be useful, although it is as well to avoid dealing on the basis of tips contained in them.

Weekly investment publications such as, in the UK, the *Investors' Chronicle*, *Shares*, and *Investors' Week* are worth a read; *The Economist* is a personal favourite of mine, although relatively few of its articles have a specific relevance to investment.

You may also want to trawl for ideas in foreign publications, notably perhaps those relating to the US market. Publications like *Business Week*, *Investors Business Daily*, and *Barrons*, a tabloid weekly of legendary influence in the US investment scene, are available in the UK.

There is an important point to make about press coverage of the investment scene – be certain to distinguish between information and opinion.

The value of a wide range of reading is that it broadens the exposure you get to information and ideas on investment. For example, profiles of companies in the *Investors' Chronicle* often contain charts and salient accounting information. It also has frequent articles about investment in unit trusts, bonds, and other types of investment.

You need not agree with or even pay attention to the magazine's view about a particular share to get value out of that article. The same applies to articles in other publications.

What might all this cost? For many years I have both written about and practised the art of investment, using many of the publications mentioned. My monthly paper bill is currently in the region of £50–60. Magazine subscriptions come extra, although publications like the *Investors' Chronicle*, *Shares*, *The Economist*, and *Business Week* often do cut-price deals for a long-term subscription.

However, remember that with the advent of the world wide web, access to online editions of many newspapers and magazines is free, and their archives can also be searched for articles on specific topics and companies.

This can cut down substantially on the need to subscribe to many different newspapers and magazines.

Newsletters

There are any number of newsletters published about the investment scene. They normally have a stock selection system or a particular speciality, recommend selected shares and contain periodic updates on their progress, as well as pontificating about events of the moment.

One problem about newsletters, apart from their cost (typically, £100 a year each), is the self-fulfilling nature of some of their recommendations. The fact that recommendations contained in newsletters are being mailed out to several thousand active investors each week or each month and are often in smaller companies with a restricted liquidity in their shares, means it is not uncommon for newsletter recommendations to move a share price markedly.

Most newsletters operate either on the basis of a portfolio selection system – picking shares that fit certain predetermined criteria – or else have a particular specialization. *Techninvest* is a good example of the latter, a specialist newsletter about high technology shares. It is highly thought of. The important thing is to find the newsletter that works for you, rather than to subscribe to a large number.

Books

Books on investment have enjoyed something of a renaissance in recent years with a number of popular titles being published for the first time and old ones revived. There are books that deal with every part of the investment scene, but those written by or about successful practitioners in which they describe their experiences are perhaps the most valuable for the first time investor.

I have already mentioned *The Money Game* by Adam Smith (Vintage Books, 1976). Some other good ones are: two books by Peter Lynch, *Beating the Street* (Penguin, 1989) and *One up on Wall Street* (Simon & Shuster, 1993); two books by Jack Schwager, *Market Wizards* (NYIF, 1989) and *The New Market Wizards*, a series of interviews with top share traders (Wiley, 1992); and two by George Soros, *The Alchemy of Finance* (Wiley, 1987) and *Soros on Soros* (Wiley, 1989).

It is a good discipline for the new investor in shares to read at least one quality investment book a month. Visit any successful private investor, and you will see that more often than not their bookshelves are full of books about the art of investment.

However successful an investor you become, there is always room to learn more from the experience of others.

Print-based reference material

Even the newest of newcomers to the investment scene will be aware that the big institutional investors – banks, insurance companies and pension funds – have a wealth of information at their disposal on which to base their investment decisions. Fortunately when it comes to information, quantity does not necessarily equal quality. It is perfectly possible for the average investor to make an informed decision about picking out individual shares with the aid of just a modicum of reference material.

One indispensable aid to successful investing in shares is the *Company Guide*, published by HS Financial Publishing, a compendium of basic financial information on all listed companies, which also includes addresses and telephone and fax numbers and a variety of other data. Armed with this publication, which currently costs approximately £105 per year for four quarterly issues, the investor is equipped to telephone or fax companies to obtain copies of annual reports and other background information.

The other guide that might be worth subscribing to, and which seasoned private investors swear by, is the *Estimate Directory*. This contains regularly updated details of the forecasts made by City analysts for the vast majority of listed companies, as well as other information derived from this data and a simple share price chart of each company. An annual subscription to four quarterly issues costs around £130.

HS also publishes *Company REFs*, a book of key accounts ratios for leading companies and this is very useful for those looking for a short cut to the financial number crunching that investigating shares in depth can entail. This is also available in CD-ROM format on either a monthly or quarterly basis and costs around £675 per year for the monthly edition.

Though the cost of all this information may sound daunting, some of it represents the 'luxury' end of the market for those with cash to indulge their investing hobby. Those who want to keep the costs down can manage perfectly adequately with less. In addition, as will be examined later, these services can be duplicated at much lower cost over the internet, possibly at the cost of a small additional monthly subscription.

Software and data

The largest cost item for any serious private investor used to be getting hold of up-to-date information on share prices during the course of the trading day, and also information on prices and trading volume in a form capable of being downloaded into various types of investment software.

The business of computerized investing, what software packages are available, how to get hold of regular price data, as well as the internet and world wide web and how they can help with access to relevant information, are all covered in later chapters of this book. But suffice to say that changes in the attitude of stock exchanges towards the commercial use of price information, and the advent of the web as a delivery mechanism have resulted in data costs coming down sharply in price.

Real time (i.e. constantly updated) price displays – typically delivered via a broadcast system that utilizes your household TV aerial – are still fairly expensive and clearly unnecessary if the investor is out at work all day. For the retired and self-employed, whether or not they are worth having depends on their cost relative to the size of funds available for investment and therefore the likely gains to be made in any one year.

Once broadband services such as ADSL become widely available at modest cost it is likely that internet-based price services may well replace those delivered in this way at a fraction of the cost.

Even so, true real time data (some services are updated continuously, but delayed by 15 minutes from real time) still costs, and exchange fees for use of the data are levied on top. Some financial website operators are taking steps to try and circumvent this, and online brokers like Charles Schwab and E*Trade are starting to offer sophisticated streaming price services for a modest monthly fee.

The norm for services like this is that they will contain all the information an active private investor needs, including the ability to create customized pages of individual shares, news announcements made by companies and various other services. These include a so-called 'limit-minder', which will alert you via a message to a mobile phone, via e-mail, or even audibly if a particular share hits a pre-programme limit. Data can usually be downloaded into various commonly used investment software packages.

While all this sounds sophisticated and exciting, and certainly will give the home-based private investor the feeling that he or she is involved in the market, my own experience has been that it can induce a feeling of pressure on the investor to deal rather more actively than might be wise.

The investment philosophy that I will put forward in this book empha-sizes the importance of selecting the correct investments for you (which might or might not be shares) and working out what they are worth, rather than looking at the money that can undoubtedly be made (and, of course, lost) by more active trading of shares.

With one or two exceptions, my best investment gains have come from careful share selection and from holding shares and other assets for relatively long periods of time – by which I mean periods of up to a year or more – rather than through shorter-term trading. This has its place, but is probably best left to the professional.

In this context, the close monitoring of price movements on a real time basis through the trading day becomes something of a distraction. For the non-computerized, a weather eye can be kept on leading shares (the top 400 or so) through accessing the BBC2 and Channel 4 teletext pages.

Digital TV services are also likely to offer free internet access, including access to financial web sites, and digital channels such as Bloomberg have prominently displayed price 'tickers'.

Financial websites and investment software are covered in more detail in later chapters, but it is worth remembering firstly that many investment software packages now contain basic data on companies, such as sales and profit figures, so some of the reference material mentioned earlier may be deemed less essential if you have one of these packages. To some degree also, price charting and company information can all be accessed via the web, making investment software of the conventional type partly redundant.

Basic costs

It is important to be realistic about how much all this will cost. Table 2.1 itemizes the prices of some of the information sources and services outlined above.

This adds up to a total of around £1,250 of ongoing costs, or under £1,000 if you choose to omit CD-REFS. In addition, the cost of an internet connection and related telephone charges could be added in. The advent of ADSL should see these capped at around a maximum of £40 a month.

If this seems a lot, it's worth remembering that doing the same exercise a few years ago would probably have brought you to a figure of more than £3,000, with appreciably less information available on tap. The internet and development in investment software has brought about a major increase in the information resources that ordinary investors can call on without breaking the bank.

Even so, for some this might still be a rather off-putting figure. So let's look at how it's possible to do the job for less. Many investors do.

Table 2.1 Investor information – basic costs

Information source	Annual cost £
Newspapers – £40 per month	480
Magazines and newsletters – say, two at £100 each	200
Books – one per four weeks, say, £10 each	130
CD-REFS (quarterly)	240
Software – budget package (one-off cost)	80
Data – including some company fundamental data	150

Assuming you have a PC, and an internet connection, all of the information mentioned earlier can effectively be accessed over the web, assuming you are not averse to reading newspapers in online format. So monthly telephone charges are all that you need pay – a likely maximum of £40 per month once ADSL is introduced.

Exactly how the internet can be used for investing is explored later in this book, but effectively all of the functions performed by investment software and personal finance portfolio tracking programs can be managed over the net, or downloaded free of charge.

The bottom line is that the *bare minimum* of annual spending is probably £500, although you may have chosen to sign up for other reasons. Forgo this and you will find you quickly come up against a shortage of either ideas or information required to make the right investment decisions in a prompt and efficient manner.

On the basis of the investment strategies and techniques described later in this book, I believe it is possible to envisage an annual return on capital invested over time in the region of 15–20 per cent, including reinvesting dividends and other investment income. So how keen you are to invest, and how cost-effective it can be for you depends on the size of the funds at your disposal.

A return of this order can in no way be guaranteed. But what numbers like this mean is that with a portfolio of say £5,000, the annual return might be £750–1,000, from which should be deducted the extra costs you incur as mentioned above. The more you have to invest, the easier it is to justify the cost of the information. The less you are investing, the more you have to think clearly about how to get the necessary information as cheaply as possible.

The real point, though, is that while the bigger the portfolio the more may well be spent on information and other resources, it will not go up in proportion. The individual with a limited amount of cash available to invest, say £2,000 or less, must recognize that he or she is pursuing a hobby, with commensurate costs that may wipe out some of the gains that are made.

For the remainder of this book, however, we will presuppose that the reader is prepared to spend at the level indicated for the basic information costs, and that he or she is prepared to pursue a strategy of actively investigating investment opportunities thoroughly. In itself, of course, this involves an investment in time which should be costed out.

To paraphrase the remarks of Lord Keynes quoted in the Introduction, playing the game does involve an entry fee.

IN BRIEF

■ Markets can be volatile, and investors are notoriously prone to bouts of fear and greed.

■ Successful investors need to cultivate patience, strong nerves, and the ability to think and act differently from the crowd.

■ The first rule of successful trading: cut losses, and run profits.

■ There is no minimum entry fee for investing, but it makes more sense if you can have worthwhile holdings in several different investments.

■ Only invest money in shares that is not earmarked for other purposes and after all other sensible financial commitments have been met. The money you use should be money you can lose.

■ Successful investment involves buying information and using tools. These cost money. Allocate at least £500 a year for print media, share price data, and/or internet connection and call charges.

chapter three

Checking out the numbers

Checking out the numbers is a vital part of any investment decision. Failure to investigate investment opportunities properly before you invest can lead to big mistakes. But the idea that this sort of research is the 'be all and end all' is wrong.

Deep analysis is all very well, but it needs to be combined with other factors: the state of the market, your own investment preferences, your risk tolerance and investment income needs, and the general acumen and trustworthiness of the management.

> Checking out the numbers is a vital part of any investment decision. Failure to investigate investment opportunities properly before you invest can lead to big mistakes.

Fundamental analysis vs technical analysis

It is well worth getting away from the rather sterile debate among the professionals in the investment game about the merits or otherwise of so-called 'fundamental' analysis and 'technical' analysis. These tags are commonly referred to in the press. You may have wondered what they mean.

In both cases these names seek to imply solidity and thoroughness. But this supposed thoroughness is often not delivered. The difference between fundamental analysis and technical analysis is roughly as follows.

Fundamental analysis

Fundamental analysis starts by looking at the underlying background to the company in whose shares you may be interested. It examines the industry it operates in, whether or not it has a competitive edge (say in terms of size, management, corporate strategy, or innovation), and looks in detail at its past financial results over a period of years. It looks (usually in great, but less convincing, detail) at how they might shape up in the future.

That is the theory. In reality much City research is simply designed to maintain the broking firm's profile in the eyes of their clients and the company itself and can be superficial and self-serving.

Technical analysis

Technical analysis contends that looking at the fundamentals is irrelevant, since all the information that is of any importance has already been reflected in the price of the shares. What matters more (technical analysts say) is the pattern of behaviour displayed by investors in the past – as reflected in the way the share price has moved as the forces of supply and demand have ebbed and flowed.

To some degree this harks back to the quote from Lord Keynes I used in the introduction to this book. The underlying merits of a share matter less than what 'the crowd' in the market believes to be the case.

'Technicians', or chartists, as they are often known, therefore spend their time performing detailed analysis, both statistical and intuitive, of trends in share prices. The objective is to come to some conclusion about the best time to buy or sell particular shares. Fundamental analysts, of course, regard them as charlatans.

This is a little unfair. While shares may be more susceptible to fundamental analysis, in the case of bonds and some other types of investment the fundamental analysis that can be done is often of a more basic nature. Shares are inherently risky: government bonds much less so. Hence the analysis that underpins trading in bonds is often more statistical. Shorter-term traders in the relatively perfect markets of foreign exchange and financial futures tend to use technical analysis, sometimes intuitively rather than formally, to make decisions.

This is not to say that all fundamentalists or all chartists agree with each other on everything either. Many fundamentalists pursue their own favoured brand of numerical analysis to the exclusion of all else, again risking not seeing the wood for the trees and being out of tune with market sentiment for long periods.

There is room for both of these approaches, and an investor ignores one or other at his or her peril. But do not worry. There is no need to go to the lengths City analysts claim to do to grasp the essence of what makes a company tick and whether its shares are good value or not. Taking a company's accounts and looking at some basic numbers is comparatively easy.

Being aware of an investment's price and how it has fluctuated in the past is also a vital part of timing purchases and sales. At the very least it may stop you buying a share, picked for good fundamental reasons, at the wrong time. Conversely, sometimes charts can give such strong 'buy' signals that they will prompt you to do further fundamental research on a share (or other investment) that you may not have considered before.

The fact that this chapter is the first of two dealing with each of these aspects does not imply that I give any more importance to one approach than the other. The essential component of successful investment is information, and how you interpret it. The more information you have, the better.

When it comes to share investing, everyday observations about well known high street names are information (moreover, information that the average professional investor may not pay attention to), price movements are information, and the numbers contained in company accounts – and analysts' forecasts – are also information. The view you might gain of the calibre of the company's executives from meeting a senior manager at the company is particularly valuable information. All of this information can and should be used to come to a judgement about a share.

And while fundamental analysts will point out that charts often give incorrect or ambiguous signals, the same can equally be said of company accounts and other fundamental information. More of that later.

Basic accounting concepts

I hope every reader of this book will come away from reading it with at least a smattering of accounting knowledge. But I will keep it simple. There are two good reasons for this.

First, the main reason is that it serves no purpose to get too embroiled in abstruse accounting topics. All you really need to know is that when you begin to find a set of accounts hard to understand, that is as good a reason as any for being wary.

Secondly, although I worked for 18 years as an investment analyst in the City, and have been a financial journalist for the last 13 years, I have had no formal accountancy training.

My point in mentioning this is simple. Understanding accounts can be easily learnt. Moreover, while I would always advocate studying a company's accounts before investing, there are subscription services, such as *Company REFs*, which are very good at calculating key ratios for you and, in the case of the CD-ROM version, allow you to screen all UK companies to find the ones that fit specific criteria.

Interpreting company financial statements is comparatively straight-forward, providing the reader has a sceptical turn of mind and some basic knowledge of the way businesses work. You do not need to be a qualified FCA to analyze a set of company accounts.

Other than a service like CD-REFS, the basic starting point is a company's annual report and accounts.

Annual reports and accounts

This is a document the companies are required by law to publish each year and to circulate to shareholders. It contains details of the company's operations over the previous year, and formal audited accounts.

The accounts contain a statement of profit and loss, a statement of the cash inflows and outflows experienced during the year – the revenue the company has received and how it has been spent – and the balance sheet, a statement of the company's assets and liabilities at its financial year-end. The numbers may be quite brief, with a lot of the detail consigned to notes at the back of the accounts.

I cannot stress enough the importance of reading these notes as part of the process of evaluating a company. Companies can and do hide embarrassing bits of detail in the notes – in the hope that they will get overlooked. Equally important, the look and feel of the document tells you a lot about the company. Good marks are awarded for simple design. Beware that small company with a big glossy annual report and lots of photographs of the chief executive.

Getting hold of a company's report and accounts is usually comparatively easy. A telephone call to the company secretary's office, or even simply to the head office switchboard (the telephone number will be in one of the reference publications mentioned in the previous chapter) will usually ensure that a copy is sent out to you, even if you do not hold any shares. Very occasionally a letter may be needed. Many companies also now have an online version of their accounts available at their website.

If possible try and get hold of more than one year's accounts. The further back you can go the better. Note also that reference books like the *Company Guide*, *REFs*, and the *Estimate Directory*, and their online equivalents, sometimes provide details of the key ratios we will talk about later in this chapter. These can be useful as an initial filter. But it is always best to look in more detail at the accounts. There is no substitute for crunching the numbers yourself.

Understanding the profit and loss account

We will now take each component of the annual report and look at them in brief to examine what they can tell us about a company.

Let's begin with our fictional company Universal Widgets to draw out some of the basic concepts.

Table 3.1 shows its profit and loss (or P&L) account.

This is a pretty standard layout for a company P&L account, although the precise terminology may vary slightly from company to company.

For instance, turnover may be called revenue or sales, interest paid may be called cost of finance, and operating profit may be called trading profit. But the logical structure as laid out in Table 3.1 will remain roughly the same.

There is one significant item missing, for which you will have to go to the notes, usually in the note relating to trading profit.

The missing item is *depreciation*.

This is the amount a company sets aside each year to replace a 'wasting' asset. Rather like depreciation on a car, the company's finance director will know that at some point in the future he has to replace a piece of machinery or a fleet of vehicles. It is prudent for him therefore to deduct from profits each year, on an instalment basis, an amount that will add up to the expected cost of renewing these assets at the end of their life.

In fact normally it is simply the original cost of the asset that is depreciated, with no account being taken of the fact that, due to inflation, the cost of replacing it may rise.

In the case of Universal Widgets we are going to assume that the depreciation this year is £5m, included in the £20m of operating expenses, and that it was £4m in the previous year. The importance of this will become clear in due course.

Before we go on we need also to look at a relatively new introduction to this category of so-called 'book entries'. This deals with the *amortization of goodwill*. Although this seems a complicated phrase, goodwill is simply the difference between the cost of acquiring a company, and the value of its tangible net assets.

Goodwill has an impact in several ways when analyzing a company, but in this instance the important point is that accounting rules now oblige companies making acquisitions to write off (or amortize) a certain

Table 3.1 Universal Widgets: Profit and Loss Account (£m)

| | Year to December | |
	2000	1999
Turnover	125	100
Cost of sales	55	45
Gross profit	70	55
Operating expenses	20	15
Operating profit	50	40
Interest paid	10	10
Profit before tax	40	30
Taxation	13	10
Profit after tax	27	20
Minority interests	2	0
Attributable profit	25	20
Dividends	5	4
Retained profit	20	16
Earnings per share (p)	12.5	10
Dividend per share (p)	2.5	2
Shares in issue	200m	200m

proportion of this goodwill each year, reducing the profits of the company accordingly. Like depreciation this is a notional amount affecting only reported profits. It is not an actual cash expense.

Let's now have a look at some of the items in the P&L account in more detail.

Turnover is simply sales revenue, normally stated net of VAT and any sales duties applicable. *Cost of sales* is the outside expense entailed in generating those sales, such as bought-in raw materials and the like. What is left is *gross profit*.

The essence of most companies is that they take these materials and process them in some way. In order to generate the sales in the first place it has been necessary for them to add some value to the raw materials. In order to do this there are internal costs – of employing people, selling the finished product, administering the business, buying machinery, and so on.

These are known as *operating expenses*. After deducting these from gross profit, we arrive at *operating profit*. This is not the end of the expense. Most companies quite rightly finance part of their trading through borrowing to fund capital investment. Provided this is kept at prudent levels and done at reasonable cost, this is perfectly legitimate. But the cost of obtaining these borrowings must be deducted from profits via the *interest paid* item.

This leaves us with *profit before tax*. This figure is the basic unit that City analysts look at, although some complexities have been introduced here recently, which we will go into later.

Companies have to pay *corporation tax*, so that too must be deducted. *Minority interests*, that is to say the interests of outside shareholders in any subsidiaries that are part-owned, must also be taken off (normally at the after tax profit level), and what is left is *attributable profit* for the ordinary shareholders in Universal Widgets.

Shareholders often expect dividends. So in order to arrive at a figure for the cash available to reinvest in the business, these payments must be deducted to arrive at *retained profits*. This is the profit kept in the business to be ploughed back for the future.

So far so good. Well, not quite. The company has actually retained more than this. The figure for depreciation (£5m in 1995) was only a notional book entry calculated by the finance director so, in cash terms, the company has in fact retained £25m, rather than the £20m shown at the bottom of the table. Retained profits plus depreciation and other similar notional book entries like goodwill amortization is actually a good proxy for cash flow, which we will discuss later on.

The *earnings per share* and *dividend per share* figures are simply the attributable profit and dividend figures divided by the total number of shares in issue, in this example 200m.

Key profit and loss ratios

Now let's look at some of the basic ratios that can be derived from these figures to give us clues about the company's performance.

Sales ratios

Sales ratios are an important figure, partly because, like cash and unlike profit, they are hard to fudge and can easily be compared internationally.

The advent of many unprofitable high technology companies in the recent boom and subsequent bust in internet stocks spawned new measures of valuation to take account of the fact that these companies were unlikely to make profits in the near future. The most common technique involves valuing them in terms of their revenue and dividing the market value of the company (its number of shares in issue multiplied by its share price) by revenue.

Paradoxically, although analysts seemingly found ways to justify ever higher valuations, using price to sales ratios is not new. James O'Shaughnessy in his book *What Works on Wall Street* (McGraw-Hill, 1994) tested post-war data exhaustively to find out which ratios correlated most closely with subsequent share price performance.

He found that the price to sales ratio was indeed one that had a powerful effect. Unfortunately for 'net' companies, his findings were that companies had to be valued at appreciably less than their sales to guarantee good performance later.

Profit margins

Like most other ratios, profit margins are a guide both to the efficiency of the business, and to the type of industry it operates in. Some service businesses, for instance, like advertising agencies or fund management firms, have limited bought-in costs but generate fee income on the back of their intangible assets – their client base and staff. Others, like supermarkets, operate on very tight margins but big turnover.

So what matters in all this is not so much the level of margin but its trend over time. An adverse trend, falling margins from one year to the next to the one after that, is disturbing and an explanation should be sought.

Margins are simply the ratio of a profit figure to sales. *Gross margin* is gross profit as a percentage of turnover, *operating margin* is operating profit as a percentage of turnover, and so on. Gross margin is a good measure to use in businesses like pub retailing, where there is a service element and a high level of bought-in products, but more normally operating margins are used.

Interest cover

The difference between operating margins and *pre-tax margins* is represented by interest. Higher or lower levels of borrowing manifest themselves in both the balance sheet and the profit statement. In the P&L account the way to measure this is to express pre-interest profit (in this example operating profit) as a multiple of the interest paid. In this case this ratio, known as interest cover, is 5 times, an acceptable level. The reason for being concerned about this measure is that an unduly low level of interest cover can leave profits vulnerable to an increase in interest rates.

Corporate tax

Current corporate tax rates are around 30 per cent, but this is sometimes reduced by overseas profits arising in low-tax areas and by the tax deductions resulting from heavy past capital investment. If the *tax charge*, the percentage of pre-tax profits taken off in tax, is significantly outside the 28-30 per cent range or has changed significantly in the past year, it is worth examining why.

Price-earnings ratios, EV/EBIT, and dividend yields

Finally, in the P&L account there are earnings and dividends to consider. Although analysts look at headline pre-tax numbers, at the end of the day it is often the earnings per share figure, or variants of it, that drive the share price. Only the more subtle analysts use other ratios based around cash flow.

Price-earnings ratio

Notwithstanding what we said earlier about the greater importance being assumed by the price to sales ratio, shares are normally evaluated on the basis of the price-earnings ratio (PER), or earnings multiple. This is the earnings per share figure – usually the forecast for the immediate coming year – divided into the share price. In this example, let's assume that Universal Widgets's share price is 250p. This means that its historic price-earnings ratio, i.e. the ratio based on its latest reported annual earnings, is 20 times.

This is relatively high by normal standards (although not compared with the egregious valuations seen in late 1999 and early 2000), but not unduly so when we consider that these earnings have risen by 25 per cent, from 10p to 12.5p in the past year, and therefore may well do so again.

Let's assume that analysts, based on their long experience of looking at the company, believe that earnings per share will grow by another 25per cent this year, taking the per share figure up from 12.5p to 15.6p. If the company is to receive the same valuation in the market when these earnings are reported in a year's time, the share price must rise to 312p.

The problem is that earnings do not always grow as the market expects. Suppose, for the sake of argument, that Universal Widgets loses a valuable sales contract and that its earnings are likely to fall back to 10p rather than grow to the 15.6p the market first expected. What happens then?

First of all, you might expect that, if the 20 times PER were maintained, the shares would fall to 200p. In fact they may well fall by more than this, because the company's hitherto solid-looking pattern of growth has been tarnished. Companies which demonstrate they are unreliable in this way normally stand on much lower multiples.

Say the multiple falls to 14 times. This means that although the slippage in earnings is only back to the prior year's level, the drop in the share price, from the original 250p to 140p (14 times the 10p earnings now expected), is 44 per cent.

This works in reverse if shares on lower multiples produce better than expected results. The shares benefit not only from the better than expected rise in profits, but also from a rise in the price-earnings ratio. There is nothing automatic about this, but it is the way the market tends to react. In some ways this is why smaller companies have their attractions. In recent years they have often been valued on low multiples and investors can do very well if they latch onto the right one. Not only do profits grow, but the company becomes better known, more widely researched, and its multiple increases.

It is important to understand this point fully before moving on, as it is basic to the whole investment process. Looking back to the different categories of shares we itemized in the previous chapter, you can probably deduce that growth stocks will tend to have higher multiples than normal blue chips, because they will have higher growth rates. As they mature, their growth will slacken and they will become blue chips.

EV/EBIT

The increasingly international aspect of investing is leading to new valuation benchmarks being used. One of these, which is quite powerful, is enterprise value (EV) to EBIT, which stands for earnings before interest and tax. Put simply though, enterprise value is the value of the company's shares in issue added to its net debt. If a company has a market capitalization of £100m and net debt of £25m, its EV would be £125m. Because EV adjusts for debt (or net cash, which is subtracted to arrive at EV), the ratio is calculated on profit before interest.

Some analysts also favour adding back depreciation and amortization too, to arrive at the ugly term EBITDA (pronounced e-bit-dah). The value of this is that companies with less debt (or more cash than debt) appear cheaper, other things being equal, and using this ratio eliminates most of the distorting effects of the differing accounting conventions between countries.

There is a danger, though, that this can be treated by company enthusiasts as an indicator of a company's financial soundness or the strength of its cash flow, which it isn't. Logically too, EV/EBIT *should* be appreciably less than the company's price-earnings ratio, because the denominator is taken before some hefty deductions, for tax and interest. A shrewd professional investor I know, for example, typically only invests in companies whose EV/EBIT is less than 10 times, a good yardstick to bear in mind.

Dividend yields

Let's not, in all this, forget about income, as some market commentators are wont to do. Many investors rely on investment income, so dividends are important too. In general the onus is on shares to perform better than more staid investments. Keeping the money in the bank or building society will normally yield lower returns than an investment in shares, because shares are more risky.

A higher return is required to compensate the share investor for the extra risk that he may suffer a total or partial loss of his capital. Part of the return from a share is measured by its dividend yield.

In the UK, dividends are paid to the investor after tax has been deducted i.e. on a 'net' basis. The investor receives a tax credit for the amount of tax deducted at source. So the income return from a share is usually calculated on the basis of the gross dividend. With the basic rate at 20 per cent the dividend payment is 'grossed up' by dividing the net payment by 0.8.

The yield is then calculated by expressing this annual gross 'income' as a percentage of the current share price. In the case of Universal Widgets, grossing up the 2.5p dividend payment by 0.8 means that the gross dividend is 3.125p. This amount represents 1.25 per cent of the current 250p share price. The gross dividend yield is therefore 1.25 per cent.

This may seem pretty puny when an investor could get maybe 4 per cent with the money in a bank high interest account and perhaps 6 per cent in a fixed interest stock. But the other component of any return that an equity investor might receive is the potential appreciation in the share price in any one year.

Let's go back to our earlier example and assume that profits grew as expected and the share price rose in line with them. The share price would have risen by 25 per cent and adding in the 1.25 per cent dividend yield on top would give a *total return* of 26.5 per cent, a very healthy return indeed.

The ratio between earnings and dividends has a bearing on this too. The less a company pays out in dividends, the more it has to reinvest in the business. High growth companies tend to want (and indeed need) to retain more of their profits in order to fund their expected growth. Yields on growth companies therefore tend to be much lower than more sedate companies, but the opportunity for price appreciation is (in theory) that much greater.

As an aside, dividend yields on shares and those on bonds have also traditionally had a loose relationship. This is expressed either as a ratio between the yield on non-redeemable gilt-edged stocks (those with no maturity date) and the yield on the FT All Share Index, or as the difference between them, known as the reverse yield gap.

The reason for the reverse yield gap being so called is that in the immediate post-war era and before, equities were considered appreciably riskier than bonds and hence had much higher yields. As post-war economic growth and inflation highlighted the riskiness of bonds' fixed returns, this gap reversed, with bonds yielding more than equities to compensate for the lack of any capital growth potential.

However, it is generally considered dangerous if the two numbers get too far out of line and gilt-edge yields roughly twice the yields on equities is probably a good long-term norm to work to.

Within companies, the relationhip between earnings and dividends is known as *dividend cover* and is worked out by dividing dividends into earnings per share.

In this example, therefore, the dividend cover is 5 times (12.5p divided by 2.5p). A dividend cover of 2.5 to 3 times might be considered normal, one of 5 times high, and one of under 2 as low.

The risk of a low dividend cover is that if profits fall, the dividend may have to be reduced. Companies with low dividend covers tend to have higher yields to compensate for this risk. High yields and low cover normally also mean that the company's price earnings multiple is low, suggesting that the market also expects it not to produce much appreciation.

But while a proportion of income stocks may go on to cut their dividends, many do not, and their prices and share ratings recover, making them good investments. This is particularly the case if their income can be counted gross and reinvested, as for instance in an Individual Savings Account (ISA).

Reinvestment of gross dividend income has a powerful compounding effect on the shareholders' returns if it is done consistently over a comparatively long period. For example, a relatively modest 7 per cent return compounded over ten years produces a gain of 97 per cent, more or less doubling your money. Over 15 years the gain is 175 per cent.

It is important to remember that the relationship between earnings, dividends and the share price is a dynamic one, and governed more by expectations of what may happen in the future than by past history. However, the presence of a good past record tends to underpin similar expectations for the future.

In fact as accounting conventions have changed, the predictability of reported earnings has fallen, making them a less reliable guide to the underlying state of the business. Analysts now frequently adjust published profit figures to get them onto a standardized and meaningful basis, stripping out items that are regarded as out of the ordinary. This can be confusing to the private investor.

In tandem with this, companies have been obliged to give a more explicit and transparent account of the way cash has flowed into and out of the business in any one year. It is to this next, very important, component of the annual report that we turn in the following section.

Understanding cash flow statements

The cash flow statement for our fictional company Universal Widgets is shown in Table 3.2.

For brevity I have omitted some of the subtotals that normally crop up in corporate cash flow statements – but otherwise Table 3.2 shows more or less how things would appear in a normal set of accounts.

Table 3.2: Universal Widgets: Cash Flow Statement

	Year to December	
	2000	1999
Net cash inflow from operating activities	46	48
Servicing of finance		
Interest	−10	−10
Dividends	−5	−4
Taxation	−12	−11
Investing activities		
Purchase of fixed assets	−30	−28
Sale of fixed assets	5	14
Purchase of investments	−6	−1
Sale of investments		
Net cash flow/outflow before financing	−12	8
Financing		
(Increase)/decrease in borrrowing	−9	4
Change in net cash	−3	4

The first figure is *cash flow from operations*. As its name suggests, this is the net amount of cash the company received from its operating activities in the course of the year. It is very important to remember that this is not the same as the operating profit struck in the P&L account. It will bear some relation to it but, as most small-businessmen will recognize, making sales and booking profits are not the same as receiving the cash.

One difference between P&L account profit and operating cash flow is depreciation which, as we mentioned before, is a notional charge that can be added back. This is to say, it does not represent an actual outflow of cash from the business.

There will be some other minor adjustments – it is normal, for instance, to take off any profit that arises from sales of fixed assets, since the revenue from the sales comes in elsewhere.

But the big factor is the *change in working capital*. Working capital is an accounting term, but in practice it means the total of stocks, and money owed to the company (debtors), minus money it owes to others (creditors). Sales and profits may rise, but money from extra sales is of no benefit to the company's cash reserves until it is collected.

Remember that we are not necessarily talking here about bad debts, but simply highlighting the point that profits recorded on the basis of invoices that have not yet been paid are not perhaps to be counted in the same way as cash that has actually been received.

Let's take our example of Universal Widgets. Its inflow of cash actually went down by £2m between 1999 and 2000, despite the fact that operating profits went up from £40m to £50m. If we assume that depreciation didn't change much, what has happened to cause this?

One reason could be that although the company has been efficient at making sales, it may have achieved this by giving its customers extended credit terms. Or it may simply have been less efficient than before at collecting its debts. Similarly its suppliers may have tightened their terms of trade and the company may have had to pay up faster for its raw materials.

This is not necessarily a remarkable state of affairs. But it is definitely a bad sign if the cash inflow from operations is radically different to operating profits. I have seen examples of companies reporting steady increases in profits but, each year, reporting much lower cash inflows, or even outflows. Needless to say, such situations cannot continue indefinitely.

Looking further down the cash flow statement we can see interest and dividends taken out. These may differ slightly from the P&L account figures because of a difference in the timing of dividend and interest payments relative to when the company's financial year ends. For instance, companies normally declare two dividends a year, an interim and a final. The final dividend will be declared when the results are published (obviously this will be after the company's financial year-end) and paid a few weeks later – perhaps three months into the company's new financial year.

The dividend entry in the cash flow statement may well be a combination of the current year's interim payment and the previous year's final dividend.

Taxation used to be paid significantly in arrears and differed from the P&L account figure which stated the amount expected to be paid on the year's profit when the time comes to settle up with the taxman. Now that corporation tax is paid quarterly, companies have had to surrender some of the cash flow benefits this regime provided. Differences between reported tax and tax paid are likely to be less than in the past, because the payment will be more current than before.

You can see by simple subtraction that after taking off interest, dividends and tax – all of which can be regarded as cast-iron obligations – Universal Widgets had £19m left in 2000 but £23m in 1999.

This is the cash available to reinvest in the business. In many companies this will simply be used for the *purchase of fixed assets* either to replace existing plant and machinery that has worn out, or to put up a new factory. Offsetting this can be disposals of fixed assets, which bring in cash. Some fixed assets may no longer be needed and can be sold. Whether a profit is earned on the disposal is less relevant. What matters is the cash coming in.

Surplus cash flow may also be used to acquire *investments*. These can represent a variety of things. In Universal Widgets's case, it could be a small stake in Consolidated Flanges, a company with whom it has a long-standing relationship. Or it may be some other type of investment necessary to the smooth running of the business. It is here, under the heading *purchase of subsidiaries*, that an acquisition would be recorded.

After taking out the net amount of purchases and sales of fixed assets and investments, we are left (in this example) with a *cash outflow before financing* of £12m in 2000 compared to an inflow of £8m in the previous year.

Now turn back to p. 49 to contrast this with the profit and loss account in Table 3.1.

In terms of profit, everything looks hunky-dory. The cash flow statement shows otherwise, illustrating the drawback of looking solely at earnings per share and profits to evaluate a company.

In this particular case, the cash deficit in 2000 had to be financed somehow, either by borrowing, or by the company dipping into its cash reserves. As it happened, it chose to do both – with cash falling by £3m and borrowings rising by £9m.

Before we look at the balance sheet, you may have noticed that it should be possible to arrive at a per share expression of cash flow and to compare this with the share price, as we did with earnings. There are differences of opinion about which figure to take, but provided a consistent figure is taken, it does not much matter about the precise definition.

The options are really either to take cash flow before investing activities – that is operating cash flow (the top figure) minus interest dividends and tax – or to take what is sometimes called *free cash flow*. This is the figure for cash flow before investing activities, minus the level of fixed asset purchases necessary to maintain the fabric of the business.

Since this latter amount is difficult to estimate, if opting for the free cash flow measure it is probably simpler just to take purchases less sales of fixed assets and knock this amount off cash flow before investing. Some figures for free cash flow exclude dividends. This is because it is not an unavoidable payment, like interest and tax, but at the discretion of the management.

Either way, dividing whichever figure is chosen by the average number of shares in issue during the year will give a per share figure that can then be compared to the share price, and with the conventional earnings per share figures. Sharp divergences in the trend between the two need to be investigated further.

As a postscript to the dot com bubble, some readers may have noticed the term *burn rate* cropping up. This is the rate at which a (usually loss-making) company is using up its cash. The normal way of expressing this is to take cash and relate it to cash operating expenses (gross profit less operating expenses, excluding any book entries). The resulting rate is expressed either as a monthly figure, or as the number of months (or in the worst case, weeks or days) before the company runs out of money.

This is a good point at which to look at the balance sheet, and the ratios that can be calculated simply from the figures contained within it.

Understanding the balance sheet

An accountant will always say that a balance sheet is simply a snapshot of a company's assets and liabilities at a particular point in time (the day the company's financial year ends).

It should surprise no one that a company's assets and liabilities, the money it is owed, the money it has to pay out, its borrowings and its cash reserves, all change from week to week and month to month, and that the timing of a company's year-end is sometimes dictated not only by tax considerations but also by which time of year will show its financial health at its most robust.

Table 3.3 shows Universal Widgets's balance sheet for 1999 and 2000.

There is another important feature of company balance sheets. This is that the difference between one year's and the next's is inextricably linked with the flows of cash into and out of the business.

We saw in the previous example that the company's cash flow from operations differed from its operating profit, because the latter took into account movements in working capital – notably leads and lags in the payment of invoices by customers and of bills owed to suppliers.

Similarly, the amount retained from profits each year goes over to the balance sheet as a credit and becomes part of the company's reserves.

However, before getting onto this subject let's take the balance sheet item by item and look at what each item means.

The *consolidated balance sheet* is the one to look for in a set of company accounts, because that is the one that includes the company and all its subsidiaries. Accounts sometimes also include the parent company balance sheet. This can be ignored.

Looking at the balance sheet item by item, *tangible assets* are self-explanatory and are often represented by property and plant and machinery.

Table 3.3 Universal Widgets: Consolidated Balance Sheet

	As at 31 December	
	2000	*1999*
Fixed assets		
Tangible assets	250	220
Investments	10	10
	260	230
Current assets		
Stocks	25	20
Debtors	35	25
Cash	12	15
	72	60
Creditors		
Due within one year	40	45
Net current assets	32	15
Total assets less current liabilities	292	245
Creditors		
Due after more than one year	80	55
Provisions	10	10
Net assets	202	180
Capital and reserves		
Shares capital	10	10
Share premium account	52	52
Capital reserve	40	38
Profit & loss account	100	80
Equity shareholders' funds	202	180

Intangible assets are now usually included. These are often items which have a value, but one which is hard to measure. They can include contracts, mailing lists, brand names and the like.

In the current asset line we have *stocks*, which needs little further explanation, *debtors* (money owed to the company), and *cash* – again needing no explanation.

Creditors, money the company owes to others – bills for raw materials, duty to the government, perhaps a dividend to shareholders and so on – are typically not split up on the face of the balance sheet, but the detail given in a note. This is a touch inconvenient. The aim is to separate out short-term borrowings, trade creditors, and the rest.

Net current assets are simply current assets less current liabilities.

Total assets less current liabilities – sometimes called *net capital employed* – is another handy measure, the usefulness of which we will come to later. *Longer-term creditors* more often than not will be represented by borrowing and the detail again hidden in a note.

Provisions represent cash the company may feel it will have to pay out at some future date and against which it is setting something aside. The use of provisions, especially in the context of takeovers, can be controversial. This aside, though, many companies quite properly make provison to pay deferred tax – a tax liability likely to occur at some date in the future.

What is left over after all these deductions is termed *net assets*. In effect, they belong to the shareholders in the company and are therefore sometimes called *shareholders' funds*, or shareholders' equity. They are represented by the nominal value of the company's share capital, the share premium, which represents the value of shares issued at greater than the shares' original nominal value, and the company's reserves, including its accumulated retained profits.

In all of the examples given above, it is worth remembering that although we have used the example of a fictional engineering company here, the method of looking at and appraising a company does not change significantly because of the industry it operates in. Cash flow remains of vital importance to any business, as the most recent examples of failed dot com businesses demonstrate. Cash is king, as an old phrase goes, and nowhere more so than in companies that have few tangible assets and negative cash flow.

There are a number of basic ratios that we will look at initially (we will look at some more complex ones in Chapter 10).

Key balance sheet ratios

The main ratios I want to look at now are gearing, return on capital and current asset ratios.

Gearing

Gearing is often used as a measure of the financial health, or rather financial risk, of a company. The normal definition is total borrowings minus cash expressed as a percentage of net assets. A typical gearing ratio might be in the 30–50 per cent area. A figure of 60 per cent may not cause too much lost sleep, especially if the business concerned is a stable cash producer, but gearing levels close to or in excess of 100 per cent tend to be viewed with suspicion. This is because more often than not they make the company concerned vulnerable to rises in interest rates.

Similarly if interest rates are expected to fall, the shares of a more highly geared company may rise disproportionately, because as interest payments fall profits will rise, other things being equal. Balance sheet gearing is the counterpart to the interest cover in the profit and loss account. This is sometimes called *income gearing*.

Let's have a look at Universal Widgets's gearing figure. Assume for the moment that all of the figures for creditors, both within current liabilities and in longer-term creditors, are represented by borrowing. The numerator of the equation would be 40+80–12, the £12m figure being the cash that is deducted before we divide the result by net assets. Hence gearing in this case is 108/202 or about 53 per cent.

Return on capital

Another crucial measure of how well a company is doing is its return on capital. This shows the profits being generated by the business and compares them to the invested capital in the business. The convention is to take profit before interest and express this as a percentage of net capital employed, that is total assets less current liabilities.

If this figure is less than the long-term cost of capital then there is clearly something wrong – because it is obvious that the company is not earning enough to sustain itself.

To calculate return on capital we need to go back to Table 3.1, the P&L account. Taking profit before interest as the top half of the equation and dividing this by total assets less current liabilities gives a ratio of 50/292 or 17.1 per cent. This would be regarded as satisfactory but not exceptional. Many companies manage to generate returns on capital in excess of 20 per cent or even 30 per cent, although the figure tends to be distorted by the timing of any revaluation of property assets and the like.

Profit before interest is taken as the numerator because net capital employed includes borrowings as part of capital, and therefore the interest attributable to it should not be deducted to arrive at the return.

The measure that excludes borrowings and interest is called *return on equity* (ROE) and is often defined as pre-tax profit divided by shareholders' funds and expressed as a percentage. Some analysts, myself included, take this a stage further and use after-tax profits as the numerator of the equation. See Chapter 11 for a more detailed explanation of specific ways in which this method can be used to value shares.

The purist approach would also take both of these calculations one stage further by calculating return on capital and return on equity using as the bottom half of the fraction the average of two years' capital or share-holders' equity, reasoning that this better represents the capital that was in use during the year and which therefore generated the profit figures that are the top half of the fraction. It is hard to argue with the logic of this, but it makes the calculation somewhat cumbersome.

It is more important perhaps to ensure that the bottom of the fraction includes net assets, including intangibles and any accumulated goodwill written off.

Companies have to state this last figure somewhere in their accounts and the logic for including it (and thereby lowering the return on equity figure) is that, whether it has been written off or not, it represents share-holders' money that management has spent, usually on acquisitions, and hence on which it should earn a return.

As a rough yardstick if management is not generating a return on this basis significantly above the yield on a long-term, gilt-edge stock, then shareholders have a right to be very wary indeed. Most of the great stock market performers of recent years have after tax ROEs in excess of 20 per cent.

In Universal Widgets's case, if we assume for a moment that its accumulated goodwill written off is £48m this takes its adjusted shareholders' funds up to £250m. Attributable profit is £25m so after tax ROE is 10 per cent, respectable but not spectacular.

Current asset ratio

Last but not least, companies live or die by how quickly they get in their payments relative to paying their bills and by how much liquid resource they possess. One way to measure this is known as the current asset ratio. This is simply current assets divided by current liabilities. In the case of Universal Widgets the figure is 1.8 (72/40).

A more robust ratio to use is known as the *acid test* ratio. This is defined as current assets excluding stocks divided by current liabilities. This gives, in the case of our example, a ratio of 1.18 (47/40).

The reasoning behind this definition is that in extreme circumstances a company will find it easier to recover its other debtors than to realize the balance sheet value of its stock, which may only be in partly finished goods.

If a company is viewed as being a forced seller of its stock, for example, it may have to discount it deeply to get any value for it, another reason for excluding it from this ratio, which measures the extent to which debtors and cash cover the money required to pay off short-term creditors.

Lastly it is of course possible to express shareholders' funds as a value per share and compare this to the share price. This is known as book value or *net asset value (NAV) per share*. The shares in issue at the year-end are often used for this calculation. In this instance the book value is £202m (net assets) divided by 200m shares, or 101p per share.

How is the company performing?

As I mentioned above, there are a number of more sophisticated ratios that can also be used, and we will cover these in a later chapter. Nonetheless the indicators described here will, when taken together and when viewed over a period of time so that a trend can be established, give a powerful sense of how a company is performing.

Are its margins rising or falling? Is it maintaining its rate of earnings growth? Is the trend in its cash flow at variance with the trend in profits? What level is gearing and has it been rising or falling over time? Is return on capital and adjusted after tax return on equity at a respectable level and has that been rising or falling over time? And what does the current part of the balance sheet look like and how has it been moving?

For those of a mind to do so, most of these calculations can be programmed into and saved in a simple spreadsheet that can be used over and over again. Readers can find a blank spreadsheet with formulas already filled in available for download at my website www.linksitemoney.com.

Boring though it may seem, I believe the relatively modest amount of time taken to extract the necessary numbers to calculate these ratios is time well spent for any investor. There is really no substitute for it.

Let's just recap and summarize the basic parameters needed to value a share:

- *Price-earnings ratio (share price divided by estimated future earnings).* Compare this with earnings growth and look for a PER significantly less than the expected rate of growth and that experienced in the recent past.
- *Yield (grossed-up dividend expressed as a percentage of the share price).* Good growth stocks will almost certainly not have high yields. And of course yields rise and fall over time along with the general level of interest rates.
- *Total return.* What really matters in share investment is the likely price appreciation plus the return from the dividend. This is called total return.

Estimate the appreciation by assuming that the company will stand on a similar PER to the current one in a year's time if profits come out as expected, and then add this figure to the anticipated yield.

■ *Cash flow.* Check that the company is not booking illusory profits by comparing cash flow from operations with operating profit. The figures need not be identical, but look for a divergence in trend.

■ *Balance sheet.* Look at balance sheet ratios like gearing and current asset ratios in the context of the likely economic environment. High gearing may be an advantage if rates are likely to come down. If the environment is starting to get rocky, companies with liquid balance sheets will do best. Check that return on capital employed and adjusted ROE are at a respectable level.

Universal Widgets – buy or sell?

Let's look at how Universal Widgets stacks up on these criteria, assuming for the moment the price is 250p.

Consider the facts:

■ The shares have a historic PER of 20 times, but growth has been good and is expected to continue at 25 per cent. The PER/earnings growth ratio (sometimes called the PEG factor) is therefore less than one – a plus point.

■ The yield is low, under 2 per cent, but if the company maintains its growth path and the PER holds up, total return is going to be well in excess of 20 per cent.

■ However, cash flow is not healthy and is sharply diverging from the trend in profits. This could mean the profits are being massaged. This is a black mark.

■ Balance sheet ratios look healthy with gearing not unduly high. The current end of the balance sheet looks reasonably liquid. Return on capital and return on equity are satisfactory but not spectacular.

■ There isn't a lot of asset support for the share price. The price of 250p compares to the NAV per share of 101p.

Few shares that are worth buying have no minus points. What matters is the weight you give to the pluses and minuses respectively. But in the end you have to come to a decision one way or the other.

As I said earlier, we need not make this decision in isolation. It is equally important to look at the way the share price itself has been moving and what that can tell us about the possible future course of the shares. We will look at this aspect of investing in the next chapter.

Analyzing bond fundamentals

Last of all, we have focused in this chapter more or less exclusively on shares, but bonds can be analyzed too. In the case of a government bond, whether it appears cheap or expensive rests on the view you take about the government's standard of economic management, and in particular the outlook for inflation.

The market's view of this can be gauged by the difference, or spread, between the yield on the bond and a widely recognized global benchmark, such as a US Treasury bond with the same length of time to go to repayment.

There are several independent agencies that rate bonds on the basis of their credit quality, using both financial analysis and interviews with management to determine what rating should be placed on the bonds. Ratings, which essentially attempt to judge the bond issuer's ability to pay the interest and repay the principal on the bond, are generally given in the form of letters, with AAA being better than AA, which is in turn better than B and so on.

Analysis of this sort comes into its own in the corporate bond market, although government bonds also have different ratings.

It is self-evident, for example, that Russian government bonds would sell on a much higher yield than UK gilts, for instance, because of the poorer economic record and consequent greater risk of default.

As with corporate bonds, government bond analysis focuses, rather as in fundamental analysis of a share, on the prospects for the company and the industry in which it operates. But it does this from the more pointed view of the likelihood or otherwise of the company defaulting and, in this instance, where the bond stands in the repayment pecking order in the event of a liquidation.

In bonds, yields explain most things. Differences in yields between similar bonds of different companies reflect the market's view of the credit quality of the company.

Clearly, simply because a bond stands on a large spread over, say, US Treasuries does not necessarily mean the bond is either cheap or expensive, in much the same way as a high price-earnings ratio does not necessarily mean a share is expensive. In the case of a share, profits growth may be such that the high PE ratio is easily supportable: in the case of a bond, a big spread over the benchmark may simply mean that the market has taken an unduly pessimistic view of the bond's credit quality.

Even if you are only interested in investing in a company's shares, it is important not to ignore this information completely. A deteriorating rating on a company's bonds suggests that a company's balance sheet may have become more stretched, for example.

IN BRIEF

■ Analyzing the fundamentals of company accounts is an important part of selecting shares. Basic accounting knowledge can be easily picked up.

■ Key measures of profitability are profit margins. These are the pencentages the various levels of profit represent of sales turnover.

■ Understanding cash flow concepts is central to investment. Cash flow can diverge significantly from profits and is almost always a more reliable indicator of a company's financial health.

■ It is important for investors to understand the meaning of key balance sheet ratios like gearing, the acid test ratio, return on capital and return on equity.

■ The importance of all financial ratios is related to the trend they exhibit over a period of years, rather than their absolute levels.

■ Valuing shares is best done by comparing price-earnings ratios with expected earnings growth, by comparing PE ratios and dividend yields with other similar companies, by comparing the share price to the underlying value of the company's assets, and by looking at return on equity relative to fixed income investments.

■ The total return from an investment is measured by looking at its share price change plus its dividend yield. The income component of this equation can be significant and should not be ignored.

■ Bonds can be analyzed in terms of the size of their yield relative to a given benchmark, and on the basis of credit quality, as perceived by rating agencies.

Analyzing price movements – timing your trading

Share price charts have an important role to play in alerting the astute investor to shares that look interesting and might warrant further research.

Furthermore, interpreted properly, they can prevent an investor from making a badly timed decision to buy or sell. Reasons which may look sound enough based solely on fundamental analysis can be overridden for a period until the charts look more auspicious.

Even though a share may look attractive, it could well be cheaper next week or next month, and using charts to get a feel for how the share price has moved in the past is a useful aid to better decision making.

There are those who believe that the charts are virtually all you need. For the moment we will disregard that view, although it does have some merit when trading particularly homogeneous products on a very short time scale.

I have always preferred to view technical analysis (charts) and fundamental analysis (number crunching and ratios) as two sides of the same coin – both equally important.

We covered the basics of fundamental analysis in the last chapter. My aim is to do the same with technical, or chart, analysis in this chapter.

Just as there is a huge volume of written work on fundamental analysis, so the literature on chart analysis is equally comprehensive. Price charts have been used for as long as there have been centralized markets for trading a commodity. Some techniques, such as candlestick charting (see later in this chapter), are known to date back as far as the seventeenth century.

What has more recently sparked both professional and private investor interest in technical analysis is the ability offered by computers to chart share prices and their movements quickly and easily without fuss or repetitive manual updating. There are professional chartists who still like to keep a number of charts by hand, to 'get a flavour' for the way the markets are moving, but most individual investors are likely to find this approach unappealing.

We will look at what investment software packages do, and how they can help the investor, in Chapter 8. First it is necessary to have some understanding of the basics of technical analysis.

First principles – understanding market psychology

As we saw in Chapter 2, one of the hardest aspects of investing is to discipline oneself not to fall prey to normal human emotions when buying and selling shares. Pride and hope have no place in investment decisions. Investing must be dispassionate.

For many, this is a hard skill to acquire. Human emotions do play a part in the market. It is the quirks of human behaviour that can be observed in the share chart prices move.

The easiest way to explain this is by an example. Let's look at this in stages.

Stage One.   Let's say that you bought 1,000 Universal Widgets shares at 100p. Imagine that the investment goes well and over the next few months the shares rise to 140p.

Stage Two.   Having made 40 per cent on your money in a matter of weeks you might consider selling, but before you can, however, the market price starts falling back towards 100p, coming to rest at around 120p.

No point selling now, you tell yourself. Wait until the shares go back up again.

Stage Three.   Let's say that the shares do just that. But as they approach 140p for the second time you have an interesting dilemma. When they reached this price before, some selling came in which depressed the price. Better to get ready now to sell if the shares hit 140p.

This intention to sell and the many similar ones made by other like-minded investors make the likelihood that the shares will bounce back down from the 140p mark all the stronger. Almost, in fact, a self-fulfilling prophecy.

How other investors view the market can reinforce this too. Let's have a look at the situation from the standpoint of a different, and less fortunate, investor.

Imagine that he originally *bought* the shares at 140p a year or so back and had seen them fall back to as low as 100p in the meantime. He did not follow our earlier advice to cut losses quickly, but held on hoping the shares would recover. But as they approach his initial buying price, the point where he can get out of the shares at no loss, the temptation to sell is strong.

Imagine now that *you* successfully bought your Universal Widgets shares at 100p and sold them at 140p.

After selling at 140p the shares drifted down again and now stand at close to 100p. The temptation to buy again to try and repeat the exercise is overwhelming, particularly if this cyclical pattern has been repeated more than once.

The very fact that several investors think this way and buy at around this price means that the shares will 'bounce' up once they hit 100p, perhaps triggering more buying interest from people who missed hitching a ride last time round. By the same token they may later bounce down from the 140p level for the reasons described earlier.

This mixture of the herd instinct and conditioned reflex can be very apparent on share price charts and buying and selling can be timed to profit from them.

Some companies, generally the more mature blue chips, have share price charts that display pronounced cyclical patterns as the shares move in and out of favour with investors. The points at which investors collectively pause and think (and act) are known as support and resistance levels, for obvious reasons.

How simple technical analysis works in practice

The operation of support and resistance levels is illustrated by the chart of the Nikkei shown in Figure 4.1. The Nikkei is the main Japanese stock market index.

Figure 4.1 Nikkei – support and resistance levels

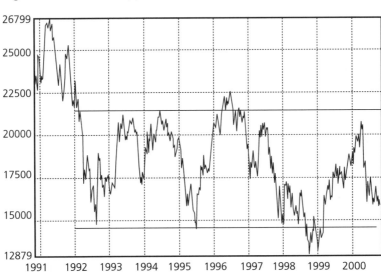

Look at the period in the chart from 1992 onwards. After having habitually bounced up off the 22,500 area in previous years, the index broke down through the support level decisively in early 1992 and quickly fell to hit a new support point around the 15,000 mark midway through the year.

Notice also how in subsequent years, despite several attempts, the index failed to penetrate back above the 22,500 resistance level (the area of the earlier broken support level). Similarly, the support level of around 15,000 was tested several times and (more or less) held firm. Buyers have tended to 'buy the market' aggressively when the index hits 15,000 and have sold when it gets above the 20,000 to 21,000 level.

The objective of technical analysis is to assist in spotting the points at which profitable trades like this can be made. The decision need not be made irrespective of the fundamentals. Chart analysis can be used to time more precisely the purchase of a share (or the market as a whole) if you have, for instance, already decided it looks attractive on fundamental grounds.

Most technical analysis techniques are really geared to spotting turning points – sometimes called 'reversals' – and making sure the investor makes the decision at the right time when these occur. I mentioned earlier in this book the need for investors to have patience. Normally this means the patience to stick with a share until the idea behind a purchase bears fruit. But it can equally mean being patient enough to ensure you don't hurry to buy a good share, but wait instead for the right price.

The method of using support and resistance does not work in all cases. Underlying fundamentals can change quickly and, if they alter in a major way, all bets are off. Trends and cyclical patterns are not necessarily reliable, and certainly do not hold good for ever. When they do change, it is no good expecting the old patterns to re-emerge. A fundamental reassessment has to be made with the old assumptions cast aside and a new strategy formulated.

Trends

Even in the case of an acknowledged growth stock that investors might feel should have a steadily rising price, it is important to remember that shares do not go up in a straight line. Often in instances like this they rise and fall successively, but each successive high point is higher than the previous one and each low also higher than its predecessor. The technique can also be applied to market indices.

Professional investors may even sell a share they like on fundamentals if they think the shares have got ahead of themselves, and buy back when they think they have lagged behind. For private investors, dealing costs can sometimes make this a less fruitful exercise.

The process works in reverse too, where prospects appear to be deteriorating. The underlying trend may be down, but the pattern will be a zigzag rather than a straight line.

A good way of following a trend is by drawing one line through successive highs and another through successive lows. This should produce two roughly parallel lines, a trend channel, delineating the boundaries of the pattern. It is important not to invent a pattern where none exists, but in many shares an established trend can be clearly marked out.

Look at the charts of the FTSE-100 index since 1988 (Figure 4.2) and the Sterling/US$ exchange rate since October 1999 (Figure 4.3). These are as good an example of an uptrend and a downtrend as you might expect to see. At the beginning of Figure 4.3 it is possible to see that the £/$ rate bounced down off the $1.65 level as the 'stale' buyers – who were stranded by the earlier drop in price – scrambled to get out.

In Figure 4.2, the long uptrend in the FTSE-100 index is clear, although closer inspection of the most recent period would probably indicate that the market has finally run out of steam and may soon break downwards in a decisive way.

Figure 4.2 FTSE – uptrend

Figure 4.3 £/$ – downtrend

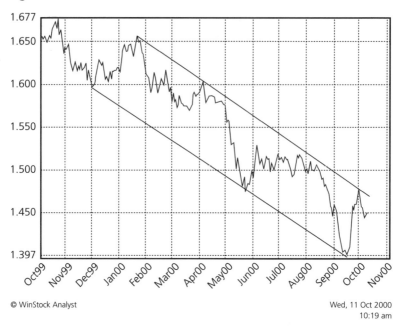

© WinStock Analyst

Wed, 11 Oct 2000
10:19 am

All of these charts are basic line charts. They simply show the closing prices of the shares, indices or currencies on successive days. But there are other types of chart format which display different information. These are outlined in the next section. As we look at them, keep in mind the ideas of trends, trendlines, support, and resistance.

Different chart types

Line chart

Line charts are a simple way of recording one piece of information: the progress of a share as measured by its closing price each day. But there are many other aspects of the way a share price moves that it is useful to know too. For instance, it's good to have a record of the range of prices at which the share traded in the course of each day, and something which shows the volume of shares traded.

Bar charts

It is (or should be) intuitively obvious that if a significant move in a share is accompanied by a high level of trading activity, then that counts for more than if the same move occurred on next to no shares traded. If a lot of people are putting their money where their mouth is, it's usually worth paying attention.

US chart books often contain charts which display this information. They are known as bar charts. Bar charts show the daily high-low represented by a solid vertical line, with the closing price represented by a horizontal notch on the bar at the appropriate point. Volume is normally shown at the bottom of the page by a vertical bar. Figure 4.4 shows a simple daily bar chart for ICI.

Figure 4.4 ICI – daily bar chart

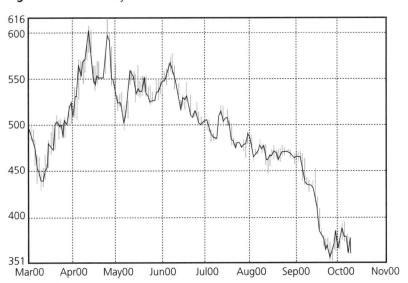

© WinStock Analyst

Wed, 11 Oct 2000
10:45 am

Candlestick chart

A variation of the bar chart is the candlestick chart. This is constructed so as to give even more information. The candlestick is formed from two lines superimposed on each other. A thin line indicates the day's high-low range, while a thicker line shows the difference between the opening price and the closing price. By convention, if the shares have risen the candle is white, and black if the price has fallen, although many chart packages use blue and red respectively to signify this.

Candlestick charts were first developed in Japan in the seventeenth century to plot the movement in the price of rice, and it is obvious from this brief description that they give more subtle degrees of information on movements in the price in the course of a single day than either of the preceding examples.

The other facet of candlesticks is that there are a large number of permutations of behaviour that can be illustrated by the charts, to many of which is ascribed a particular significance and (this being a Japanese invention) an evocative name. Figure 4.5 shows the candlestick chart for ICI for the same period of time covered by Figure 4.4.

Figure 4.5 ICI – candlestick chart

© WinStock Analyst

Wed, 11 Oct 2000
10:29 am

Point and figure chart

Another variant is the point and figure chart. Point and figure charts work on a different principle to the other charts described so far. They attempt to concentrate on the direction of a particular trend rather than the time it takes to reach fruition. They also have a method for filtering out insignificant movements in the price of a share.

The convention is that upward moves are presented by a column of crosses and downward moves by a column of zeroes. Figures crop up periodically in the chart – 1, 2, 3, and so on – to represent the start of a new month – January, February, March etc. With point and figure charts, therefore, it follows that if a trend continues unbroken – i.e. the price moves up steadily, perhaps by different amounts each successive day with an occasional day with no change – irrespective of how long the process takes, the move is simply represented by a column of crosses (i.e. a single vertical line). There is also normally a minimum threshold movement of a few pence, below which nothing is recorded.

The charts tend to look somewhat different to normal line charts and bar charts. Extended upward or downward moves look more dramatic. Periods of indecision, with the shares gyrating up and down, produce broader patterns of noughts and crosses across the face of the chart.

Price relative chart

Lastly, many investors follow price relative charts. These show the price of a share relative to the movement in an index, normally either a market average or the index for the sector of which the share is a part. For instance, the price relative of Sainsbury might be calculated either with respect to the FTSE-100 or the FT All Share Index, or else relative to the Food Retailing subsector index.

A price relative chart is calculated quite simply by dividing the one into the other, normally dividing the price of the shares by the value of the appropriate index on the same day. The interesting aspect of a chart like this is that it gives a continuous guide as to how well or otherwise a share is performing relative to the chosen benchmark.

If the share price is rising faster than the index, or falling less slowly, the price relative line will have a positive gradient, if the reverse is the case it will have a negative slope. Only if the shares are moving precisely in line with the benchmark will the line be horizontal. The most obvious use of a measurement like this is to spot when a share is moving out of (or back into) favour. This happens when the gradient of the line changes from positive to negative (or vice versa).

Care needs to be taken in making judgements on this score, though. What the private investor should be interested in is absolute performance.

Holding a share which outperforms because it goes down less than the market as a whole is a turn-off for most private investors. Positive relative strength is only really of interest to the investor if the general trend in shares is upward.

Interpreting the charts

More generally it is through their interpretation of charts that technical analysts often come in for criticism. There are any number of patterns that can be thrown up by charts, and these are often given arcane names, producing a mystique that some feel gets in the way of rational interpretation. Hence 'double tops', 'head and shoulders tops', 'saucer bottoms', 'pennants', 'flags', 'wedges', 'triangles', and so on.

It is not so much the detection of the patterns on charts that is controversial, but the ascribing of predictive value to them, often to the exclusion of any fundamental analysis.

In some instances, however, they seem to work. This, and chart inter-pretation in outline, can be explained by means of an example. Take a 'head and shoulders top' of the sort displayed on the chart of GUS shown in Figure 4.6.

Figure 4.6 GUS – 'head and shoulders top'

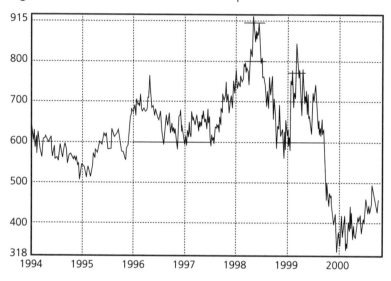

© WinStock Analyst

Wed, 11 Oct 2000
10:52 am

I have drawn horizontal lines on the chart to show the presence of the head and each shoulder in the example. The left 'shoulder' was formed in the 18 months from the beginning of 1996 between 600p and 700p, the 'head' between 800p and 900p in 1998 and the right 'shoulder' between 600p and 750p over a period of about 12 months from October 1998.

In this example, the so-called neckline is at 600p, with the shoulders and the head clearly visible above it and to the left and right. The theory is that if the share price breaks down through the neckline, then the downward move in the shares from there onwards will be numerically equivalent to the distance from the highest point on the chart down to the neckline.

In this example a decisive break down through 600p would suggest a drop in the shares from 600p to just under 300p, the high having been just over 900p. It is also sometimes argued that the size of the downward move is related to the time period over which the top formed, in other words by the width of the formation as well as its depth. In this instance, however, GUS hit a low point of around 318p, more or less vindicating the first part of the theory, but doing so very quickly indeed.

While it may be tempting to dismiss all this as so much mumbo-jumbo, the fact is that rules like this often do work precisely because enough people in the market, professionals and amateurs alike, follow charts and react to their signals. This tends to make reality conform to the theory often enough for zealous chartists to retain their enthusiasm.

Before moving on from these different chart types to consider the various indicators that can be derived from share price data and the uses to which these can be put, it is worth making one general point.

Many chart software packages (see Chapter 8) now provide the tools for charting and analyzing share price movements, but also fundamental data such as sales, profits, and dividends. This reinforces the view that neither 'fundamentals' nor the share price action should be viewed completely in isolation.

There is also the very sensible point that the more information you can assemble the better your decision is likely to be.

This is true even if charts alone are used. No investment decision should ever be made on the basis of a single chart or indicator in isolation. Different statistical indicators can be used for different purposes, but ultimately the best decision is likely to be made when several indicators flash a similar signal.

Moving averages and variations on the theme

It will probably surprise no one that share prices have always had a tendency to move around from day to day in a seemingly random fashion.

These day-to-day fluctuations, or 'chatter', in the price of a share are distracting to investors. They may alternately become encouraged on an up day, discouraged on a down day , and just end up puzzled.

One reason for the seeming randomness is that the market can exert a pull on a share price contrary to the way it might otherwise have moved. Produce some good news for a share on a day when the index falls 150 points, and the result may be a small fall in the share price. Conversely, bad news issued on a day the market as a whole is strong might lead to no change in the price.

Large blocks of shares crossing the market on a particular day can distort the price, as can the positions that individual market-makers hold. The unwinding of large positions by market-makers often leads to sharp, and unpredictable, changes in the price of individual stocks.

Moving average

In order to get a clear picture of how a share is moving, investors need to strip out these extraneous movements. One of the best ways to do this is via a moving average. The idea is that the share price each day for a period of days is taken and averaged.

Going back to Universal Widgets, let's say that the closing price on ten successive days was as follows (in pence): 105, 106, 107, 107, 106, 100, 99, 103, 105, and 107. The average of these ten days is 104.5. Now let's say that on day 11 the price moved up to 110. The average of this price together with the preceding nine days is 105. It is possible to work this out by adding up all ten numbers and again dividing by ten. But the same effect is gained by taking the previous total and adding or subtracting the difference between the new day's price and the one 'dropping off' the other end of the sequence, and then dividing by 10.

Now imagine this process being continued day after day for several months, with each day's price being added on, the tenth one back on the previous sequence being dropped off, and the result being averaged.

From the previous example it can be seen that, despite fluctuations in the price, the change in the moving average from one day to the next is comparatively small. The raw price zigzags around the average. If the moving average line is viewed on its own it will represent a smoother picture of the underlying movement in the shares, with the day-to-day 'chatter' stripped out.

Moving averages can be calculated over a variety of time periods. The principle is that the shorter the period used for the calculation, the closer the moving average will correspond to the underlying price. The longer the period, the smoother the trend.

For technical analysts and investors alike the significance of moving averages lies not in viewing them in isolation, but in watching how they interact both with the underlying price, and seeing how two moving averages of the same share price, but of different time periods, interact with each other.

One approach is to take the price and compare it with a long-term average, for instance the 200-day moving average. A more typical method is to identify when a shorter-term moving average crosses a longer-term average when both are moving in the same direction.

Different pairs of time periods are traditionally used, the 20-day and 50-day averages are often compared, for instance, or the 30-day and 90-day. Better signals may be given in some stocks with different pairings of numbers.

The crossing points of moving averages are illustrated in Figure 4.7 showing GUS for the period from May 1998 onwards.

Figure 4.7 GUS – moving averages

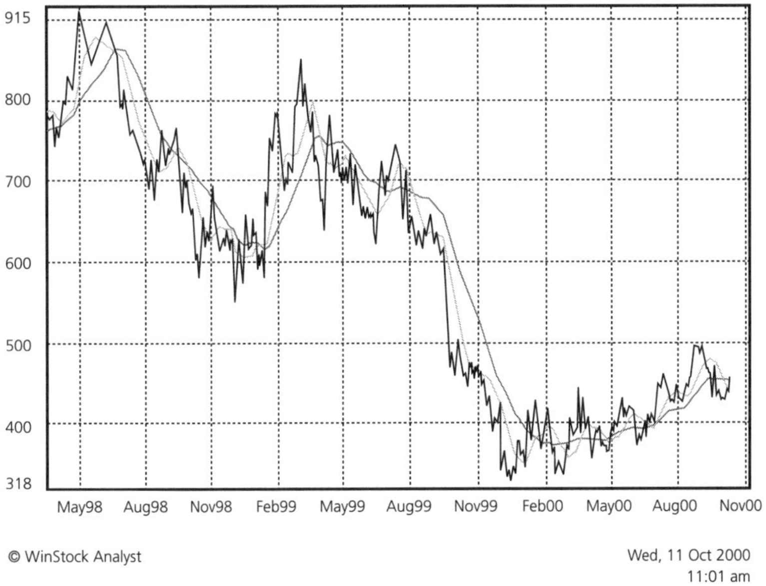

© WinStock Analyst

Wed, 11 Oct 2000
11:01 am

As an illustration of the supposed predictive nature of moving averages, look at the period around January 1999. Here it can be seen that the shorter average is moving up through the longer-term average and that both are themselves rising. This is normally construed as a very positive sign and is known in technical analysis circles as a 'golden cross'.

The drawback of this approach is that if there is not much of a gap between the averages, in this case only 30 days, the lines tend to intertwine and distinguishing which line is moving where is more difficult. In the chart, this can be seen to be the case for much of 2000. Different pairings are sometimes used to get around this, typically 30-day and 90-day averages.

If longer time periods are involved the two lines can be distinguished more easily, but the drawback is that the signal of any turning point will be given that much later. Shorter-term pairings, on the other hand, may be quicker on the draw but will lead to an excessive number of futile trades which go nowhere and result only in high dealing costs with little to show for it.

MACD

Observing moving averages, especially on shares that have displayed clear cyclical patterns in the past, can work well, but perhaps not by waiting until the signal is given. By then it may be too late, and the lion's share of the anticipated move may have occurred.

One way of attempting to get some early warning that something may be afoot is to measure the fluctuations in the gap between two moving averages.

An indicator that does this is known as the Moving Average Convergence and Divergence indicator, or MACD. The principle is as follows: the difference between the two averages is drawn as a line chart, but reduced to a base level of zero.

A simple MACD for GUS is shown in Figure 4.8. Referring back to Figure 4.7, it can be seen that turning points in the shares are indicated by extremes in the MACD as or before the share price reacts, although the relationship is far from precise.

Figure 4.8 GUS – a simple MACD

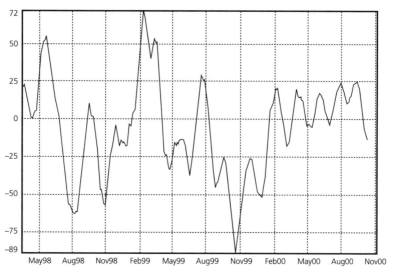

© WinStock Analyst

Wed, 11 Oct 2000
11:08 am

OBOS

There are other ways of measuring momentum using moving averages. One of the simplest and most popular is the Overbought/Oversold (OBOS) indicator. This measures the difference between the share price and a moving average.

The particular type of moving average chosen is very important in this context. Too short term an average (say 20 days or less) will produce a wildly fluctuating OBOS indicator. A much longer-term average (say 90 days or more in duration) will move so slowly that the OBOS will simply tend to resemble the moves in the underlying share price.

Surprisingly often, individual share prices will exhibit a particular character. They will move either tightly or loosely around a medium-term moving average, with the price often swinging back once a particular maximum divergence is reached.

Look at Figure 4.9, which shows the OBOS indicator for GUS, based on a 50-day moving average. As can be seen quite clearly from this chart, if the shares diverge by more than 15 points from the moving average on the upside, or about 20 points on the downside, a reversal is normally likely.

Figure 4.9   GUS – OBOS based on 50-day moving average

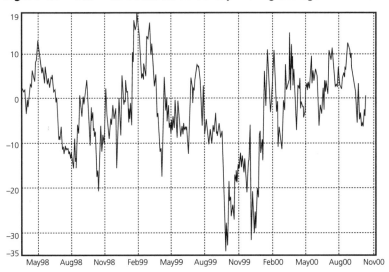

© WinStock Analyst

Wed, 11 Oct 2000
11:11 am

The reversal in the indicator need not represent a marked change in the share price. The longer the shares stay at a new lower level, the more the resulting gradual reduction in the moving average will narrow in the gap between it and the share price and so eliminate the seemingly oversold indication of this chart. Where the OBOS indicator can work well is when it is looked at in conjunction with other indicators, including the current position of the underlying share price relative to past strong support and resistance points.

Momentum and how to gauge it

As most experienced market professionals will tell you, shares develop a momentum of their own. Spotting when upward or downward momentum is flagging is a good way of spotting the potential for a reversal in the share price, especially when used in conjunction with other indicators.

Those close to the market, traders who follow the prices of a small group of shares on a minute-by-minute and hour-by-hour basis, are the most likely to be attuned to changes in a share's momentum. But the phenomenon of share price momentum can be graphed.

The best analogy of momentum is a person bouncing up and down on a trampoline. The upward bounce will be quick in the early stages, slowing down rapidly as the maximum height is reached, and then reversing quickly as gravity takes hold. Hitting the trampoline on the way down there will be a sharp drop in momentum back to zero and then an acceleration in upward momentum as the trampoline's springs do their work.

There are shares that are particularly prone to displaying these up and down movements, and there are also specialist (and expensive) software packages that can identify precisely how these cycles of momentum are formed. They then aim to profit from this knowledge by using it to fine-tune buying and selling decisions.

Momentum indicators

More common momentum indicators can be just as good as the specialist software packages, even though they may use less sophisticated mathematics. A simple momentum indicator will plot the moving change up or down in a share price over a period of days. A 21-day momentum chart, for instance, will aggregate the gains and subtract the losses seen in the share price over a 21-day period. The following day will drop the earliest change off and add in the new one. If the gain in the latest day outweighs the one made in the day now 'dropping off', the indicator will rise.

The 21-day momentum indicator for GUS is shown in Figure 4.10. It suggests that points of plus or minus 20 seem to represent the extremes, although it is hard to ascribe any long-term predictive power to this.

There are variations on the momentum theme.

Meisels indicator

This indicator – named after its originator Ron Meisels, a Canadian stock-broker – simply adds up the number of 'up' days and takes away the number of 'down' days over a specified period – ignoring the size of the change that might have occurred in the price on any day. Taking, say, a ten-day moving period, the days when there are a net six plus or six minus days are comparatively rare. Out of ten days, for instance, this could only happen if there were eight up days and two down days, or vice versa.

Figure 4.10 GUS – 21-day momentum indicator

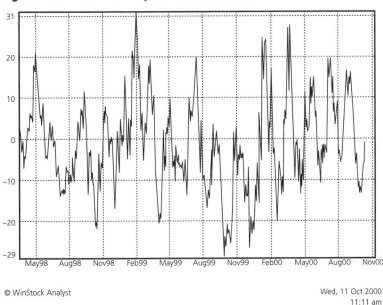

© WinStock Analyst

Wed, 11 Oct 2000
11:11 am

When used in conjunction with other indicators, and support and resistance levels, the Meisels chart hitting plus or minus six can provide a signal of a turning point.

RSI

A more sophisticated momentum variant is the Relative Strength Indicator (RSI), sometimes called the Rate of Change (ROC) chart or the Welles-Wilder Index, after its inventor.

This works on the same principle as the Meisels indicator, but aggregates the price changes over the period (normally 14 days). The index is then plotted as a percentage. If more than 70 per cent of the aggregate change is upward, this is generally considerd a sell signal. Conversely a buy signal is generated if fewer than 30 per cent of the last 14 days' changes have been up (or 70 per cent have been down). The signal is given when the indicator begins to reverse from this overbought or oversold territory.

The RSI oscillator is valued by technical analysts because, in a stock with pronounced cyclical tendencies, it tends to peak slightly ahead of the share price. No indicator works every time, but in conjunction with other measures, it can be a useful guide to timing trading decisions.

The RSI pattern for GUS is shown in Figure 4.11.

Figure 4.11 GUS – RSI pattern

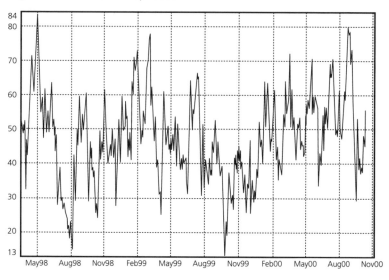

© WinStock Analyst

Wed, 11 Oct 2000
11:11 am

The 70 per cent level on the upside seems to provide an appropriately limited number of turning points and the latest one shown on the chart coincided with a short-term peak in the share price. But generally the signals have lacked precision, often signalling a change of direction a little too early.

Stochastic indicator

Another indicator that works well with share prices displaying strong cyclical tendencies is the stochastic indicator. Stochastics is a branch of statistical theory. But the idea behind it in this instance is comparatively easy to grasp. It measures the variation of a share price over time in relation to the high and low point for a particular period.

The explanation is as follows: at any one point in time a share price will be sitting somewhere in a range of prices for, say, a 14-day period. The current price may be the highest point the shares have reached in the 14-day period, or it may be in the middle of the range of prices seen, or it may be at the lowest point. The stochastic calculation simply expresses the difference between today's price and lowest point for the period as a percentage of the difference between the high and low for the same period.

Let's take an example. Say that Universal Widgets's price over the last 14 days has ranged between 200p and 250p and the current price is 240p. The stochastic for this particular price is 80 per cent. The price is 40p more than the low point for the period, 80 per cent of the range of 50p over the period.

If on the following day the price moved up to 245p and the range did not change, then the stochastic measure would be 90 per cent (45/50 times 100 per cent). From this example it can be seen that when the price is at the high point for the chosen period, the stochastic, will be 100 per cent and when it is at the low point, the stochastic will be zero. Fluctuations will be between these two limits.

Figure 4.12 illustrates a simple stochastic series for GUS for the period from July to October 2000, together with a smoothed 'trigger'. As with moving averages, combinations of smoothed values can be used to produce a trigger effect to aid decision making.

Figure 4.12 GUS – stochastic indicators

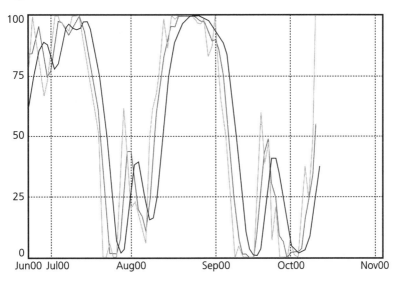

© WinStock Analyst

Wed, 11 Oct 2000
11:11 am

In the case of this example, the points where the two smoothed lines intersect at or close to zero or 100 appear to coincide almost exactly with turning points in the chart. In the four successive instances indicated on Figure 4.12, acting on the information would have provided the opportunity to sell at 460p, buy at 425p, sell at 490p and buy again at 425p over the course of three months.

As is also the case with moving averages, another valuable use of stochastics is to highlight divergence. If a share price moves up strongly but the stochastic fails to react, this may be seen as a sell signal, a sign that underlying momentum of the shares is contrary to that indicated by the share price movement.

By the same token, a share price slump not accompanied by a significant move in the stochastic could be a sign that things are changing for the better.

Charts vs fundamentals

It should be obvious from the above that there is more to charting and technical analysis than meets the eye, and that the criticism that charts are simply concerned with the arcane identification of patterns in random movements of the share price is ill-informed.

> Share prices can clearly be subjected to sophisticated statistical analysis and many traders can and do, with experience, make profitable trading decisions based on charts.

Share prices can clearly be subjected to sophisticated statistical analysis and many traders can and do, with experience, make profitable trading decisions based on charts.

My own experience as an investor is that charts have worked well for me from time to time in certain phases of the market and in particular when I have combined them with detailed fundamental analysis. Though trading solely on the basis of charts can and does work for some, a major difficulty for the private investor is finding the time to sit watching a trading screen all day in order to spot profitable opportunities as they unfold. For those who are prepared to do this, online dealing and the advent of cheap real-time price information can make this a profitable activity if followed in a disciplined way.

However, professional traders work on the tightest of margins and for the enthusiastic amateur in many cases the incidence of dealing costs and the difference between the bid and the offer price can sometimes make frequent trading of this type a rather difficult way to make money.

Nonetheless it is possible to use charts to make medium-term trading decisions, and to use computer systems to take the donkey work out of scanning the market for stocks that fit particular statistical patterns.

We will look at the merits of different share price charting packages and how to download data for them in Chapter 8.

But, assuming you have found a share to trade, the next chapter deals with how to go about selecting a broking firm through which to deal.

■ Technical analysis, the study of share price movements, is an important part of timing the purchase and sale of shares that may have been picked out through fundamental analysis.

■ Human psychology and conditioned reflexes play a part in the workings of technical analysis. These are often manifest in 'support' and 'resistance' levels at particular points in share price charts.

■ Shares often move up and down in powerful trend channels. A break-out from a trend channel is considered a significant event, heralding a change in direction.

■ There are many different types of price chart, often displaying subtly different variations of a basic pattern.

■ Moving averages are a way of eliminating random short-term fluctuations from a price chart. The intersection of moving averages of differing lengths can be a significant indicator of changes in direction.

■ Momentum, the difference in speed with which a share is moving in a particular direction, is also used to time share purchases and sales.

■ Using charts to time purchases and sales can be a frustrating business. It is particularly important not to use a single indicator as the guide, but to have it confirmed by several others.

■ Using charts actively can induce over-trading. It is important to take into account dealing costs when working out the likely benefit of acting on a particular chart signal.

chapter five

The mechanics of dealing

For those who have never done it before, the process of dealing can seem part of the mystique of the stock market. Phoning up your broker or logging into an online dealing system, giving the order to buy or sell your shares – what could be more exciting?

Nothing could be further from the truth.

The exciting part of investment is picking the right share, watching it rise, and selecting the right time to sell. The intricacies of how the deals are accomplished are mildly interesting but, once set up, are simply part of a routine that every investor becomes used to.

In short, it's what you buy (and sell) and when that's important.

The best way of looking at dealing is to use an analogy with retailing. There are many different types of shop. There are specialist boutiques, large expensive department stores, cut-price supermarkets, and many variations in between. And, of course, you can always buy online.

There are shops where you are encouraged to seek advice and where the assistants are helpful and attentive – but where the merchandise is usually more expensive – and those where you might go because you know exactly what you want and a keen price is what you are looking for. You might buy through an online store because of the convenience it offers.

One of the factors that has traditionally put many people off the investment scene is the idea that share dealing is somehow the preserve of the rich, not something that 'ordinary' people can indulge in.

The City bears its share of the blame for this. Certainly it was once the case that City brokers did not want to take on clients who were anything other than seriously wealthy. The idea of blue-blooded brokers having to deal with the man in the street with his inconveniently small lots of shares was anathema.

But times change. The opening up of the City to external competition, and the mass privatizations of the 1980s, and more recently the advent of cheap online dealing services, have brought many people into the share-owning arena for the first time, each with their own modest requirements for buying and selling shares.

The result has been some demystification of the City and its intricacies, and a lessening of the feelings of apprehension that many would-be investors used to experience when contemplating buying and selling shares. In the last year or so the growth of the day-trading phenomenon has, if nothing else, brought with it a real sense that share dealing has been democratized. Now you don't have to be rich to be able to make or lose money trading shares.

In addition, the advent of the Financial Services Act in 1986 has meant that brokers were more tightly regulated. This does not stop share investments falling in value, of course. But it does mean that the investor is unlikely to be the victim of fraud or to lose money because his broker goes out of business. The client's relationship with the broker is enshrined in a legal agreement which defines the rights and obligations of each party.

What this means is that the other more important aspects of choosing a broker – the level of service you feel you require; whether or not there are any specialist areas in which you might like to deal; settlement arrangements; whether or not you need advice – can rightly come uppermost in the decision-making process.

Let's therefore have a look at some of the issues involved in deciding between different types of broker, and some of the questions that need to be asked and answered.

An honest broker ...

If you read any nineteenth century novel, whether written by Dickens, Trollope or some other author, a stockbroker is usually depicted as someone untrustworthy, devious, and even dishonest.

This gave way, typically in the 'Roaring Twenties', to an image of stockbrokers as tough and ruthless manipulators of markets, who sucked small investors into stocks at ever higher prices and then exited themselves just before the bubble burst. More recently, in the 1950s and 1960s stockbroking became the epitome of suburban respectability, even to the point where lush suburban areas became known as the 'stockbroker belt'.

More recently still, the image is of high-powered dealers paid 'telephone number' salaries and bonuses, and winning and losing millions (or even billions) – aided by sophisticated computer programs – as an increasingly volatile market moves up and down on a whim. Indeed for online traders, the only interaction is with a computer screen that gives the dealing price and a limited time to decide whether or not to accept it.

While all of these images contain some elements of fact, none is the whole story. There is no point denying that insider traders do exist now as in the past, that some stockbrokers even now have a less savoury reputation than others, and that – as the example of Nick Leeson demonstrated – for the high-fliers it can (and occasionally does) all go horribly wrong.

But just as there are accountants and solicitors whose work is less than satisfactory, and those who operate on the fringes of the law, they do not represent the vast majority of their professions. It is the same with stockbrokers. The vast majority of brokers, and perhaps especially those looking after private clients, are normal professional people dedicated to doing the best for their clients.

This is not to say that there have been no changes in the way the City has operated over the years. The advent of a greater degree of competition combined with the abandonment of the right to have fixed commissions in the mid-1980s, has led to a shake-out in the services provided by different broking firms. The end result has been specialization by City houses. The broad division is along the lines of the clients they serve. Many broking firms, especially the larger ones, have opted only to service clients at the investing institutions and big companies.

The institutional investment and corporate finance business has often been combined with market-making and activities known as proprietary trading (where the firm risks its own capital trading in the markets).

Not only does structuring a firm like this involve high risks and high rewards, but overheads are also high because the firm concerned requires the services of many hundreds of highly paid professional staff and heavy investment in telecommunications, computer systems and other equipment.

At the other end of the scale is a large number of smaller firms, often based in the regions, sometimes with several branches, but with an office in London. These firms have typically chosen to specialize in dealing with private clients almost to the exclusion of other types of business.

Because firms of this nature normally fulfil a straightforward function i.e. to act as their client's agent, they do not suffer the conflicts of interest that bedevil the larger integrated securities houses (sometimes called investment banks). For many of the latter firms, a private client business is either absent, or viewed rather as an afterthought and certainly not integral to their business.

Private client brokers are not without their power in the market. Many have substantial numbers of clients and the collective funds of all these individuals can run into billions. Some private client brokers have also built niche corporate finance businesses specializing in providing advice for the smaller companies that are also viewed by the big boys as too insignificant to bother with.

But the revolution in the City in the past few years has brought other changes, including the creation of wholly new firms to service the private client market. These firms specialize in offering a highly efficient no-frills service and are often based in low-cost, out-of-town locations, maintaining efficient links to the market but able to offer discounted commission rates.

The growth of firms of this type has been facilitated by the fact that since the market 'went electronic' in 1986, there has been no need for brokers to be physically located in the City of London in order to be able to transact business.

Last of all, the past two or three years has seen huge growth in the number of brokers offering online dealing services, using the internet to link their clients to market-maker systems, and thereby allowing clients to input orders and deal without any manual intervention. The advantage of services like this is price: commission rates at the time of writing are as little as £10 per trade irrespective of size.

Services like this have also grown up that offer the ability to trade in both the UK and certain overseas markets (the USA, France, Germany etc.) from the same account. The advent of web-based information sources means that it is as easy for an investor to get information on Microsoft as Marks & Spencer, and in turn almost as easy to make a decision to buy or sell the shares. You may prefer only to deal in UK shares, but the point is that if you want to spread your wings and deal in other markets, the mechanics are now comparatively easy.

As well as the different types of broking firm – large integrated houses not much interested in private clients, private client specialists, and the large-scale no-frills dealing services – there are also a variety of different services open to the individual wanting to deal in shares.

... but which service to choose?

In the past broking services started from two assumptions. They are based on views that are still common, but now a little outdated. The assumptions are that:

■ the broker is likely to know better than the client which shares are likely to go up and down
■ everyone is likely to benefit if private client funds are managed collectively.

The belief behind both of these views is that the private individual is not really interested in the machinations of the stock market and would much rather delegate the job to a professional. This view is now patently outmoded.

Outdated or not, it gave rise to the idea that the ideal and most economic structure for a private client broking firm is to have a relatively modest number of extremely wealthy clients (at the very least in the millionaire category) and for the broker to have absolute discretion as to how their funds are managed. This broker would probably only take on new clients by personal recommendation.

At the other end of the scale the newest category of broker is one who offers no advice, and is indeed precluded by regulatory statute from doing so, and simply transacts the deals as instructed by the client in the most efficient manner and as cheaply as possible. This broker will deal for anybody. These no-frills services have extended quite naturally into online dealing services, which in turn have been facilitated by changes in the settlement regime which have made administering a broking account much easier.

These represent the two extremes. In fact there is a range of permutations of style of service in between them. Table 5.1 lists the range on offer.

Table 5.1   Broker services – what they offer

Type	Advice	Dealing	Remuneration
Discretionary	After the event	At broker's discretion	Fee
Portfolio advice	Comprehensive	At client's discretion	Fee + Commission
Dealing advice	Investment only	At client's discretion	Commission
Execution-only	No	At client's discretion	Commission
Online	No	At client's discretion	Commission

Wholly discretionary

The wholly discretionary service means that the broker makes all the decisions for the client, acting on his or her behalf and only informing the client after the event. This has some advantages. The broker may be able to act quickly to take advantage of market opportunities and perhaps apply for exciting new issues on behalf of a group of clients, issues that an individual might ordinarily be precluded from investing in directly.

For many investors the idea of surrendering total control is rather unnerving, and it is a moot point whether or not the performance of some brokers is any better than the investor might be able to achieve on his or her own with a little bit of effort.

One plus point for discretionary services of this type is that the broker is typically remunerated on the basis of an annual fee related to the total value of the portfolio. If the shares the broker selects do well, then his fee will rise. This provides a worthwhile incentive to get things right for the client and to a degree counters the concern that the account will be needlessly 'churned'.

Portfolio advice

Here the broker is made aware of all aspects of the client's personal financial circumstances. Investment objectives will be set jointly and periodically reviewed. The broker may then be given limited discretion, or may offer advice to the client on how best to meet these objectives. In particular there may be guidance on how best to invest in order to minimise any tax liabilities the client may have.

The charges for this type of service are normally a mixture of a fixed fee plus dealing commission, with supplementary charges sometimes made for services such as valuations and the preparation of tax statements for the Inland Revenue.

Dealing advice

This is the stockbroking service that many experienced investors will be familiar with. Here the broker earns most of his remuneration via dealing commission but will periodically inform the client when he has a particularly interesting investment idea, or a recommendation on a particular share.

Commission will be charged at a standard rate and the client will have a designated contact at that particular broker with whom he can build up a relationship and who may be contacted from time to time for advice.

The point about this arrangement is that the relationship must be a two-way one. The client will wish to feel that he or she is getting a good service from the broker. And equally the broker will need to feel that the client is not wasting time and that orders result periodically from the service he gives. More frequent dealing on behalf of the client may be rewarded by the client getting a more thorough service from the broker, with the broker initiating calls disseminating information.

Basic research may be offered as part of the package. But the service will not as a matter of routine include any aspect of personal financial advice or tax minimization. These services can be offered, but would be the subject of extra charges.

Execution-only

The wholly new aspect to broking services introduced since the deregulation of the City in the mid-1980s is the idea of an execution-only broker.

Here the client is offered simply a dealing service with no information or advice other than the quotation of a dealing price. On occasion research may be offered on a cash or subscription basis, but the rationale of the execution-only broker is that the absence of any advice means that dealing charges can be kept to a minimum.

This type of service has proved very popular indeed with experienced investors who by and large pick their own shares, do their own research, and are prepared to accept the consequences of making their own decisions. They have also been extensively used by investors who have acquired small parcels of shares, perhaps as a result of privatization issues and simply need a broker occasionally when the time comes to sell a particular investment.

There are many brokers and share dealing operations advertising execution-only services, but not all of them offer truly discounted commissions. The choice is such that, if this is the route you choose to go, there is everything to be gained from shopping around and choosing the broker that offers the best combination of services at a price you are prepared to pay.

Online services

Online dealing services have grown from execution-only services but it is worth bearing in mind that, convenient though they are, they do differ, in terms the commission they charge, the efficiency of their systems and the way in which orders are transmitted.

Some big online brokers have suffered, at times of high levels of market activity, from being so swamped with orders that computer systems have been unable to cope. A smaller firm may offer just as good a service without these problems of size.

Some firms offer additional subscription based services to clients, but with the volume of information available for free on the web, the added value of some of these offerings is questionable. Some firms link your dealing to an existing bank account: others use a separate money market account. Some firms will allow you to deal in certificated form: others will not. And so on.

Every broker's charging structure is different, but a rough guide would be as follows. A wholly discretionary service might be charged out on the basis of an annual 3 per cent fee related to portfolio value. A middling dealing with advice service might bear commission at 1.5 per cent of the amount of money involved in a particular transaction. An execution-only broking service would charge a flat rate commission on all transactions falling within a certain band, resulting in a commission charge of 0.7 per cent or sometimes a bit less. Some execution-only brokers operate low rates for frequent dealers and have an extra low rate for a closing transaction (i.e. a sale following an earlier purchase) completed within a certain length of time.

Commission rates charged by online brokers vary considerably: some brokers operate complex tariffs with a combination of a minium commission level and a sliding percentage scale of charges, while the more enlightened simply offer a flat fee per trade irrespective of size. Some charge as little as £10 per deal. Most brokers have an account administration fee on top, which typically amounts to about £50 a year. Table 5.2 shows details of the services and charges of leading online brokers.

Table 5.2 Online brokers and their charges

Name	URL	Annual charge	Basic commission rate
Abbey National	www.sharedealing.abbeynational.co.uk	0	£16
Barclays	www.barclays-stockbrokers.co.uk	0	1%
James Brearley	www.jbrearley.co.uk	£25	£20
Cave and Sons	www.caves.co.uk	0	1.50%
Charles Schwab (Europe)	www.schwab-worldwide.com	£20–120	0.90%
Comdirect	www.comdirect.co.uk	£25	£12.50
DLJ Direct	www.dljdirect.co.uk	0	0.75%
Egg Invest	www.egg.com	£60	£9.99
E*Trade	www.etrade.co.uk	£50	£14.95
Fastrade	www.fastrade.co.uk	£20	0.50%
Goy Harris Cartwright	www.ghcl.co.uk	£35	£20
Halifax Sharedealing Ltd	www.halifax.co.uk	0	£12.50
Hargreaves Lansdown	www.h-l.co.uk	£50	£9.95
iDealing	www.idealing.co.uk	£20	£10
Killik	www.killik.co.uk	0	1.25%
myBroker	www.mybroker.co.uk	0	£25
Natwest Stockbrokers Ltd	www.natweststockbrokers.co.uk	0	1%
Nothing Ventured	www.nothing-ventured.com	£50	0.80%
REDM	www.redmayne.co.uk	£60	0.50%
Selftrade	www.selftrade.co.uk	0	£12.50
Sharecentre	www.share.co.uk	£5	1%
Sharepeople	www.sharepeople.com	£50	£17.50
Stocktrade	www.stocktrade.co.uk	0	0.40%
Stock Academy	www.stockacademy.co.uk	£40	£15
TD Waterhouse	www.tdwaterhouse	0	1%
Virgin	www.virginmoney.com	0	£14.95
Xest	www.xest.com	£45	£14.99

The 'job spec' for your broker

The advent of much stricter regulatory controls on brokers, as well as the comprehensive training and examination regime that now exists for City personnel at all levels, means that while many people once chose brokers solely on the basis of personal friendship or word-of-mouth recommendations from trusted friends, this no longer applies.

Many brokers still do get new clients in this way. But, provided some elementary precautions are taken, it is perfectly possible to choose a broker dispassionately and to pick one whose services are precisely right for you. Indeed there are strong arguments in favour of not choosing a broker because of a personal relationship or as a result of the recommendation of a close friend. If things subsequently go wrong, personal animosity may be the result.

How does the individual investor, who may not have dealt in shares before, go about choosing a broker? You can of course simply log onto an online broker's site and start from there. But if you prefer not to deal online, a good starting point is a list of private client brokers produced by APCIMS. APCIMS (tel: 0207 247 7000) is the Association of Private Client Investment Managers. The list gives details of individual broking firms including phone numbers, addresses and brief descriptions of the type of service offered.

From this list some initial selections can be made simply by answering for yourself a couple of elementary questions.

The questions to ask, assuming you don't want to use an online dealing service, are as follows:

Question 1. Should I choose a small firm or a large one? The answer to this is not straightforward. Large firms will normally have more robust finances and perhaps be better equipped to deal with all aspects of the service you may require. On the other hand, a smaller firm is better able to offer an individually tailored and more attentive service. Also, do bear in mind that your bank may also operate a dealing service for customers. On the whole, these can be expensive although HSBC's Teletrade service is, in my experience, the exception that proves the rule.

Question 2. Should I choose a local firm or a London-based one? This question really applies to investors who live outside London. My own preference here would be to go for the local broker, provided you are satisfied that it can offer an equivalent range of services to a London-based broker, including the full range of dealing services and facilities to trade in a variety of different securities, not just straightforward equity shares. Many do.

Local firms have the advantage of being on the spot, so that any problems can be sorted out with a visit to the firm's office. They may also have a particular niche in researching the affairs of local companies, and have better information on these companies than some larger firms. Because of the electronic nature of the market, having access to the full range of prices and information on the wider market and its constituents does not present a problem for a regional broker.

The next step is to whittle down the likely list to a handful that are hard to separate on most other criteria.

The way to do this is by specifying the types of services you would expect each firm on your 'shortlist' to be able to provide.

The following factors are particularly important (and the reasons are pretty obvious). If you have not decided in advance to go the execution-only route, the firm you choose should be able to offer these services:

■ a full range of dealing services, including discretionary, portfolio advice, normal dealing with advice, and execution-only (both online and off-line)

■ commission rates competitive with the best in the market

■ a dealing service in traded options

■ a dealing service in overseas stocks

■ a dealing service in fixed-interest stocks and convertibles

■ an efficient nominee service or CREST individual membership

■ approachable staff with a good telephone manner

■ the ability to transact orders in the course of a single telephone call

■ the ability to provide portfolio valuations if requested

■ the ability to provide managed or self-select ISAs on competitive terms if required.

This 'job spec' for your broker raises a number of points that can be dealt with in turn.

Working out what you need

In the first place it is important to have the opportunity to switch from one type of service to another without the inconvenience of having to change broker to do so. It may be, for instance, that an individual begins as a 'dealing with advice' client of a broker and then, gaining confidence in the market, progresses to greater independence with a lower cost 'execution-only' service.

It goes without saying that commission rates should be competitive, though it is perhaps not always necessary to choose the broker offering the lowest commission rates.

When it comes to share dealing, as in most other aspects of life, you do get what you pay for. But equally it is important to weed out those firms offering an unreasonably expensive service. Some of these firms may pitch their commission charges high simply to discourage relatively small-scale investors, and it is as well to be alert to this.

Dealing service in areas other than straight UK equities should ideally be part of the service. Buying gilts is normally fairly straightforward with most brokers, but it is certainly possible that at some stage the investor may also want to deal in traded options (these will be discussed in brief in Chapter 7), and the ability to do this without being forced to change brokers is important.

It is vital, for some types of option transaction for example, for the broker to be the same one through whom one would deal in the ordinary shares of the same company. Not all brokers deal in options, so this is an important point to check.

Similarly the investor may want the flexibility of being able to deal in other markets if need be. These might include, for example, buying American stocks, or French shares. A broker should be able to offer a service that enables this to be done with the minimum of fuss, with details like safe custody, registration and currency all taken care of. Some online brokers are now starting to offer this.

The ability to deal in non-equity share investments is offered by most UK brokers. There may be times, for instance, when the client needs to buy fixed-interest investments such as government stock, corporate bonds, or convertible bonds.

Essential features of a broker nominee

Next on the list is that the broker should be able to offer an efficient nominee service. This is a mechanism by which the investor buys a particular share, but the purchase is registered in an account in the name of the broker's nominee company. This enables the broker to handle the administration of the stock concerned with much greater ease. CREST individual membership, available for a few pounds a year, operates in much the same way, and is administered by the broker on the client's behalf (with the important difference that, unlike many nominee set-ups, your name is preserved on the register, meaning that a company you invest in will be able to communicate with you directly, sending out annual reports and other information).

Though some investors still prefer to keep paper certificates, as settlement times shrink the luxury of transfers being sent back and forth in the postal system is less feasible and may require specially extended settlement times to allow for possible delays. These will cost the client more. In short, opt for electronic settlement and the system will be speedier and cheaper. The efficiency of brokers' nominee accounts does vary, however, but investors need feel no warier of having their stock in this 'dematerialized' form than they would having their money in a bank.

Charges related to nominee accounts are likely to be linked to the number of stocks being looked after, but should not be more than say £10 stock per year.

Nominee arrangements or CREST individual membership are now the norm in the City, particularly so since the advent of electronic settlement. Non-nominee arrangements are the exception rather than the rule and settlement through these non-standard channels costs more. This is likely to be even more the case with the coming of so-called T+3 (settlement on the third business day following the trade) electronic settlement in 2001.

Though the efficiency of a nominee service is hard to gauge until it has been used for a while, an efficient nominee should work invisibly, with the client feeling he is still the shareholder and is in control of the nominee account, which the broker is administering on his behalf, rather than the other way round.

To sum up, the essential features of a broker nominee are as follows:

- The nominee account can be linked to a high interest bank account.
- Surplus cash earns interest.
- That the account is designated in the client's name and not 'pooled'.
- The investor receives normal company documentation (i.e. annual reports) promptly.
- The investor can attend company AGMs without additional charges being levied.
- The option exists to switch to CREST individual membership.
- The nominee account activity is conducted for a nominal fee.
- Details required for tax returns are provided promptly.

An important test of a good broker is that their staff are approachable without being overly familiar, and that they are efficient, courteous and professional, putting the client at ease when he or she calls up, offering the appropriate level of advice unobtrusively, and dealing efficiently.

Dealing services also vary enormously in speed and efficiency. While it is acceptable to have to hang on to get through to a busy dealing desk at peak times in the market, an inability to get hold of a dealer at any time is inexcusable. In most cases the dealer should be able to transact the deal while the client is holding on. This is especially true of execution-only brokers, many of which use automated computerized order-entry systems connected to major market-makers. In other cases, the broker should undertake to transact the order and report back by telephone within a matter of minutes if the client requests it.

Some brokers operate through a system of telephone order-takers who then collate orders and transfer them to the dealing desk some time later to be executed. The client does not get an immediate report back, and only discovers the dealing price when the contract note arrives in the post the following day. While many individuals accept service of this type as a fact of life, it is not necessary to settle for this, and the ability to report back that a deal has been done in a timely fashion should be perfectly compatible with, and indeed a particular feature of, execution-only broking services.

Online services, as noted previously, vary in the way they work, a few still operating by (in effect) the client e-mailing orders to dealers, or at least doing so for certain smaller stocks. But most are now standardized on automated execution, giving the client a firm dealing price when the order is input and a few seconds during which the client must confirm that this is acceptable. If the order is confirmed, the deal takes place instantly.

Clients sometimes want to know what they are worth and should also be able to order standard portfolio valuations if required. These days, however, it is easy enough to keep track of a portfolio of shares using a computer spreadsheet and a copy of the *Financial Times*, or else by using one of the web-based portfolio tracking services (see Chapter 9). A statement of tax credits on dividends on shares held during a tax year should be provided by the broker as a matter of course. You will require this to be able to complete your tax return. Small charges may be made for such services.

Lastly, the broker should be in a position to offer the client the facility to invest in as tax-efficient a manner as possible. In particular, most brokers offer the facility for the client to own shares through either a managed or self-select ISA run by the broker. Most brokers offer services of this type, but it is again as well to check that the charges made – which can vary considerably – are competitive.

How to choose

The whole premise of this book is that it is perfectly possible for an individual to make his or her own decisions about investing on the basis of publicly available information and without excessive spending. In addition, it is worth bearing in mind that most private client brokers will only offer the discretionary and portfolio advice style of service to individuals with substantial sums to invest. In this context the word 'substantial' means a minimum of £100,000, and in some instances probably rather more than this.

What this means is that, to all intents and purposes, for the individual with, let's say, £10,000 or less to put into the market, the choice comes down to the dealing with advice or the straight 'execution-only' service, either in its online or off-line versions. My own preference is for the execution-only type of service in virtually all respects.

> It is perfectly possible for an individual to make his or her own decisions about investing on the basis of publicly available information and without excessive spending.

However, it is perfectly normal for the first-timer to want to have some initial guidance in how to deal and on the ins and outs of the market. It is possible to some degree to get this from an execution-only trader, who may be able to help with factual questions. An execution-only broker is, however, precluded by City regulations from offering any sort of advice. So do not ask an execution-only dealer for views on where the market is heading, or what he thinks about a particular company. He will not be allowed to help.

But, for most investors of an independent turn of mind (and an independent turn of mind is a prerequisite for being a successful investor), execution-only dealing fits the bill perfectly.

There is one exception to this. This concerns dealing in traded options.

We will cover this aspect of the stock market in a little more detail later in this book. But at this stage let's just say that the newcomer to the options market will benefit from having a measure of advice for the first few trades, before switching to an execution-only service at a later date.

Paradoxically, option trading is one area of the market where doing one's own research is essential, but some preliminary hand-holding may be necessary. Even with a good idea, many investors buy the wrong type of option, lose money and are put off trading options for life because of it.

In the end, the reason for choosing one particular broking firm over another will be an entirely personal one.

The best way to go about it is to contact several either by letter or telephone (or e-mail) and request further information. Most brokers have a brochure which they will send out to prospective clients. Compare them (or in the case of online dealing services, their websites) carefully, noting any additional charges hidden in the small print.

Consulting the pages of the *Financial Times* or the *Investors' Chronicle* should yield a satisfactory number of names and phone numbers. A standard letter sent to each one is probably the best approach and minimizes the feelings of apprehension that someone new to the market may feel about telephoning a broker 'cold'.

My preference would be to ask for a face-to-face meeting before signing up. It is always good to get a visual feel for the nature of a particular operation: how friendly the staff are, how efficient and functional the offices (you do not want your commissions paying for unduly lavish offices), and how efficient the broker's systems are. Having said that, for some online brokers, this may not be particularly practical, or indeed enlightening.

Many brokers include a questionnaire with their brochure which will help the potential client decide what type of service he or she requires and help the broker to decide what type of service it will be economical to provide. It is important that you are not persuaded by the broker into signing up for a level of service with which you are not happy.

Once the final shortlist has been whittled down to one, and this fact communicated to the broker in question, the normal next step is to fill in a client agreement form.

This establishes client records for the broker, and will include such details as your address, telephone number, bank details, and so on. It also represents a legal agreement between the broker and client, establishing the rights and obligations of both sides. The client agreement is required under City regulations and is designed to safeguard the interests of the client by establishing the ground rules of the relationship at the outset.

Among other things it assures the broker that he will be paid for stock purchased by the investor, and vice versa. It will also be used to set up such details as a nominee account and, if necessary, a bank account linked to the dealing account.

Once this form is completed and the paperwork has been processed, the client will be informed in writing and given an account number. If the account is an execution-only one, there will be no designated contact but the client will be given a number, often a toll-free one, to call when he wishes to place an order.

The really important point about all this is that the process of dealing should not get in the way of investment decision making. The investor must be comfortable with and confident that the broker will execute the deals promptly and efficiently.

Calling your broker should become a routine matter that can be done with confidence. Making the right investment decision is the important part of the process. The physical act of dealing should be no more complicated than ringing a theatre box office or an airline to book some tickets.

How to deal ... and what happens afterwards

Dealing in shares is essentially simple, whether online or not. What follows is an approximation of what should happen.

Ring up the broker, give your account number to identify yourself, say you want to place an order. The dealer will ask what you want to do.

Let's say you want to buy 1,000 shares in Universal Widgets.

Enquire what the price is in Universal Widgets. The dealer will check the price on his market price display screen. Say you know that the price is around 200p. The dealer will check the price and give two figures. The lower price is known as the bid price and is the price at which you would be able to sell: the upper, or offer, price is the price at which you can buy.

The difference between the two is the spread, representing the 'turn' the market-maker keeps for making a continuous market in the shares. The dealer comes back on the line and says '198–202'.

You ask the dealer to buy 1,000 shares.

In an online dealing service you would log into the site using your user ID and password and call up the price normally by inputting the appropriate three or four letter 'ticker code' or the company name. The price quote will be as above. Fill in the on-screen dealing ticket.

The dealer will ask if you want to place a limit on the price at which you want to deal, in case the price has moved in the few seconds that have elapsed since the price was checked. Placing limits is not, in my view, a particularly good idea unless the share price is gyrating wildly. You have made the decision to buy and your objective is to buy the shares in the market at the best price available at that time. Wanting to set a dealing limit may be a sign that you are less than wholly convinced that the decision is the right one.

You can simply say 'buy (or sell) at best' – or in the case of an online service, enter your PIN number and hit 'confirm' – and the broker (or automated online service) will execute the order for you there and then. In the case of a conventional broker, you can either hold on while the order is done, or ask that the dealer rings you back with a report on the price at which he has dealt. Before transacting the order the dealer should always read it back to you for confirmation. 'Buy 1,000 Universal Widgets at best'. The report will simply come back: 'Bought 1,000 Universal Widgets at 202p'.

What should happen next is that in the following morning's post (or by e-mail) you will receive a contract note stating the time of the deal, the number of shares involved, the price, commission and any other charges, and the net cost to you of a 'buy' order, or the proceeds of a 'sell' order.

Assuming that your broking account is linked to a bank account, your account will simply be debited with the amount stated five business days (or three when T+3 settlement comes in) from the date of the deal. Sale proceeds will be credited in the same way. A few online brokers credit or debit the account quicker than this. The broker, assuming you have an account with the nominee, will send statements of your nominee account holdings from time to time. All that remains to be done after that is to keep track of the price via teletext, the web or a newpaper every day to see how your shares are doing. Table 5.3 shows a step-by-step summary of placing an order.

Table 5.3   Placing an order – a step-by-step summary

	'Voice' broker	*Online broker*
Step 1	Telephone broker	Log in to secure website
Step 2	Ask dealer for price	Check price online
Step 3	Place order with dealer	Fill in online dealing 'ticket'
Step 4	Confirm order with dealer	Press confirm button, enter PIN
Step 5	Wait for report	Deal details confirmed
Step 6	Contract note by post	Contract note by e-mail
Step 7	Account debited/credited	Account debited\credited

The advent of paperless settlement through the CREST system has meant that it has become more important for private clients to have nominee arrangements with their brokers. Contract notes will still be issued and these, together with the periodic statements of holdings that are issued to clients as part of the CREST system, represent all the proof the client needs to demonstrate that electronic records are correct. Share certificates will eventually become a thing of the past.

When share settlement on trade date plus three days (T+3) arrives, alternative arrangements will continue to be made available for those who wish to settle on different terms and who wish to remain outside the paperless system, but those options are likely to be relatively costly.

Although many private clients, especially the more elderly, are not keen on nominee arrangements or the idea of 'paperless' settlement, the system will prevail and those new to the investment game are unlikely to give it a second thought.

So far we have looked at how the market works, what personal skills and physical tools the investor needs to be able to make investment decisions, and how to appraise shares using both fundamental analysis and share price charts. We have also, in this chapter, looked at how to choose a broker and the mechanics of buying and selling shares, and at how these deals are settled.

It is time now to look at how to build up a sensible portfolio of shares and measure its performance. This is covered in the next chapter.

I N   B R I E F

■ The mechanics of dealing are mundane and should be put in perspective. The important aspect of investment is how you select a share and how long you keep it, rather than how you buy and sell.

■ There are several different types of broking service. The more the broker holds your hand, the more he will charge. If you are connected to the web, online dealing is cheap and convenient.

■ The premise behind this book is that the reader will be capable of making his or her own investment decisions and therefore can opt for a low-cost, execution-only service – either online or off-line.

■ Charges vary and it is worthwhile shopping around. Beware of hidden extras.

■ It is essential that investors pick a broker that has a well-organized, properly protected nominee service, or one that offers CREST membership. This simplifies the administration of share transactions considerably.

■ Choose your broking firm carefully, if necessary through a personal visit.

chapter six

Portfolio building blocks

made the point earlier that the amount the average investor should have available to invest in the stock market is governed by the need to have a spread of investments to limit risk.

Good investment is not simply about picking shares at random and hoping for the best, but having a strategy that suits you, that plays to your strengths and that conforms to the sort of risk levels appropriate to your financial situation and that you feel comfortable with. Risk can be tailored in a number of ways, not only in your choice of different shares, but in the types and size of companies in which you invest, and by investing in other types of security.

In this chapter we are going to look at the reasons why this is important, and how to go about building up the right mixture of shares and other investments.

Although ordinary shares may seem the most important and eye-catching component of the investments you may have, they are likely to be only a part of your overall assets.

> Good investment is not simply about picking shares at random and hoping for the best, but having a strategy that suits you, that plays to your strengths and that conforms to the sort of risk levels appropriate to your financial situation and that you feel comfortable with.

For instance, just as we might look at a company and examine whether it has liquid assets or not, or how much borrowing it has relative to its assets, so the individual investor needs to construct a personal balance sheet to determine what type of investment strategy is most appropriate.

Your personal balance sheet

Let's take a couple of examples to make this clearer.

Fictional Investor Number One

Like our earlier example of Graham Average he might, say, be a 50-year-old married professional person. Perhaps he works as a self-employed consultant. His children are grown up and no longer a drain on his income.

He lives in a house that is worth £250,000 on which, because it was bought many years previously, the mortgage is only £50,000. He recently inherited a property worth £75,000 (currently rented out). From the sale of his stake in an earlier business venture he has capital of £50,000. His income from consulting and his wife's earnings comfortably cover all his outgoings. He is contributing to a personal pension. This is invested in a unit-linked vehicle and has a value of £200,000.

What investment strategy should this person pursue? To determine the right course of action we need to work out what net assets he has already.

These can be listed as follows:

- equity in the main property of £200,000
- equity in the inherited property of £75,000
- free capital of £50,000
- £200,000 invested in a pension fund
- last but not least, no immediate requirement for investment income.

What do these figures tell us? One fact is that the free capital that might be available for share investment represents quite a small proportion of the overall total. This individual's total assets are in excess of £500,000, but only £50,000 of that is actually available in cash.

Another important fact is that the pension scheme assets are likely to be conservatively invested. Though individual circumstances differ, there is by and large a duty on pension fund managers to invest conservatively. In addition, as a self-employed individual, our investor may feel that investing surplus cash in extra pension contributions is the most tax-efficient way of investing.

The proportion of any individual's assets invested in a pension fund also matters in another way. It is likely that the pension portion of the assets will be invested in a mixture of leading blue chips on the one hand, and government stock or safe fixed-interest investments on the other. What this means is that it is possible to take the view that the investments one makes oneself can in consequence be somewhat more adventurous.

In this instance, we could question whether or not keeping the inherited property is a sound investment decision. It may be being rented out to give an overall return of say 8 per cent, but the individual needs to be conscious that in an era of low inflation its value may not rise and its total return may therefore be inferior to other forms of investment. So whether or not to keep this property is an investment decision in itself.

The conclusion from this brief resume is that this individual could profitably invest in smaller growth companies and other more speculative investments. The stable, though arguably unexciting, return from property and the fact that the pension fund assets are also invested conservatively, combined with the absence of any requirement for income, leads to this decision.

Fictional Investor Number Two

Like our earlier example of Aunt Agatha, she is a widow who has a modest pension, just enough to live on, but somewhat less than she was accustomed to before her husband died. Let's look at her assets:

- The pension brings in an income of £500 per month.
- She owns her own home, a modest house worth £100,000.
- Her husband's life assurance brought her a capital sum of £200,000.
- There is an obvious requirement for investment income.

It can be seen quite clearly here that the circumstances are entirely different. It is important to this investor that capital is preserved, but also that it generates income, whereas our self-employed professional has plenty of income and assets already locked away in conservative investments.

So, given the relatively low return from property, it would be sensible for this individual perhaps to move to a smaller property, and release some capital for further investment. Her investment decisions may also be influenced by whether or not the pension is likely to rise with inflation. If not, some route must be found to produce an inflation-proofed investment income while attempting to preserve capital.

These examples also highlight that no single investment philosophy can suit all investors. While one investor may decide that a patient value-orientated long-term approach is best, or may want to invest in growth stocks, as investors get older their requirements change. Investing long term is little use to a person in his or her 70s and 80s, and equally, investing in low-yielding growth stocks is unlikely to make a lot of sense for someone who needs investment income to live on.

Beware of market gurus who seek to suggest their patented 'one size fits all' approach is the only way to go. There are plenty of investment styles to choose from: choose one that suits you best and is right for your own financial circumstances and appetite for risk.

Risk

Periodic gyrations in the market, the recent boom and subsequent bust in small internet companies being a case in point, only serve to illustrate how risky the stock market can be.

Defining risk can be difficult. What is risky to one person may not be to another. From an objective standpoint, and in the opinion of many market observers, risk equates to volatility. In other words the more the price of an investment swings around within a given period, the greater the probability that you might end up losing money at the end of it.

The ideal for many investors – and incidentally the rationale for investment vehicles such as hedge funds – is to generate the maximum amount of return from and investment for the minimum amount of risk.

This is easier said than done. But what all investors have to come to terms with is that there is a link between the return that an investment generates and the risk involved. The higher the return offered or perceived, the higher the likelihood of some loss of capital. As the disclaimers on most forms of investment say: 'the value can go down as well as up'.

There is also a link between liquidity and return. Liquidity is the ease with which an investment can be turned into cash without penalty. The best illustration of this is the difference between the interest earned in a so-called high interest bank cheque account, and that earned on, say, a building society deposit that requires three months' notice. When I last checked, for example, the former offered annual gross interest of 1.7 per cent and the latter 6.5 per cent. The difference represents the price of instant liquidity.

Also, remember that many investments, such as property, are relatively illiquid. They may offer a seemingly high return but they have to be sold through a cumbersome and time-consuming process. Or if you want to sell quickly to a cash buyer, you may have to accept a lower price. Neither can property be part-sold. Either you sell all the property, or you don't sell. No way has yet been found to sell half and keep half, as share investors sometimes do to lock in part of a gain.

Lack of liquidity in a share is unlikely to trouble most modest private investors. However, smaller company shares are harder to buy and sell in quantity than those in leading companies, for obvious reasons. This is often manifested in greater volatility and in a wider spread between the bid and offer prices quoted for the shares, which can affect the profits or losses investors make.

One of the other key elements to investing is compounding. The theory runs something like this. If you consistently invest your gains back into the market year after year, you will benefit in a major way from the compounding effect generated by having increasing amounts to invest.

Reinvesting your gains means that future gains are based on a bigger pool of capital, which in turn generates a higher level of monetary gain even if the returns earned each year stays constant. All the better too if this can be done in a tax-efficient environment.

This is OK in theory, particularly for those who need to 'get a life'. In practice many investors choose to spend their investment gains on other things: a new car, a holiday, their daughter's wedding, or something else. And why not? For most normal human beings, the object of their investments is to give pleasure rather than achieve the maximum gain possible before they die. Beware of arguments that rely soley on compounding.

Overall portfolio strategy

Although this book started from the premise that investment in shares should only be conducted with money surplus to immediate requirements, it can be seen that in reality the process isn't really as simple as that.

You need to set out a coherent portfolio strategy at the outset and try and stick to it. The nature of the strategy will be determined by your temperament, the money you have available, and your other assets.

Key strategic decisions need to be made at the outset taking the following questions into account:

- How big are your stock market investments to be in the context of your money assets?
- Ditto equity in property and accumulated pension contributions?
- Are your investments required to produce income while preserving capital?
- Are your investments required to be liquid enough to cover unforeseen events?.
- Do you want to let your gains compound, or spend them?

Let's assume for a moment that you are in the position of our first individual. Reasonably well set up, you have decided in principle to invest your surplus £50,000 in small companies in the hope of making better-than-average returns.

What is the next step? Well, one advantage that private investors have is that they don't need always to be 'in the market'. The professionals have to invest come what may, because they have regular and substantial flows of cash that must be allocated to some form of investment. The investor, pondering what to do with some surplus capital, faces no such pressures.

Market behaviour – general rules

The first point is to make sure that the timing is right for investing in shares. Bear in mind that the stock market normally anticipates (or, as the professionals say, 'discounts') events that are likely to happen in the future. The economy may be booming, but if the market – that is, the aggregate of all investors, both professional and private – comes to believe that boom is soon likely to turn to bust, then the market will begin to fall.

Market timing is a big subject in itself, and being too cautious is a recipe for missing out on substantial potential gains. But there are certain good indicators of different phases of the market that should be kept in mind.

It is as well, for example, to be aware of the following points:

- Sustained increases in interest rates are generally bad for markets.
- The prospect of steady interest rate reductions is bullish.
- Periods of great popular interest in stocks and shares generally presage a downturn.
- Ditto speculative excess, such as the early 2000 bursting of the dot com bubble.
- Buy bonds when interest rates are high, the economy stationary and some topic other than the stock market is dominating the conversation
- Buy shares soon after the above, when bond prices start to rise.

Let's short-circuit this process and say that our investor has decided that the time is right and that he wishes to get involved in the shares of smaller speculative companies, mainly because he has no need for income, has a good level of tolerance for risk and because all his other investments are relatively conservative.

This is not the end of the story, however, because normal prudence suggests that risk can be reduced without sacrificing much return by simply diversifying one's holdings among several different companies.

Controlling risk

Although each of the companies in which the investor chooses to invest may be risky individually, it is possible to structure things so that the risks inherent in each one are offset, or at least reduced, by the spread of investments chosen. This is basic investment theory, long since accepted by almost everyone.

It sounds obvious. In other words buy shares in, say, six different companies and risk is automatically reduced. Right?

Wrong.

It is vitally important to make sure that the constituents of the portfolio are as diverse as possible. Why? Because if that isn't the case, the adverse factors that affect one will affect the rest.

Say, for instance, you believe that a particular drug company has developed a cure for cancer. You believe the share price will go sky-high once the news is released.

Now think about it a little more. It could be good to hold the shares, but it might be risky if at the same time you hold shares in other drug companies.

Why? Well although the other shares might move higher in sympathy, they could be developing competing products that would suffer if their competitor proved to have the magic cure. Equally, if the drug proves not be effective, or has unfortunate side effects or provokes the authorities to regulate the entire drug market, all the shares in that sector will suffer.

The best strategy in these circumstances is therefore to pick the best share in each of a number of different sectors, rather than to go all-out for one particular area. In other words, as the statisticians would say, avoid having two shares whose businesses are closely correlated.

This has to be tempered by the fact that different groups of sectors do move in sympathy at different phases in the market's cycle. For instance, those sensitive to interest rates tend to move first, followed by consumer goods, manufacturing, and finally – late in the cycle – commodity-based companies. But this formula does not work in every cycle, or at every point in every cycle, and companies within sectors can of course buck the overall trend.

While good investments tend to have in common the fact that they offer 'something new', the nature of that special ingredient can differ in the case of different shares, and mixing different types of unique selling point in different shares may also help to lower risk.

For example, let's say you have four shares. One is a drug company with a new wonder drug; the second is a down-at-heel manufacturing company with a dynamic new chief executive; the third is a pub company benefiting from structural changes in its own industry; and the fourth is a bus company benefiting from privatization. We have something new in all cases: innovation; management change; structural change; and legislative change.

All are legitimate reasons for investing, and all the companies are in different industries; and most importantly none of the potentially adverse factors for one is likely to affect the others.

To sum up, the main guidelines for controlling risk in relation to diversification are as follows:

- Own a mixture of shares and other investments.
- Own several different shares.
- Own shares in different industries.

■ Own shares in large companies and small companies.

■ Have a standard dealing 'unit' for each share.

■ Have a fixed pain barrier at which you will always cut your losses.

These other forms of control are outlined next.

Other forms of control

A further aspect to portfolio diversification is that buying a single category of share can increase risk, and rewards. For example, smaller companies' shares tend both to rise and fall faster than the market as a whole. Smaller companies generally outperform over time, but tend to do particularly well in the later stages of bull markets, and perform badly in bear markets. Simply buying smaller companies alone can increase risk.

This is not to say that the risks are not worth running.

Having a disparate portfolio when investing in smaller companies is prudent, because too great a concentration can be disastrous. But a conscious decision to invest in smaller companies, because you feel the market is likely to be buoyant and smaller companies have been left behind, is certainly a legitimate one.

It should be recognized, however, that this tactic involves a greater degree of risk than, say, mixing some small company investments with those in the shares of bigger, more solid organizations.

There are some other important aspects to portfolio diversification and risk control.

One is to make sure at the outset that each investment is of a standard size. In other words, you should have a standard dealing 'unit'. If you have £40,000 to invest and want to invest it in a maximum of eight companies, make sure each investment is roughly £5,000.

This simplifies making decisions, particularly if investments fail to perform, since the decision making process is not complicated by the fact that different portfolio constituents are of markedly different size. Those with £5,000 to invest might use units of £1,000.

Equally it is important to have a pain barrier, or 'stop-loss', a point beyond which an investment is automatically sold without a second thought. In my own investment decisions I have tended recently to work with £5,000 dealing units and more often than not to sell if any investment loses more than £700. If you have made the decision to buy correctly, then a 10 per cent plus fall in the price should not happen.

Cutting losses is a vitally important part of successful investing. Indeed it is no exaggeration to say that how you handle losses has a major bearing on the overall returns you make. Think of it as being like managing a five-a-side football team where you have an unlimited number of substitutes. Your shares (or other investments) are the team's current players. It is clearly not right to substitute the players who are playing well. Get rid of those who are looking tired as soon as possible and try new ones.

Cutting losses is of course not without cost. For a start there are dealing costs to consider, and also the influence of the difference or spread between the market-makers' buying and selling prices.

Table 6.1 shows stop-loss levels for shares of different prices. The influence of dealing costs and the bid-offer spread in the stop-loss process is clearly shown.

For instance, using a 10 per cent stop-loss, the overall effect of cutting a loss on a £5,000 investment with the shares priced at 50–54 would be in

Table 6.1 Impact of bid-offer spread and dealing costs on stop-loss position

These are the prices at which you can deal (illustrative):

Dealing spread on your investment in a:		50p stock is	250p stock is	500p stock is
		48 to 50	247 to 250	495 to 500
Stop-loss 10% below middle price is:		45	225	450
But allowing for spread, on a:				
£5,000 deal	...sell at...	44	223	447
	so loss is...	£600	£540	£530
£3,500 deal	...sell at...	44	223	447
	so loss is...	£420	£378	£313
£1,000 deal	...sell at...	44	223	447
	so loss is...	£120	£108	£106

So total loss on a 'stop' set 10% below original offer price is:

Loss	50p stock	250p stock	500p stock	Adding dealing costs of
Dealing unit				
£5,000 Absolute	£690	£630	£620	£90
%	13.8	12.6	12.4	
£3,500 Absolute	£473	£431	£366	£53
%	13.5	12.3	10.5	
£1,000 Absolute	£155	£143	£141	£35
%	15.5	14.3	14.1	

Dealing costs (typical 'voice' broker):

	Purchase £	Sale £	Stamp duty £	Total £
	50	15	25	90
	20	15	18	53
	15	15	5	35

the region of 14 per cent – after allowing for the spread and dealing costs. Dealing costs are a comparatively minor part of this equation. There is really no way round this problem.

The other side of this particular coin is that if an investment rises sharply in value, it is also important to keep an eye on the balance of the portfolio and also to have a care that being over-dependent on the fortunes of one share, however well it is performing, also introduces risk into the equation.

This is a good problem to have, of course, but thought should be given to making sure that there is a strategy in place that covers how and when to sell if its performance starts to falter.

My own favourite method, if you are fortunate in having a share that doubles in value, is to sell half your holding at that point, recouping your initial outlay and leaving the rest of the shares in the books 'for nothing'. This takes the pressure off any subsequent decisions you may need to make.

In theory, of course, if you still believe in the share and have no other good reason to sell, then some might say this decision is a bit of a cop-out. But it is equally valid to say that it is simply a prudent way of managing your money and that you may be able to pick another highly successful investment with the funds you release in this way.

As an aside, of course none of these methods has much relevance if you are set on day-trading. For the uninitiated, day-trading is simply buying and selling within the day to generate lots of small profits. Ending each day holding no shares means that day-traders are less prone to being upstaged by external events – good or bad – taking place outside of market hours. On the other hand each trade has to be done at minimum cost. The current UK regime, with stamp duty on share trading, militates against really active day-trading and it is, in my view, a hard way to make a living.

All of the decisions and techniques mentioned above: what type of strategy to follow; what level of risk you can tolerate; and how to be disciplined in the way you manage your investments are all important irrespective of the type of shares or other investments you invest in.

Many of the most successful investors have been very broad-minded in the type of investments they choose, mixing and matching shares, bonds, options, property, private equity and so on. You will work out your own investing style as time goes by. It may be scrutinizing charts, looking for new technologies, exploring asset situations, or some other method.

Once you do find something that suits the way your mind works and you are successful at it, my experience suggests that you depart from it at your peril. I have always been fairly good at spotting undervalued small companies and by and large much less astute when it comes to trading shares in big companies. I have made money by trading property, but have had little consistent success at reading the bond market. I am less than comfortable valuing technology stocks. Find your 'thing', and stick to it.

With that, it's time to look at the various building blocks you can use in your portfolio. (The next chapter will give some real-life examples of how they can be used in practice to maximize your returns.)

The building blocks

In Chapter 1 we touched on the wide variety of shares available. Blue chips, smaller company shares, commodity shares, and so on. But shares are only one aspect of investing, and you may want to put your money into other types of investment. A well-built portfolio can produce steady gains with the minimum of tinkering, and can help you achieve certain important financial goals, such as generating income, or producing a specified target return at a fixed time in the future. Here are some of the building blocks you can use, their advantages and their risks.

Blue chips

Most investors start out buying the shares of big companies because they are names they know. And at certain times in the market cycle, blue chips do best. However, as Jim Slater puts it so memorably, 'elephants don't gallop' and on the whole investors ought to get better returns from carefully selected smaller companies. One advantage of blue chips is that options are available in the largest companies, allowing investors more flexibility. For simple market exposure, however, a tracker may offer better value, especially for investors whose intention is simply to buy and hold.

Advantages: Provide exposure to growth in profits and dividends at large listed companies. Narrow dealing spreads and good liquidity. Options often available on these shares (see below).

Risks: Tend to be more closely correlated with the market than smaller companies. Some blue chips have been appalling performers because of management failings.

Uses: Central core of portfolio.

Smaller company shares

Astute investors can do well by picking out good smaller companies. Returns can be substantial provided you follow a disciplined approach. The main reason for this is that small company shares tend to be under-researched and therefore their value may get out of touch with reality. Small investors can gain a real advantage here, especially if they have specialist knowledge of the industry in which they operate. Management of companies like this may be more amenable to answering questions from small investors.

The drawback to a strategy that involves smaller companies is that patience is required as they tend to move infrequently, but in big jumps when they do. Many investors wrongly shy away from smaller companies, but if an individual's other investments are in more conservative stocks and bonds, then smaller companies can be a good way for individual investors to play the market.

Advantages: Less familiar and probably under-researched by brokers, and therefore a greater likelihood that they are incorrectly valued. Usually simple businesses, and therefore easier to grasp. Management may be more amenable to contact with investors.

Risks: Greater risk of failure. Shares may be less liquid and spreads may be larger, especially if the shares fall into the 'penny share' category. Unlikely to be big income generators.

Uses: Significant part of portfolio, especially if other investments are very conservative.

Investment trusts

Investments trusts have a long and distinguished history and can be a good way for investors to get instant diversified exposure to a market, especially if the trust can be bought on a significant discount to assets. However, this may reflect lacklustre management, so some care needs to be taken to ensure that the trust's performance has been up to scratch in the past. If it has, investing like this is a good alternative to a portfolio of blue chips. Some investment trusts also offer specialist exposure to areas that are otherwise hard for the small investor to access – venture capital, certain overseas markets, and so on. In addition, many investment trusts operate savings schemes that allow an investment to be built up gradually with minimal dealing costs.

Advantages: Allow investors to gain exposure to a broad spread of investments through one share. Some allow access to specialist areas that may otherwise be closed off. Liquidity of shares varies with size of trust.

Risks: Share price depends both on the value of underlying assets and the varying premium or discount to this value that the trust's shares sell on. The trust's manager may move, or the trust may change its objectives.

Uses: Either as a substitute for a portfolio of blue chips, or as a means of gaining access to a promising area or market that would otherwise be difficult to enter.

Gilts (government bonds)

Often thought of as being for 'widows and orphans', bonds are not risk-free. Their prices are affected by perceptions about future trends in interest rates and inflation. The only guarantee is that the income will be paid on particular days and the nominal value of the stock you have bought will be repaid at a fixed point in the future. If you pay over the odds for your holding, you may not get back your entire investment at maturity: £90 nominal of stock may cost you £100, but you will only get £90 back on redemption.

Advantages: Produce fixed and therefore known income delivered at pre-set times with absolute security. Index linked bonds produce a fixed income adjusted for inflation. Highly liquid with narrow dealing spreads.

Risks: Price rises or falls inversely to general level of interest rates and other market factors. Bonds with longer to run to maturity tend to be more volatile in this respect.

Uses: For producing income, especially inflation-proofed income, or as a counterweight to speculative investments elsewhere in portfolio.

Corporate bonds

More fashionable of late, corporate bonds have grown in popularity as investors have sought higher yields. Usually purchased in the form of bond funds, investors are spared undue credit risk as a result of the diversification that such funds offer, but don't expect big capital growth in addition to a high yield.

Advantages: As with gilts, but with the proviso that security depends on the perceived credit quality of the issuing company. Hence corporate bonds tend to have higher yields than government bonds.

Risks: Risk of default is higher. If the company defaults, interest may not be paid and the amount invested may not be repaid in full. Bond prices are subject to the vagaries of interest rates and also to perceptions of the state of the corporate bond market and the credit quality (financial standing) of the issuer. Normally only accessible to private investors via corporate funds and hence subject to charges, and dependent on the quality of the managers.

Uses: For investors seeking extra yield who have a reasonable level of tolerance for risk.

Convertibles

Convertibles are a specialist area of the market and only a limited number of them are available. If a stock you are interested in has a convertible issued, then this may be worth looking at as an alternative to the equity, especially if you are cautious about the market.

Advantages: Usually issued by companies, these are corporate bonds that contain an option to convert into shares at a specific price for a period of time. They produce reasonable fixed income until conversion and the presence of the option provides some element of gearing to upward movement in the share price.

Risks: Conversion option may prove worthless. If so, the investor will simply be left with a low yielding bond in a poorly performing company. Limited choice. May be more difficult to deal in, especially through online brokers.

Uses: Cautious means of investing in a particular company.

Zero coupon bonds

Frequently issued by investment trusts, these have a fixed life and are normally bought at a deep discount to their redemption value, with the return being produced by a gradual uptrend in price as maturity approaches. The return is in effect the compound rate of growth needed to get from the price you pay to the redemption value of the bond over the number of years of life still outstanding when you bought it. Because they have a relatively low monetary value for much of their life, changes in expectations about interest rates can have a disproportionate effect on their value in the market. If held to maturity, however, they make a good and reasonably predictable investment.

Advantages: Return is concentrated in the form of a reasonably predictable capital gain if the bonds are held to maturity, and so may have tax advantages for certain investors. Long-dated zeroes have a high level of gearing to interest rate movements.

Risks: Have to be held to maturity to extract most benefit. Tax regime may change to neutralize their benefit.

Uses: Typically employed by higher taxpayers who wish to save for a specific future event. Often used in school fees planning.

Cash

Cash is king. Investors should always have a certain amount of cash available just in case an excellent investment opportunity comes along, but if you are very negative on the market, switching into cash is the easiest way to protect yourself. Bear in mind, however, that interest rates on cash held on demand are very low. To earn more interest, you may need to give a longer notice period, thus sacrificing liquidity.

Advantages: No risk of loss. Absolute liquidity if held in a bank current account.

Risks: Value will probably be eroded by inflation.

Uses: Contingencies, or if particularly bearish on the outlook for the market.

Gold

Gold is for the deep pessimists among us, those who expect the Apocalypse and reason that an internationally acceptable commodity like gold will be the only investment that holds its value if economic activity collapses, currencies are debased, companies default, and governments renege on their debt.

Advantages: Internationally accepted and a perceived store of value. Can be purchased in coin form. Portable.

Risks: Price governed by supply and demand. No income. Requires secure storage.

Uses: Hold if expecting deep bear market and severe deflation.

Property

Property is regarded by professional investors as a legitimate investment category and offers the possibility of both capital gain and income generation at yields significantly higher than conventional fixed-income investment. Watch out for holding costs though: if you have tenants, you need to provide for wear and tear and commission for an agent to collect the rent.

Advantages: Hedge against inflation. Can be rented out to provide income. Supply is restricted.

Risks: Property values not transparent and heavily dependent on fashion and location. Illiquid. You need large amount of money to buy, and borrowing to invest is unacceptably risky.

Uses: Can be an alternative to shares. Residential property prices are usually a good indicator of the overall health of the economy.

Tracker funds

Trackers mimic a particular index and so represent a good way for investors to achieve broad exposure to the market without buying lots of different shares. Costs are low. Index trackers may not follow the market with exact precision and index constitutions and their weightings are changed from time to time.

Advantages: Mimic the movement in the market. Low charges. Can be hedged using options.

Risks: No opportunity for exercising stock selection skills. Index weightings may change without much warning.

Uses: Alternative to portfolio of blue chips.

Unit trusts

Very popular means of investment by the general public, but suffer from some drawbacks, most notably that managers may move. Charges are also high, as are spreads, although OEICs, a new type of fund, offer a single buying and selling price.

Advantages: Wide variety of both general and specialist styles. Fund performance and portfolio details readily available.

Risks: Manager may change without warning. Spreads may be significant, and charges can erode gains in value.

Uses: Alternative to a portfolio of shares or as a way of accessing a particular niche market or sector.

Venture capital

Venture capitalists invest in young private companies and make their money when the companies mature and either float or are taken over by a trade buyer. Returns on this so-called private equity investing have historically been good – in the 20 per cent per annum area – but the opportunity to invest in this way is usually only open to those with big money to invest. Private equity also depends for its existence on healthy public stock markets. Private investors can invest via specialist funds or listed private equity management companies like Candover and 3i.

Advantages: Generally high returns if held for the longer term.

Risks: Illiquid. Can have poor returns in early years. Usually only accessible via venture capital trusts or listed investment trusts of the fund manager.

Uses: To improve long-term portfolio returns.

Hedge funds

Despite a lurid history, most hedge funds are dedicated to producing modest absolute returns with minimum levels of volatility, irrespective of underlying market conditions. Most investors can only access them through specialist 'fund of funds' products although there are moves afoot to create tracker funds based around recognized indices that mimic the performance of a group of leading funds in each subset of the hedge fund market.

Advantages: Moderate returns with low volatility (if properly managed) and generally uncorrelated to the conventional stock market. Variety of styles available.

Risks: Illiquid. Can 'blow up'. Normally only available to private investors of modest means through managed 'fund of funds' products.

Uses: To improve long-term returns independently of movements in the stock market.

Options

Options offer investors the right but not the obligation to buy (a call) or sell (a put) a specific parcel of an individual share or index. Because of this they can be used to speculate either on a price or a price fall, giving geared exposure. Alternatively they can be used in conjunction with a holding in the underlying shares around which the option is based, to produce additional portfolio income through a process known as covered call writing.

Finally, they can be used to provide insurance. The holder of a portfolio of blue chips can hedge against a fall in the market, without having to sell shares and perhaps incur capital gains tax, by buying an index put option. This will rise in value if the market falls, offsetting any losses the investor may incur elsewhere.

Advantages: Can be used to provide geared up exposure to a directional movement in a share or index, as insurance, or to produce additional portfolio income. Flexible.

Risks: Not available for all shares, and of limited duration. Can lose entire amount invested if predicted event does not materialize in time. Spreads can be wide, especially on low-priced options. Not all brokers deal in options.

Uses: As pure speculation, or (in a different way) for 'insurance'.

What next?

The point about enumerating these various choices is to show that there is more to investing than simply buying shares in a big company with a well-known name. Each type of investment carries its own different mixture of risks and rewards and it is up to you to work out how this fits in with the other investments you have, especially say the equity you have in your home, or the value of your pension fund, and work out from this what level of risk you are comfortable with and what sort of return you wish to aim for.

As a rough guide, the following table of 'best buys' may help (see Table 6.2).

Table 6.2   Best buys in different circumstances

Best income:	gilts; corporate bonds
Most secure:	gilts; cash
Best hedge vs deflation:	gold
Best hedge vs inflation:	property
Best 'halfway house':	convertible bonds
Best 'instant' diversification:	trackers; investment trusts
Best capital growth:	zero coupon bonds; smaller company shares

The next chapter explores in more detail the mathematics of combining some of these investments by looking at some real-life examples.

I N   B R I E F

- There is more to investing than buying shares. Make sure you check out all the available investment choices.

- Be aware that there are different dealing costs, spreads and charges on different investments, and different levels of risk.

- Work out, bearing in mind your other assets and your temperament, what level of risk you are comfortable with.

- Find an investing style that suits you and stick to it.

- When investing in shares, always cut losses quickly and run profits.

Designing your portfolio

Investing is not about holding just one share through thick and thin. There are choices to be made in terms of the different shares you might hold, different types of investment apart from shares, and how you go about selecting and monitoring your investments. If you do not pay attention to this aspect of investing, in the longer term your performance will suffer

Simple strategies for maximum return and minimum risk

This book aims to examine all aspects of investing, not just buying and selling shares. Even if all you want to do is invest in shares and related investments, you need to understand the basics of building and managing a portfolio. We covered some of this in the previous chapter. We now look at some concrete examples of how different investments can be combined.

The reason for this is simple. It is impossible to discuss the concept of portfolio diversification without mentioning the role other types of investment can play in adjusting the risk in a portfolio to more acceptable levels or in improving the income generated from your investments.

When making a statement like this the implicit assumption is that the risk should be reduced, but it is possible to use alternative forms of listed investment to *increase* the risk profile, and therefore the potential return, on (say) a portfolio of unexciting blue chips, or indeed to keep the risk level constant while increasing portfolio income.

We will therefore look briefly first at the various different types of investment alternatives to ordinary shares and their role in increasing or reducing portfolio risk.

Let's start from the assumption that the investor has £50,000 to invest in total, and currently has £30,000 invested in a mixture of large blue chip companies and more speculative smaller companies. If this sounds too large a figure, it could just as easily be divided by ten, and the same principles would apply. Some of the diversification strategies that could be pursued and their impact on portfolio risk and income are outlined below.

Strategy One. Cash – keep the balance of £20,000 in a bank deposit

This strategy has the advantage of retaining liquidity in order to increase investment in other areas at short notice if the need arises. Interest rates on bank deposits are, however, lower than virtually all other forms of fixed interest investment. And simply leaving cash in a bank deposit has little impact either way on actual portfolio risk, although there may be an opportunity lost in not investing it in something more enterprising.

If you expect to stay out of the market for some time, it is possible to earn extra income by locking up your money for longer. Interest on 90-day notice accounts is higher than instant access ones. It is also possible to shop around for higher rates at the newer online banks, and some broker money-market accounts offer rates that are higher than normal current accounts.

But this is only a matter of degree. Cash is essentially dead money and will probably be eroded by inflation if you do not put it to productive use.

Strategy Two: Gilts – invest the balance of £20,000 in government securities

Government securities, or 'gilts', are fixed interest stocks issued and guaranteed by the British government. To recap on what was explained earlier in this book, they return a fixed income, with interest normally paid twice-yearly. Stock is available in both a fixed-term and undated form, and in a variety of maturities with strictly fixed interest or in a form where interest payments are linked to the RPI, so guaranteeing to preserve the investor's capital.

The yield on a government security, and indeed on any fixed interest investment, can be calculated in two common ways. One (as described earlier) is known as the running yield, which is simply the annual gross income expressed as a percentage of the price of the security.

The other is known as the redemption yield, or yield to maturity, which takes into account the running yield, and any capital gain or loss that might result if the security is held all the way to maturity and interest on income assumed to be reinvested. If a stock is bought at below its face value and held to maturity, when it is repaid at par the redemption yield will be higher than the running yield (vice versa if it is acquired when the price is above par).

Using gilts as a complement to a portfolio of equities has a number of implications. Equities (and for that matter fixed-interest investments) are at risk if interest rates rise. Higher interest rates choke off economic activity and lower the relative attractiveness of the normally lowish yields on ordinary shares. And, since the income on gilts is normally fixed, if interest rates rise and bond yields rise in sympathy, the effect is for gilt-edge security prices to fall (see Table 7.1).

However, an astute choice of maturity date can limit the risk. Let's say, hypothetically, you are happy with your share portfolio and have significant gains on it. You do not wish to sell and realize the gains, but you want to limit the overall risk that interest rates might rise over the next two to three years.

Buying a government stock that stands below par but which matures in two or three years time will guarantee an eventual capital gain which will offset at least some of the fall in equity values in the meantime if rates rise, while in all probability giving extra income at least equivalent to that on the equity portfolio.

Let's look at a current example. At the time of writing, the Treasury 5 per cent stock of 2004 stands at 97.24, i.e. 2.76 points below par. The stock has a running yield of 5.14 per cent (being 5/97.24), but the redemption yield, including the two percentage point plus appreciation in the run-up to maturity, is 5.81 per cent.

It can probably be seen that, in its most extreme form, buying gilts simply equates to keeping cash on deposit. But a wise choice of stock, maturity date and the position of the price in relation to the par value (normally stated as £100 per cent in the case of gilts) can produce a much more creative solution to the risk problem.

It is also worth noting that the yields on certain gilts can reveal a number of other facets of the market and the economy. There is an historic relationship, for instance, between the benchmark 20-year gilt yield and the yield on equities. In the years before equities grew in popularity, yields on ordinary shares were higher than those on gilts, and this disparity was known as the yield gap.

Table 7.1 Impact of differing returns on gilts vs equities

Portfolio type	Amount	Features/ assumptions	Capital gain	Income	Total return over two years Absolute	%
Shares	25,000	7% compound p.a. gain; 3% yield	3,623	1,553	5,176	20.7
Gilts	25,000	12% gain over 2 years; 6% p.a. yield	3,409	3,400	6,809	27.2
Combined	50,000	As above	3,623	4,053	11,085	22.2

Now, it is more common for equity yields to be below gilt yields, and this relationship (as alluded to briefly in Chapter 3) is known as the reverse yield gap. Its position at any one time can tell us a lot about the relative over or undervaluation of equities relative to gilts, and therefore whether to skew one's investment strategy towards one or the other. Another good guide is the shape of the yield curve. This shows the redemption yields on gilt edge stocks ranked by maturity date (see Figure 7.1).

Figure 7.1 UK gilts yield curve

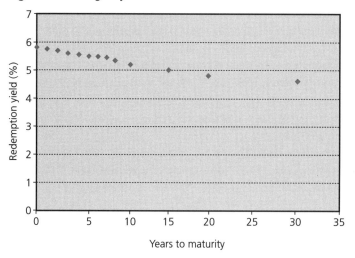

Years to maturity

The normal situation is for the yield curve to slope upwards from left to right. Investors normally demand higher yields for stocks that have longer to go to maturity, because they are at risk of price fluctuations in the meantime for longer. If the curve is too steep, this probably indicates that short-term interest rates are unsustainably low and can only rise, depressing the market in shares.

Conversely an inverted yield curve, as in the example above, where short-dated yields are higher than longer-dated ones, may mean that short rates can only come down, or that the long end of the gilt market is vulnerable (yields will rise and prices will fall). In the case of the UK, the price of long-dated gilts has been driven up and hence yields driven down, for two reasons. One is that tight control of public spending has meant the government has issued less stock to pay for its expenditure. The other related reason is that this reduced supply of stock has forced pension funds, who need to buy the stock to meet their long-term obligations, to pay higher and higher prices.

By the same token, the yield on undated gilt-edge stocks (currently around 5 per cent) is normally reckoned to be a proxy for what is known as the risk-free rate of return. Government stocks are believed to be as near riskless as it is possible to get, and therefore the yield on Consols or War Loan, uncluttered by calculations on their position at maturity, is viewed as the purest of benchmarks. The current yield gap between 2.5 per cent

Consols (4.97 per cent) and the FT All Share Index (2.14 per cent) is 2.83 per cent. The risk-free yield is more than double the yield on the equity market.

In fact the real risk in holding gilt-edge stock is that inflation erodes the investor's capital. To offer investors protection in this respect, the government has issued index-linked stocks, where the interest payment is connected to movements in the RPI.

This means that the difference in yield between an index-linked stock and a fixed-interest stock of similar maturity will be a guide to the market's view of the likely future trend in inflation. For instance, at the time of writing, the yield on the 2 per cent index-linked stock maturing in 2006 is 2.65 per cent, and the average redemption yield on the conventional gilts maturing in 1998 around 5.6 per cent, implying that the market believes inflation between now and mid-2006 will run at a fraction under 3 per cent.

Strategy Three: Trackers – invest the balance of £20,000 in an index tracking fund

As most interested observers of the investment scene will probably be aware, there has been an upsurge of interest in recent years in index tracking funds. These are collective investment vehicles, managing large aggregated pools of money on behalf of many small investors. They deliberately invest in such a way as to track either the FTSE-100 index, the FT All Share Index, or some other benchmark.

Vehicles of this sort represent a useful tool for investors who are uncomfortable with the level of risk they perceive to be inherent in their portfolio and who wish to change it with the minimum of fuss.

Crucial to choosing the right amount to invest in funds of this type is a concept known as the 'beta factor'. This is a statistical measurement, based on the past performance of a portfolio, that attempts to isolate that part of the performance of an individual stock or portfolio that is simply reflecting the impact of a move in the market, and the part that is specific to the stock or portfolio concerned.

Put simply, the beta factor measures the likely movement in the stock for a given percentage movement in the market. If, for instance, the beta factor on a company is 1.1, this means that a 10 per cent upward move in the market would be likely to see a 11 per cent upward move in the price of the stock (10 per cent times 1.1). Similarly, if a stock had a beta of 0.95, a 10 per cent rise in the market would produce only a 9.5 per cent rise in the price of the stock. See Table 7.2.

Organizations such as the London Business School produce tables of the beta factors for quoted companies, and indeed they can sometimes be derived in certain technical analysis packages. Simple observation of the movement in a particular share price may give one a good handle on whether or not it has a high or a low beta.

Smaller companies, more highly geared companies, and those involved in high-tech or capital-intensive industries will tend to have higher betas than those companies that are regarded as large, safe and boring, those that operate in industries normally regarded as stable, and businesses that generate cash.

So, for instance, brewers, food manufacturing companies, and broad-based industrial companies have lower betas, other things being equal, than small electronics companies, biotechnology companies, and mining stocks.

It is worthwhile taking a little time to understand the nature of the portfolio of shares you have invested and, having done this, decide whether or not you are comfortable with the level of volatility it possesses.

The point about investing part of the portfolio in an index fund is that by definition the index fund's beta will be exactly 1.0, i.e. the fund's value should rise and fall exactly in line with the market. Hence investing in an index fund is a way of raising (in the case of a portfolio with a beta below one) or lowering (in the case of a beta above one) the overall volatility of a portfolio.

One interesting phenomenon of late has been the introduction of so-called exchange traded funds (ETFs), which are in effect a tracker fund in the form of a share that can be bought and sold in the market in the normal way. Any disparities between the actual market and the ETF will be ironed out by arbitrage, and the funds have the advantage of much lower charges and better liquidity than unit trust based trackers.

Trackers are also being developed that mimic more specialist indices allowing investors to invest, for example, in a broad-based technology share index like the Techmark 100 or the Wired Index Fund, and providing a less risky (though far from risk-free) way of tapping into technology shares.

Table 7.2 Impact of index-tracking investment on volatility portfolio

Portfolio type	Amount invested	Beta	Effect of 10% gain in market	Effect of 10% fall in market
Shares	25,000	1.2	3,000	−4,500
Index tracker	25,000	1	2,500	−3,750
Combined	50,000	1.1	5,500	−8,250
Change in shares alone (%)			12.00%	−18.00%
Change in combined (%)			11.00%	−16.50%

Strategy Four: Collective investments – invest the balance of £20,000 in a unit or investment trust

The preceding strategy alluded to the fact that there are many investment choices, one of the most popular being collective investment vehicles such as unit trusts. These are open-ended pools of money which grow or contract as investors either buy or redeem units. Their value reflects the underlying portfolio.

As explained earlier, investment trusts by contrast are 'closed-end' funds, managing a fixed pool of money but whose shares are listed on the Stock Exchange. Investment trust shares often stand at a discount to the underlying value of their assets, for a variety of reasons.

My own preference is for investment trusts because of the discount factor and because of the reasonable degree of prior knowledge one has about the contents of the portfolio and the management style of the trust. That said, the unit trust industry is by far the most popular with ordinary investors.

In the context of our hypothetical portfolio adjustment exercise, there are two possible uses for unit/investment trusts. One is as a way of getting 'instant diversification'. If, for example, an investor had only (say) £3,000 to invest, the realistic alternative might be to buy two separate holdings in completely disparate companies. This would still have substantial risk. If one of the companies were to hit hard times, for example, the collapse in the share price would have a disastrous effect on the performance of the portfolio.

An alternative would be to put the whole £3,000 in a long-established broadly based investment trust or unit trust. The possibility of buying shares in such an investment trust at a discount is an added attraction to an investor who also now has the stimulus of owning shares and being able to follow the price on a daily basis.

In the case of an investor with a holding of more volatile smaller company shares, investing in a broadly based UK trust would again have the effect of diversifying the portfolio and lowering its volatility relative to changes in the market.

Investment trusts and other collective investments have another use, however. As we saw in the previous chapter, they can be used as a relatively safe means of investing in territory that might otherwise be considered unduly risky, or where the complexities of dealing and settlement effectively put them out of bounds for the private investor.

So, our hypothetical investor might be perfectly happy that his/her existing portfolio gives a good spread of exposure to the UK stock market and happy too that the level of risk and volatility of the portfolio is absolutely right for his/her needs.

But he/she also feels that (say) Latin America and Eastern Europe are likely to be the boom areas of the investment business over the next ten years and wishes to invest some of his remaining funds in these areas. It is impractical (and excessively risky) to even attempt to invest individually in these areas, but there are a number of specialist investment trusts that invest in these areas, and in which ordinary private investors can buy shares. Before doing so, however, it is essential to check out the performance of the trust, the record of the managers or fund management group that is sponsoring it, and the nature of the investment portfolio.

The process of doing this is rather similar to the process one might go through when checking out the credentials of a particular company. At the very minimum, an annual report or prospectus should be obtained to have a look at some of the detail prior to investing. It is, however, again worth remembering the axiom about risk and return.

Emerging markets, to take this example, may seemingly offer high returns, and by proxy so will the collective investments through which it is possible to invest in them. But the corollary is that the risk is also higher. It is therefore essential that an investment of this type is only contemplated when the risk in the rest of the portfolio is not particularly high. If it is, then some other form of risk-reduction strategy (either buying gilts or index tracking funds) should be considered alongside the emerging market investment.

One last word on investment trusts. Investment trust shares often stand at a discount to the underlying value of their portfolio and statistics on this are published daily in the *Financial Times*, but discount levels vary considerably, widening if the market is in a prolonged 'down' phase and narrowing as it improves. Buying investment trusts when the market is depressed can give the investor a profitable and relatively risk-free double whammy: the net asset value (NAV) of the trust will rise, say, in line with the market, but superior performance will be generated by a narrowing in the discount. This is illustrated in Table 7.3.

Table 7.3 Double-whammy effect of variations in investment trust discounts

	Starting value	Market + 10%	Market + 20%	Market −10%	Market −20%
Net asset value	100p	110p	120p	90p	80p
Discount (say)	20%	15%	10%	25%	30%
Price of trust	80p	93.5p	108p	67.5p	56p
Gain/loss (%)		17	35	−16	−30

Strategy Five: ISAs and EIS – enhance returns through tax-efficient investing.

In recent years there has been considerable growth in the use of tax-efficient savings vehicles, notably Personal Equity Plans and, more recently, ISAs. Each tax year (so far) up to £7,000 can be invested in an ISA. Husbands and wives have separate allowances so a married couple in theory could invest at the moment up to £14,000 a year in these vehicles. Gains on the shares held in an ISA are free of capital gains tax while dividends are free of income tax, provided the investments are held for a minimum of five years.

There are drawbacks, however. Firstly, if you opt for a managed ISA, say one linked to a unit trust or investment trust, there are significant initial and ongoing yearly charges which deplete some of the benefits.

Even in self-select ISAs, which do tend to be less costly in this respect, there are charges for dealing. The advantage of an ISA, however, is that it enables the investor to reinvest dividend income tax free. If the shares concerned are held for a long time the compounding effect of this can be substantial.

There are pluses and minuses to ISAs as a means of portfolio diversification. The first is that their value depends on the individual concerned being a taxpayer. It is also generally considered unwise to let tax considerations drive investment decisions, and the long-term nature of ISAs rather argues against much of what this book is about, namely selecting good undervalued shares and holding them until their potential has been recognized and then selling them.

It is possible to do this within an ISA, but ISA funds must always be more or less fully invested. There is no sitting on the sidelines if you expect the market to fall. Having said that, unlike PEPs (where there were restrictions on investing outside of shares) bonds and other forms of investment (cash, life funds etc.) can be included in an ISA, making them more flexible, if somewhat more complicated to understand.

Many people simply opt each year for a single maxi-ISA, either self-select or via a unit trust. However, the ability to include income generating corporate bond funds in an ISA, means that real tax-efficient diversification is now possible. Remember though that the ongoing level of charges (typically 1 per cent of portfolio value per year) tends to have a dissipating effect on the performance of the ISA, and the investor should check this out carefully before committing money to one.

A further disadvantage is that if funds are withdrawn from an ISA before five years are up, tax becomes payable and this has an inhibiting effect if funds are required to meet unexpected contingencies. In other words, the higher return available on an ISA over and above similar non-ISAed investments, essentially reflecting the impact of the tax relief less the charges made, has to be traded off against the reduced liquidity implied by the fact there are penalties for early withdrawal.

Another tax wrinkle to bear in mind is that gains on conventional investments can be rolled over and gains tax deferred by reinvesting the funds in 'unlisted' investments, such as securities quoted on the Alternative Investment Market. Tax becomes payable once such investments are sold, but it is a way of postponing the incidence of a tax bill.

For those seeking serious equity-based tax efficiency, Enterprise Investment Schemes (EIS) are a possibility. Here the investment is generally a higher risk unquoted vehicle, but investors are allowed to deduct the entire investment from their tax bill, a useful concession for higher rate taxpayers. Once the investment has been held for five years, any gains, say if the investment floats or is taken over, are capital gains tax-free. There is much higher risk in an investment like this, and very limited liquidity, and indeed no guarantees that the shares will ever 'exit' once the qualifying period is up.

Readers should bear in mind the general advice to make investment selections objectively without taking too much notice of the tax status of particular categories of investment. Better to select a good stock that rises in value and pay gains tax, than select a poor one that has tax-exempt status but which falls in value.

Strategy Six: Options – enhance returns through traded options

As we outlined in a previous section it is perfectly possible for an investor to be concerned that the profile of his portfolio is not risky enough. In other words, he or she may feel that the market looks set for a rise but his/her own shares are too safe and therefore offer too little prospect of a good return.

It might be, for instance, that the investor has pursued a conservative investment strategy in a period when the market has been drifting but now feels that an upswing is in prospect and therefore the current rather conservative holdings need spicing up a little.

While it is of course possible to do this by selling the existing holdings and buying new, more speculative ones, this strategy incurs dealing costs, may attract capital gains tax, and will also mean that the investor has the bid-offer spread to overcome before the new investments begin showing a true profit.

The traded options market can be used in a variety of ways to counteract this problem and open up the possibility of enhanced returns.

Trading in options is a huge subject and readers interested in pursuing this topic further are urged to read up on the subject in more detail before beginning to trade. My book *Traded Options: A Private Investors' Guide* (FT Prentice Hall, price £18.99) gives a comprehensive introduction to the subject, complete with worked examples.

In brief, however, options can be used in a number of ways. Buying a call option (that is to say, an option to buy shares at a specific price for a specified period of time in the future) involves the investor in a limited outlay but, if he/she is correct in his/her judgement about the market and a particular share, then using an option is a relatively inexpensive way of backing this judgement without disturbing an existing portfolio. See Table 7.4.

The investor will retain greater flexibility if he/she buys a call option that is in-the-money, that is to say where the exercise price of the call option is below the current market price – so that the option already possesses some intrinsic value.

In addition, an option with a long time to expiry will be more expensive, but it does offer more time for the buyer's judgement to be proved correct.

If the judgement is wrong, in terms of direction, timing or both, the investor stands in theory (and in practice) to lose the entire amount spent on the option, but this is the limit to the loss. It is worth remembering, however, that the value of the option when purchased by the investor is likely to include some so-called time value, that is to say the price of the option will be greater than its intrinsic value.

This time value clearly becomes worth less and less the nearer the option gets to its expiry date. At expiry, the value of the option will simply equate to its intrinsic value, if any.

An example of the way gearing works on options is shown in Table 7.3. It can be seen that the overall beta factor of a portfolio will be increased materially through the purchase of, say, a call option.

Options can also be used in other ways. For instance, as an investor you may have decided to take a profit (or cut a loss) on a particular share, but you still wish to retain some protection in case the share rises after the transaction has been completed.

Buying a call option achieves this objective.

Option contracts are denominated in lots of 1,000 shares, so selling say 5,000 shares but at the same time buying five contracts in a call option with an exercise price close to the price at which you sold, gives you protection if the price rises after you sell.

Because options are commonly used in this way as insurance, the price of an option is often known as its 'premium'. In the same way, buying a put option (an option to sell shares at a specified price for a particular length of time in the future) at the same time as buying the underlying stock buys insurance against the price falling after the underlying stock has been purchased. If this happens, the value of the put option will increase as the value of the stock falls.

Lastly, if it is anticipated that the value of particular stocks and the market as a whole will fluctuate within a narrow range for a lengthy period of time, the investor can 'write' (i.e. sell) a call option against an underlying holding. The advantage of this is that the writer of an option keeps the

Table 7.4 Impact of options on a conservative portfolio

Portfolio constituent	Beta	Starting value (£)	Value after:			
Amount Type			Market + 10% over 3 months	Market + 20% over 6 months	Market – 10% over 3 months	Market – 20% over 6 months
£4,000 Blue chips	0.9	4,000	4,360	4,720	3,640	3,280
£1,000 XYZ 160 call option (6 months to expiry)	n/a	1,000	1,720	2,400	120	0
Underlying stock price		180	200	220	160	140
Price of option		25	43	60	3	0
Combined portfolio value		5,000	6,086	7,120	3,760	3,280
Portfolio gain/loss (%)			22	42	–25	–34

premium paid by the buyer of the option, but may not have the option exercised against him if the price of the underlying share fails to move sufficiently during the life of the option.

The worst that can happen is that the share price will move in the buyer's favour and be exercised, requiring the writer to honour the option contract at the exercise price. This means in effect that the writer of the call option will sell the stock at the exercise price of the option plus the option premium.

For example, let's assume that you hold 3,000 Hanson shares. The price is 180. You do not believe the price will move significantly for the next three months. You therefore write three Hanson 180p call options for a price of 12p. It will only be worth the holder of the option exercising it if the price of Hanson moves above 192p in the next three months. If it does not, the 12p premium that you as the writer of the option have received represents additional portfolio income. If the price moves up to 200p and the holder of the option exercises the option then all is not lost. You still keep the option premium, meaning you in effect sell the stock at 192, participating in most of the rise, and come out with capital intact.

These strategies, buying call options to increase portfolio 'gearing', buying calls or puts as an insurance policy or hedge against a transaction in the underlying shares, and covered call writing are the simplest of all option strategies, but should be considered by investors looking to adjust the risk-return profile of their portfolio.

It is also worth noting that as well as options on individual stocks, it is possible to buy options on the FTSE-100 index. This is a way of gaining exposure to overall changes in the market, and may be appropriate in certain circumstances.

You may decide, for instance, that the market is headed lower. You sell your entire portfolio and buy short- or medium-dated gilt-edge stock standing below par, but you wish to insure against your judgement on the equity market being wrong. You therefore earmark a small proportion of the cash realized to buy a 'footsie' call option, with a strike price close to the index point at which you sold your holdings.

This will provide the necessary insurance for the period of the option. Note that index options of this type come in two forms, American-style exercise and European-style exercise. American-style options permit exercise at any time up to expiry. Individual equity options are of this type too. European-style options only permit exercise on the expiry day itself, and therefore have lower premiums, because the writer of the option is not exposed to the risk of exercise in the meantime.

Lastly on this subject it is worth noting that not all brokers offer a facility to deal in options, and of those that do, not all permit private investors to write options. Indeed uncovered writing of call options (i.e. where the investor does not hold the underlying stock to match the option transaction) is known as 'naked writing' and should be avoided at all costs, since it exposes the investor to unlimited risk of loss.

Before contemplating any option trades, readers are strongly urged to study the subject fully and if possible attend some of the many training courses organized for private investors.

Portfolio structure

Different types of portfolio are suitable for those with different appetites for risk, different time horizons and different income requirements, as well as for different phases of the market.

> Different types of portfolio are suitable for those with different appetites for risk, different time horizons and different income requirements, as well as for different phases of the market.

An outright bear of the market might have a high proportion of his money in cash and short-dated government bonds, with perhaps some natural resource stocks and property. Physical assets and commodities and the shares of those that extract them tend to hold up best in testing market conditions. Things to avoid in bear markets are small companies, and the favourites of the previous bull market. A later bull phase will almost certainly throw up new favourites.

A long-term bull would have a mixture of shares large and small, or perhaps a lot of smaller company shares mixed in with an index tracker.

An income seeker might have a corporate bond ISA and some higher yielding equities and convertibles. Call options could be written against the equity portion of the portfolio to generate additional income.

Those with a high appetite for risk or a sanguine long-term outlook would have more invested in smaller companies and perhaps enhance their returns by buying call options from time to time.

The percentage weightings in Table 7.5 are examples and should not be construed as recommendations. There are, in short, as many permutations of this sort of thing as there are investors. Once again it is important to know what type of investor you are, what style of investing you feel most comfortable with, what level of risk you wish to assume. Find your optimum trading style and stick to it.

Table 7.5 Illustrative percentage portfolio weightings for different circumstances

	Bear	Bull	Income	High risk
Cash	40	0	5	0
Bonds	30	0	50	0
Convertibles	0	0	20	0
Index tracker	0	20	0	0
Large co. shares	0	20	30	0
Small co. shares	0	50	0	60
Property	10	5	0	10
Metals	20	0	0	10
Call options	0	5	–5*	20

*i.e. 5% in written covered calls on sum of large company segment

The important point about all investment activity is the assessment of risk and reward, and choosing a level of risk that is comfortable and appropriate to the individual's financial circumstances and liquidity needs. The strategy adopted depends on the amount available to invest and whether income is or is not a requirement.

Those with sufficient funds to enable eight or ten shares to be acquired with £3,000–£,5000 invested in each might well stick entirely to picking out individual equities using the techniques described elsewhere in this book.

Those of more modest means might contemplate investing part of their capital in some individual equities and the remainder in a broad-based investment trust or index tracking fund. Those with a more modest amount to invest but with a taste for a greater degree of risk might invest part of their capital in an index tracking fund and give effect to views on individual shares by buying call or put options (depending on their view).

Those requiring income may invest part of their portfolio in gilts and part in high-yielding equities, supplemented when it is felt appropriate by covered call writing to further enhance portfolio income. Those pursuing simple buy and hold strategies should consider doing so through the various tax-efficient vehicles available.

Investors have to try at all times to assess whether they believe the market is likely to rise or fall and whether they are happy with the risk this poses to their portfolio, i.e. either it will fall in value, or get left behind in a rise.

Measuring gains and losses

It is important for investors to try and measure as accurately as possible what level of risk their portfolio possesses, and how it will act under certain market conditions, but also try and discriminate between temporary short-term market movements, which may be largely ignored, and major trends and changes in direction.

There is also a balance to be struck between overactive trading, which will only enrich your broker, and total inactivity, which will lead to profitable opportunities being missed. It is necessary for strict trading disciplines – running profits but cutting losses and operating a stop-loss system – to be maintained at all times. This is particularly the case if option trades are being undertaken as part of your portfolio strategy, since the limited time factor weighs heavily on the option buyer. It is also necessary to be open-minded about what you invest in. Shares are only one of the choices.

It is also good practice to measure the performance of your portfolio at regular intervals against a benchmark like the FTSE-100 or FT All Share Index, to assess how your trading is going. Chapter 12 contains the results of an analysis of my own dealing over nearly 15 years of private investing.

Analyzing your performance in this way may provoke questions as to the right strategy to follow. The necessary parameters can easily be programmed into a standard spreadsheet package, or simply kept up to date with pencil and paper. In my view the investor should know the overall value of his portfolio and the profit or loss on each of its constituents on a daily basis. Web-based portfolio trackers are also available, and are updated in real time or something close to it.

A questioning approach is always appropriate, and in particular analyzing why particular trades did not pay off, and working out what distinguishes successes from failures.

Measuring portfolio gains and losses, highlighting new opportunities through searching a database of share prices, and being aware of price movements and the opportunities they throw up are all tasks that are aided considerably by using various types of investment software and computer-based services. What each of these products and services does and how they can help the investor will be considered in the next two chapters.

IN BRIEF

- The concept of spreading risk is a vitally important part of investing.
- The degree to which investment in shares should be diversified is determined by the individual's own personal 'balance sheet'.
- Markets move in broad cycles and share investment should only be contemplated once one has understood fully the current position of the market cycle.
- It is important to avoid investing in shares whose business activities are similar.
- There are a number of ways of diversifying risk and enhancing returns. These include: gilt-edge stock; index tracking funds; unit and investment trusts.
- Investing tax-efficiently can be a significant factor in raising investment returns, but it is important not to let the tax break drive the investment decision.
- Traded options can be used in different ways to enhance portfolio income and to increase returns while at the same time increasing risk by a defined amount. Investors should read widely on this subject before using these techniques.
- It is a good discipline to measure your investment performance and to analyze your share trades to get pointers to improve results in the future.

chapter eight

Computer-aided investment

This chapter concentrates on how computers can be used to simplify and automate some of the routine tasks of investing. Chapter 9 looks in more detail at the internet phenomenon and how it (and other electronic media) can be used to obtain that all-important investing 'edge'.

For the benefit of the less technical, however, I must stress that using computers is by no means the be all and end all of investment activity. On the contrary, being thorough and exercising judgement have always been the most important aspects of successful investing.

But using computers for some of the more routine tasks is important, because it frees up the investor to concentrate on the more creative part of the process: hunting out undervalued shares and other forms of investment.

Another important consideration is that the professionals operate using sophisticated computer systems. Barings, Long Term Capital Management and other similar débâcles demonstrate that using these systems is not necessarily a guarantee of success, particularly if the information generated by them is not promptly or correctly acted on. But if the private investor wishes to compete on as level a playing field as possible, then access to timely information and the means to analyze it are important.

Lastly, the interest generated by articles in popular magazines like the *Investors' Chronicle* and *Shares* on the subject of investment software, information sources, and other similar topics makes it very clear that many private investors also see this as an important part of the discipline of investment.

Successful independent investing is all about being thorough in research, meticulous in accounting and measurement of performance, and painstaking in the identification and monitoring of trading opportunities. It is, or should be, hard work. Those who have read this far almost certainly possess the characteristics needed to succeed.

What computers do is to make these tasks a little easier.

In the past, many budding investors may have been put off acquiring investment software partly because of its cost, and particularly the cost of the data to go with it, and partly by brokers who had a vested interest – in the form of discretionary commissions, and fees earned for providing valuations and CGT calculations – in making sure that their clients stayed less computer-literate than they were.

But the cost of software and data has fallen very sharply in recent years and the increasing prevalence of no-frills dealing services has provided a powerful incentive for many investors to take the initiative in this area.

There remain some misconceptions about investment software. One is that the software packages themselves are complex and designed for dyed--in-the-wool chartists. Another is that these packages are priced outside the reach of those with a relatively low budget. Neither of these is correct. There are several good budget software packages, all of which are relatively easy to use and which provide fundamental data as well as price charts.

Most packages will work perfectly well on a standard home computer, but will require some means of updating data, normally via modem.

Monitoring your money

Before you even start selecting shares, it is important to have a means of keeping easy track of what they're worth on a day-by-day basis. One option, explored in the next chapter, is to use a web-based portfolio monitoring system. But often it's easier just to construct a simple spread-sheet to monitor your holdings and your bank balances.

How you might do this does vary from individual to individual. In my own case, as a self-employed person, I need to keep track of a variety of different things: who owes me money, what I owe the VAT-man and the Inland Revenue and so on, as well as my normal household bills and how my investments are doing. Employed individuals and retirees may have a somewhat different perspective.

The result in my case, however, has been that for day-to-day monitoring of my investments and business and personal liquidity I have used a simple Excel spreadsheet which looks something like the one shown in Table 8.1 (the numbers and stocks are fictitious).

As you can see, this has the big advantage of simplicity. I can see at a glance what my investments are worth at any one time (I rarely have more than five or six), how much profit they have made or lost, what percentage each represents of the total, and how the stock exchange-related portion relates to my cash resources, and my business debtors and creditors.

The important aspect of this is that ensuring adequate liquidity at all times is a vital part of investment discipline. I am occasionally caught out, but have never been forced to sell shares in order to meet pressing bills, a state of affairs that should be avoided at all costs.

While I have to keep close tabs on my liquidity and on who owes me money, those who have a salary or pension guaranteed to come in on a particular day each month may focus more closely on analyzing their personal spending, and keeping track of the outgoings.

There are packages – Microsoft Money and Intuit's well-known Quicken, for example – which take this approach to the 'nth' degree. In these programs regular spending and investing can be monitored, and the packages can be used to slot figures easily and quickly into tax returns.

With income tax self-assessment now a fact of life in the UK, using software like this will become increasingly important in the future.

How do they work? The core of both packages is a register that contains details of transactions in whatever bank and credit card accounts you set up in the system. Each time you write a cheque or charge a credit card, enter the details into the register along with any deposits you make and other credits. Standing orders can be set up, so that they are logged automatically by the system, or the system can be used to prompt you to record them in the register.

Table 8.1   Finance summary

Stock	Amount	Cost	Price	Value	Gain/Loss	% Value
Agricultural Agencies	10,000	5,165	0.65	6,500	1,335	38.96
Digital Properties	10,000	4,050	0.49	4,900	850	28.69
Universal Widgets	2,000	5,206	2.84	5,680	474	33.26
SE total		14,421		17,080	2,659	100
						% total
SE total				17,080		35
Money market account				600		1.25
Current account				−160		−0.33
Business account				4,500		9.35
Reserve account				1,275		2.65
Building society				13,500		28.06
Debtors				11,321		23.53
Total				48,116		100
Tax due 1 July 2001 Income			2,500	3,450		
NI			950			
VAT and other creditors				1,844		
Short-term net assets				42,822		

Periodically, usually when your bank statements arrive, the software will allow you to perform a reconciliation to make sure the system tallies with your paper record. Any transactions missing at this point – those surreptitious trips to the cash machine, for example – can then be added in to 'balance the books'. A reconciliation report can then be created, showing the current balance in the register, and what portion of it is cheques that have yet to clear, or payments that have yet to be included. See Figure 8.1.

Essentially that's it. One important feature though, is that each entry will be allocated a category (household expenses, gifts, car expenses etc.) either from a default menu or from ones chosen by you. This allows you to itemize your income and expenditure, helping you to analyze where your money's going, and to budget better. A system like this comes into its own when you have been adhering to it for a while, allowing you to track your spending and providing summary totals of items like interest income and pension payments that can be useful, for example, when it comes to tax return time.

Figure 8.1 Quicken screengrab

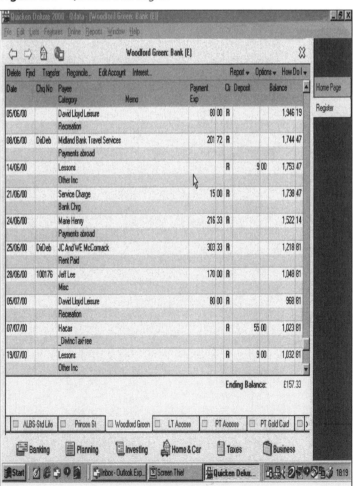

Both packages can also be used to monitor investments, setting up a similar register to that for bank accounts and logging purchases and sales. In theory too, the value of holdings can be updated over the web although in my experience this can be harder than it seems to get right, especially if some of the investments you have fall outside the normal run of blue chips. Portfolio entries have to be tagged with codes to extract updated prices. If this updating is performed regularly, the package can be used to draw basic charts plotting the progress of these different investments.

Both are relatively easy to use and will function perfectly well on 'low-spec' computers. Supporting written material such as manuals tend to be either slim or non-existent. Both programs rely heavily on on-screen help files.

The cost of the basic packages is around the £30 mark, with more sophisticated versions, which include tax software, available for roughly twice the price. Microsoft Money does, however, include one or two extra bells and whistles, including a company car worksheet and calculators for working out loan repayments.

Keeping transactions up to date is not a particular chore if it's done each day, and if you use software like this for a month or so its advantages become very obvious indeed. Eventually these programs will integrate with banking and online dealing services.

Investment software basics

Before looking at the various different categories of investment software, it's a good idea just to take a minute or two to review exactly what you might need. Table 8.2 provides a summary of the different types of packages available, together with contact details.

Think of it in terms of buying a car. How powerful a model do you need, how experienced a driver are you, what optional extras are there, how much will it cost to run, and will it fit in your garage? If you're a novice driver, a Porsche isn't a good idea – it costs too much and you might find it hard to drive.

The 'will it fit in your garage' aspect is easy. You need to make sure, like any piece of software, that you have enough space on your computer hard drive and enough computer memory to store data and run the program to best advantage. Some packages are much more memory intensive than others although on the whole they use less memory than say, a typical spreadsheet or word processing program. Data files, such as the share price information needed to generate charts and especially the fundamental information that sometimes accompanies them, can eat up disk space.

Table 8.2 Main software suppliers

Company name	Web address	E-mail address	Type of package	Price bracket	Demo available
Adest Resources	www.adest.com	na	S	High	No
AIQ	www.aiqsystems.com	sales@realtimetrader.co.uk	PT	Low	Yes
Dividend Associates	www.sharewatch2000.com	john@dividend.demon.co.uk	PFTS	Low	Yes
Equity Workshop	www.equityworkshop.co.uk	na	O	Medium	No
Grail Systems	www.grailsystems.com	sales@grailsystems.com	PFTOMS	Various	No
Indexia	www.indexia.co.uk	info@indexia.co.uk	PTOS	Various	Yes
Intuit	www.intuit.co.uk	alanross@intuit.com	M	Low	No
Investor Ease	www.investorease.com	enquiries@investorease.com	PFT	Low	Yes
Ionic	www.sharescope.co.uk	info@sharescope.co.uk	PFT	Low	Yes
Keyscan Ltd	n/a	73504.2444@compuserve.com	PFT	Low	Yes
Meridian Software	www.meridian-software.co.uk	na	PT	Low	No
Mesa	www.mesa.co.uk	na	S	High	No
Microsoft	www.microsoft.com/uk	na	M	Low	No
Nirvana Systems	www.nirv.com	na	PS	Medium	Yes
Optionvue Systems	www.optionvue.com	info@optionvue.com	TO	High	Yes
Q-Data	www.q-data.co.uk	Ruth@q-data.co.uk	PO	Medium	Yes
Sentinel Software	www.sentinelsoftware.co.uk	jenny@sentinelsoftware.co.uk	PT	Various	Yes
Sepal	www.tradeoptions.net	info@tradeoptions.net	PO	Medium	Yes
Share Genius	n/a	Tel. 0117 9571948	O	Low	Yes
Synergy Software	www.synsoft.co.uk	Steven.Marsh@synsoft.co.uk	PFTS	Various	Yes
Trade to Win	www.TradeToWin.com	Tom@TradeToWin.com	PS	High	Yes
Triumvirate Technology	www.triumvirate-technology.ltd.uk	enquiries@ttl.prestel.co.uk	PFTOS	Various	Yes
Ultra	www.ultrafs.com	steve@ultrafs.com	S	High	No
Updata	www.updata.co.uk	info@updata.co.uk	PT	Various	Yes
Winstock Software	www.winstock.co.uk	winstocksoftware@llineone.net	PT	Low	Yes

Key: P=Price charts; T=Portfolio tracking; F=Fundamentals; O=Options; M=Personal financial mangement; S=Specialist

If you're a newcomer to investing, or to charting, it's best to choose a so-called 'entry-level' package that has a variety of functions and offers easy access to data. The point about these is that you can always upgrade later. Some of the major software houses have a 'trade-in' policy that makes trading up relatively easy by letting you pay just the difference between one product and the next one up the scale.

What options do you want factory fitted? As mentioned before, increasingly investment software combines the two main themes of investing: charting (or technical analysis) – the graphing and interpretation of share price movements – on the one hand, and accounting fundamentals and company news on the other.

Many packages also offer the ability to monitor your holdings and can generate capital gains tax calculations, portfolio analyses and the like. Others may have option pricing models attached, or more specialist charting. Beginners can avoid the extras to start with.

Like cars, some software packages can be expensive to run. Importing data, rather like filling up with petrol, can be costly. See the next section for more detail on this. To start with, opt for a simple package that offers an easy means of importing end-of-day data. Again, the best plan is to start at the cheaper end of the scale and work up.

Can you take a test drive? To get a real feel for how a program works on a day-to-day basis, you need a demo. Many software companies offer these and they are a must before committing yourself.

What does the whole thing cost? Simple packages are available for well under £100. Data can be free. Alternatively a typical 'fundamentals and data' offering may have a modest one-off cost of around £50 plus data costing £10 a month. More elaborate specialist software, or programs specifically designed for in-depth chart analysis using real-time data can run well into four figures. You need experience, and possibly a dollop of training and reading, to get the best out of these.

Downloading data

Downloading price data for shares and other investments is a big subject in itself, and in the past has often caused more pain and grief for the investor than mastering the complexities of using the investment software that goes with it.

It is probably self-evident that the basis of any investment software package is its ability to build up a stream of reliable daily price information that can be stored and retrieved as necessary. More recently many programs have also begun to include fundamental company information such as balance sheet and profit data, directors' dealings and the like.

You can input price data manually from a newspaper, but doing so day after day for even a limited number of shares will quickly become tedious, while building up a price history this way on a new share you are interested in is well-nigh impossible, or at best very time-consuming.

There are successful investors who rely on the charts produced in publications like the *Company Guide*, *Company REFs* and the *Estimate Directory*, but having taken the decision to use investment software, finding an effective means of downloading a sizeable volume of data on a daily basis is an important part of getting the best out of your chosen package.

Advances in technology have made this process progressively easier and cheaper. Basic end-of-day share price data is now effectively free, but the better quality and more comprehensive the data you want to have, the more it will cost, and (in theory at least) the better the investment decisions you will be able to make. Charges are usually made for fundamental data, so if the software you choose incorporates this, you will probably have to pay a monthly charge.

The best price data of all is known by the acronym OHLCV, which stands for Open, High, Low, Close and Volume. Getting data of this type enables a number of additional and more sophisticated chart formats to be used. Even if these are not employed, volume data alone is almost universally useful in making investment decisions.

The data downloading services on offer have increased in number dramatically in recent years. Data is now available for download via teletext, direct from certain price display services, by modem from proprietary databases, via the web, and by e-mail. There are also services that supply data by weekly disk. Each of these methods has its advantages and disadvantages and these are summarised in Table 8.3.

Table 8.3 Data sources summary

Type	Free?	EOD/OHLCV?	New hardware needed?
Teletext	Yes	EOD only	Yes
Dial-in database	No	Both	No
Display services	Yes	Both	No
Disk	No	Usually EOD only	No
E-mail	Yes	EOD	No

Teletext

The telextext services of BBC2 and Channel 4 contain comprehensive share price display pages updated several times daily. Taking the two services together, about 400 shares have prices updated seven times daily, while the Channel 4 service run by Teletext Limited also has the two Teletext 2000 pages, which contain closing prices for all listed shares on a daily basis, updated late in the evening.

Various software companies have interfaces that enable the easy downloading of prices and database maintenance of price files obtained using the Teletext 2000 service.

To use teletext to download price information you need to fit your PC with a teletext adaptor card. This is a standard PC expansion card with a socket attached to take the plug from a TV aerial. The user runs a spur off the TV aerial and plugs the cable into the back of the PC. This then enables teletext pages to be displayed on the PC, and the data on them downloaded into a software package. Teletext adaptor cards currently cost in the region of £100 plus VAT.

The big advantage of using teletext is that it is free.

The drawback is that although reliability has improved over the years, a teletext user is still at the mercy of TV reception, climatic conditions and the efficiency of the TV aerial used. In the days when I used teletext to update my software, I had to spend out not only on the expansion card but also in the end on a high performance aerial to improve the quality of the reception into the package and eliminate errors in the downloading procedure.

Teletext downloads also need to be done at a certain time each day, and arrangements need to be made to automate this procedure if the user is away for an extended period, although this is not an insurmountable problem.

Finally, a major drawback to teletext is that it does not give either OHLCV or even volume data.

Modem

Downloading data by modem overcomes a lot of these disadvantages. Various proprietary databases are available that offer data by modem, particularly those for software packages that offer fundamental data in addition to price information.

Services like this used to cost a lot. Now they tend to cost in the region of £10 per month with the software that uses the data either free or available at comparatively low cost.

The drawback is that the user may effectively be locked into a particular service and price data may not be easily transferable to other software packages.

Data display services

Price display systems like Market Eye and some satellite based services enable data to be downloaded into a range of investment software packages at no extra charge. Market Eye also offers a data download-only option.

Although I have my doubts about whether or not live price feeds are really useful for anyone other than short-term traders, if you are set on one, then there will normally be no need to spend additional sums on downloading data for a chart package, provided of course you have ensured that the package chosen is compatible with the feed.

Data by disk

A few software suppliers have developed services by which a selected list of shares can be updated via a disk posted off to subscribers on a weekly or fortnightly basis. Services of this nature tend to be cheaper than online services, via modem or some other means of dial-up, but the user loses out to a degree on the timeliness of the information.

Nonetheless for those interested only in longer-term trading opportunities services of this type are easy and cost-effective to use, the new disk being simply inserted into the computer each week and the updated price files copied across into the price files stored on the computer's hard drive.

Internet-based services

This topic is covered in much more detail in the next chapter, but it is worth recording that the advent of investment-related websites has done much to democratize financial information, including price data. Many so-called 'portal' investment sites also offer charts and fundamental information, and these may enable online investors to do without conventional investment software altogether.

Data by e-mail

Some software allows price data to be delivered to subscribers by daily e-mail. Services like this have progressed considerably in recent years, allowing the updates from the data to be more or less completely automated. Services like this are often provided free of charge or for a small upfront fee, although the data involved is simple end-of-day closing prices.

One important general point relating to data is that if you are contemplating buying or using any software package, make sure that you work out in advance the cost and feasibility of getting data to use with it. Data costs can add significantly to the price of the package, and those packages primarily designed for US users may not be compatible with the common sources of data for UK or European shares.

Charting software

As already covered in Chapter 4, price charts can be of help in timing purchases and sales, even if you make your share selections on fundamental grounds. Chart movements reflect investor behaviour and not to use them, at least to some degree, could mean you miss something obvious.

Many of the purer charting packages still have an array of indicators and chart types that would be bewildering for a novice. If you're new to charting, some of the software comes with explanatory material on technical analysis but otherwise it's probably a good idea to get hold of one of the many books on the subject. The best is John Murphy's *Technical Analysis of the Financial Markets* (New York Institute of Finance). A high-priced tome at £44, but well worth the money.

An excellent basic package is Winstock's 'The Analyst', which costs around £80, although an extra £45 allows you have price data e-mailed daily. I have used this package over some years and it works very well indeed. E-mail updating is now wholly automated. The charts in Chapter 4 were generated using the Winstock package.

Other basic charting packages include Updata's Invest. This is very much an entry level package, with most users converting to the much more expensive Trader program. Indexia's Intro, which works in a DOS environment, albeit on a normal Windows operating system, is also easy to install and use. Indexia allows easy upgrading to its two more expensive packages, by letting users pay the difference. For technical analysis purists, Indexia II Plus, the top-end package, is probably the best value on the market.

In general terms, with chart packages the principle is that the more chart types and indicators the package has, the more expensive it will be, and the more likely it is to be used in conjunction with a real-time feed for heavy-duty trading.

If your taste is for the more esoteric, there are specialist packages around for Gann analysis, for Elliott Wavers, for those addicted to sine wave analysis, and for market timers. For the most part, however, these packages are US orientated and on the expensive side and configuring them for use with UK data can be problematic.

Ultra Market Adviser, for example, an excellent market-timing product, only has US data at present, but the package's developers in Texas are thought to be looking at the possibility of also getting hold of UK data for the package. See Figure 8.2.

Figure 8.2 ULTRA screengrab

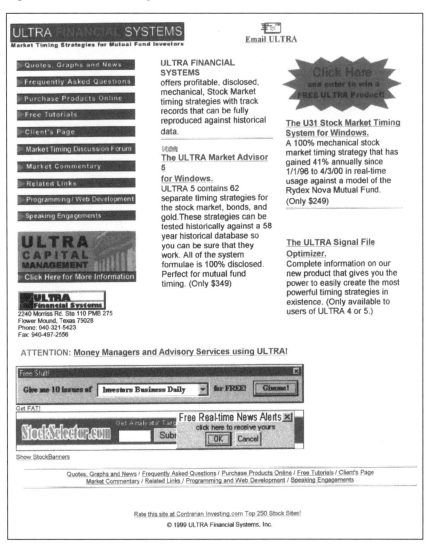

Software with fundamentals

Software that contains both price charts and fundamental data has struck a chord with investors in recent years. Rightly so, investors feel able to make better judgements about shares with the benefit of fundamental information, however rudimentary it may be.

Software like this that includes accounting information makes no pretence that the numbers contained are comprehensive, simply that it is conveniently arranged and that it's easy to switch between charts and fundamentals.

Apart from basic stock market data such as PE ratios, PEGs and yields, it tends also to include consensus earnings estimates, information on directors dealings and, in some cases, recent news items. Sources vary, but data is normally drawn from HS Financial Publishing or, in the case of news, AFX.

Ionic Information's Sharescope package, in particular, has developed sophisticated uses of the data. Sectors and indices, or specially created portfolios, can be analyzed using a 'data mining' tool that integrates both price-related parameters such as volatility, a limited number of technical indicators, and accounts items of various descriptions, with the results displayed in a near-3D format.

The tool is unique in a budget priced software product. In general, within the software, tables of price and fundamental data can be put together easily and displayed or exported to Excel for further analysis.

Synergy Software's 'Portfolio Evolution' is a somewhat more comprehensive package when it comes to fundamentals, with more detailed P&L and balance sheet information set out in a standardized, easy to use format, with tabs for each subset of information, making it easy to analyze an individual share in detail.

In Synergy's case, the drawback of pulling in such a large amount of information is the time then required for updating, especially if you forget to do it regularly and you have a less powerful computer. Share price histories are easier to get at than in some packages and the chart offering arguably more sophisticated.

In terms of price there is little to choose between the two packages. Sharescope has a one-off cost of £80 and then data at £12 a month including VAT. Synergy charges £144 per year for a bundled package of software and data, to all intents a data cost of £12 a month excluding VAT.

Where products like this score is in allowing easy tabulation and analysis of large quantities of basic data, and then allowing it to be exported to a spreadsheet for further analysis.

Sharescope, for example, can justly claim to have pioneered the inclusion of fundamental data in investment software. Whether you use this package or one of the alternatives depends essentially on your style of investing: Sharescope offers a more quantitative approach, other packages, such as Synergy's, may be better for investigating individual shares in more detail.

Options software

We looked in Chapter 7 at how options can be used in the context of organizing a portfolio with the correct level of risk. Options software is a special sub-group of the investment software scene.

There are two main types of option software. On the one hand, there are option pricing models. These allow you to input the various parameters of a particular option – underlying price, strike price, expiry date, volatility, cost of money, dividend payments and so on – and work out either an option's implied volatility from its market price, or the fair value of the option at a given volatility level, and other useful statistics.

Then there is software for managing deals and charting trading strategies. If you are buying more than one option as part of the same trade, or using options in conjunction with a holding in the underlying shares, software like this makes it easier to keep track of what's happening.

If this sounds complicated, not to mention expensive, remember that simple option pricing software is available free of charge or as low-cost shareware over the web. But you do get what you pay for. Commercial packages tend to have more features.

LIFFE has a directory of information that includes details of some popular options packages and technical analysis software. You will probably need to investigate several to find the one that's best for your needs. The following are a few examples.

Option Evaluator from Source Code Software is a Windows-based 'option pricer', somewhat more sophisticated than those available on the web. One useful feature is the ability to calculate volatility from an inputted stream of share prices or index values. It also allows for different option pricing methods to be selected and will graph projected profitability.

SG Options is a DOS-based package written by Bristol-based Geoff Bacon (tel: 0117 957 1948). Priced at a modest £85, the DOS package will take end-of-day prices via a compressed computer file from the LIFFE website and plug them into the model. The software is an option pricer with some extra functions built in. These include graphing of various option parameters as well as working out and monitoring strategies. Data can also be entered manually.

The DOS construction means the package works very quickly and takes up minimal disk space. A Windows version currently under development is likely to be a little easier to use, however, with some extra features including quick select buttons for picking strategies.

Sepal Software's Optionbase software (tel: 01707 276156, or www.tradeoptions.net) is a similar DOS-based package with much the same features, although the price is a somewhat heftier £228 including VAT. This software does allow you, however, to manipulate various param-eters (such as time to expiry) from the same screen and see the effects instantly. Generally, however, the software is more complex to use than the SG Options package.

Indexia's Option Trader product (tel: 01442-878015 or www.indexia.co.uk) is designed to work with the firm's various technical analysis packages but will function as a stand-alone program if users are comfortable with it not calculating the underlying share volatility. If the package is used with one of Indexia's mainstream products, however, this important calculation is done automatically from the data in the chart software.

The option package is also available at half price to existing users. For a new user buying the group's entry-level Intro chart package and Option Trader, the total price is about £250. The whole set-up runs under DOS, although it is installed within Windows and will work perfectly well on any Windows machine.

As in Indexia's case, some other option programs are designed to work at their best as part of an established technical analysis software suite. They can be expensive, however.

Omega Research (www.omegaresearch.com) is another good example. Its Option Station software, for example, is designed to work in conjunction with Tradestation, its top-end technical analysis package. It costs an extra £750 on top of the chart software, which itself costs some £1,500. Though it can be used separately, it pretty much ranks as the Rolls Royce of option software.

For those with a more modest budget, Omega's Supercharts software offers a reasonable compromise, providing technical analysis of the underlying shares and an option valuation package as part of the same system. Trendline (tel: 0208 367 8808) and Grail Systems (tel: 0208 940 9244) are among the UK suppliers of these packages, a full list of which can be found at the Omega website.

The basic advice, however, is to start off with a cheap and cheerful solution using either a free or shareware package. At a later date you can always then graduate to a more expensive one if you feel your trading needs that extra edge.

Cost comparisons and functionality

Comparing software products is a difficult exercise, but in broad terms you get what you pay for. While we have given some price indications in the preceding sections, since each software product is subtly different from the next, the relationship between the price of each package and what it does is less clear.

The more complex and more expensive systems are less suited to newcomers to the investment scene, and demand a lot of time and attention to extract the best value. This can include reading, training courses, and a lengthy period of familiarization with the software.

Table 8.2 shown earlier gives a price band for each product, broadly corresponding to the entry-level, mid-range and advanced-level subdivision that most of the big software suppliers operate. There are a number of systems, however, where payment is on a subscription basis, normally bundled in with data provision.

In terms of what the products do – their 'functionality' – the general rule is that the more expensive the system, the more technical indicators it will have and the more sophisticated its additional capabilities. These might include, for example, market scanning and automatic testing of trading methods. However, even basic systems for beginners – particularly those produced by major suppliers such as Indexia, Synergy and Updata – have an adequate number of indicators for all but the most enthusiastic chartist or hyperactive trader.

Over and above these technical indicators (which are difficult to specify precisely in a table), most products will handle routine portfolio management tasks including the recording of transactions and dealing costs, and the ability to keep a running cash account. A few can automate capital gains tax calculations.

As noted previously, transaction monitoring need not be regarded as an essential component to a particular software package, although most have it (in some cases in only a rudimentary form). Some programs have the ability to export data into a spreadsheet or into an alternative personal finance monitoring system such as Quicken, thus obviating the need for an integrated portfolio management module anyway. Functionality like this tends to be included because some do find it easier if the facilities are all available in the same package. It's a matter of personal choice.

As explained earlier, the incorporation of fundamental data is a feature of a number of packages. Often this would not be the main purpose behind an investor's purchase of such a program, and products do differ in the amount of data they incorporate. In some it can be as basic as simply recording dividend yields and PE ratios, in others the information is more sophisticated.

Systems differ too in the different ways of downloading data that they support. Teletext download options are available for most budget-priced packages, but the data available through teletext is of less use in more sophisticated programs, which require OHLCV data. Several budget packages also include a 'data by disk' service, which is one way that software suppliers can gain a stream of revenue from a single purchase. These options, however, often represent a comparatively inexpensive way of getting the most out of the systems.

In the case of the mid-priced and upper-range packages, more data options are available. These include taking data from services such as Market Eye, satellite services, those using radio and pager technology, data by modem and e-mail, and data from the internet and world wide web. In general terms the more sophisticated the package the more flexible it will be in accepting data in different formats. Most allow the importing of data in ASCII format, however, and many US packages accept data in the format used by Metastock, one of the best-selling packages worldwide and something of an industry standard.

A rational strategy is for an investor to select a budget package from a supplier with a clearly defined 'ladder' of products through which a user can upgrade. The initial download option can either be via teletext or another economical data source, for instance by e-mail or through the internet. As the user becomes more familiar, upgrading to a more sophisticated package can then be done at relatively low cost, and the option of more comprehensive data downloading can be explored.

Private investors are increasingly using investment software to keep track of their investments and to help them make trading decisions.

IN BRIEF

- Private investors are increasingly using investment software to keep track of their investments and to help them make trading decisions.

- The investor has a choice between using a spreadsheet package in conjunction with a simple chart program, or buying a package that has both functions combined.

- Investment software is available in a range of prices, from under £100 to over £1,000. In recent years, budget software packages have become available that also have fundamental information on companies.

- Portfolio management modules contained in investment software packages enable the user to record and analyze transactions, to keep track of their cash balances and investment profits and losses, and to produce valuations and Inland Revenue-acceptable capital gains tax schedules.

- Charting modules in investment software packages contain a variety of chart indicators. The more expensive the package, the more indicators it will usually contain.

- Mid-range and upper-priced packages often include software that enables the indicators to be fine-tuned to suit different shares, and which enable the database to be scanned for shares that meet particular technical criteria.

- Downloading data into investment software packages can represent a significant extra cost, but is usually worth it. Data is now much cheaper than it was and delivered by a variety of means, of which the most reliable involve either a dial-in database or receiving data by e-mail. Good quality data has the potential to improve investment decision making.

- The best strategy for the newcomer to investment software is to choose a basic package with a low cost data download option, and then upgrade later if necessary. There is generally no penalty for upgrading.

- As the investor graduates to more complex packages, there is a hidden extra cost in terms of the extra time needed to learn about and get the best value from these packages.

The online investor – shares and the internet

The average private investor would need to be remarkably reclusive not to have heard of the internet at some point over the past few years. 'Surfing the net' has become an overused buzzword. Newspapers are devoting increasing amounts of space to the subject. Many web-based businesses have floated on the stock market, although their fortunes have been mixed.

There are now more than ten million regular internet users in the UK, and probably as many as 100,000 investors now deal regularly with online brokers, with many more using the 'net' to research investment choices of all types.

What this chapter aims to do is to give a brief outline of how you can use the internet to give you that all-important investing edge. It is worth taking this seriously because the web has a huge quantity of investment-related resources available free of charge.

Getting connected

Existing net users can skip this section.

The essentials for getting connected to the internet are a computer with a reasonable amount of free hard drive space, a modem and a telephone line.

Any would-be internet user needs to open an account with an internet service provider. There are a large number of service providers around, the important point being to choose one that enables you, the user, to dial into the service using a local telephone number. Most major providers have local call 'points of presence' in major towns and cities around the country.

Table 9.1 shows a range of UK-based internet providers.

Once the account is opened, the service provider should supply software enabling you to access the internet easily and efficiently.

It is important to remember that the speed with which downloading information (web pages, files, software etc.) can be accomplished is really dependent not on the power of the computer you are using, but on the capacity of your modem.

The ideal compromise between speed and cost at the moment is a modem that runs at 56,600 bps. As a rough guide this will enable connection to an internet service provider's computer and permit the downloading of 100,000 bytes of data in about 30 seconds. Hence a file that is 1.3MB in size might take around seven minutes to download from a remote computer.

The cost of the whole exercise is less than you might think. There are 'free' service providers around, although they tend to charge heavily for support. Many other service providers (especially those who provide their own content in addition to permitting web access) work on the basis either of simple time-based charges for online usage, subject to a monthly minimum, or charge a flat fee (normally around £10 a month) for unlimited use.

Table 9.1 UK-based internet service providers

Top 10 free ISPs		
Provider	*URL*	*Tel.*
Screaming.net	www.screaming.net	(0800) 376 5262
Cable & Wireless Internet	www.cwcom.net	(0800) 092 3013
Madasafish	www.madasafish.co.uk	(09010) 222324
UK Online	www.ukonline.net	(0845) 333 4567
Freeserve	www.freeserve.net	(0900) 500 049
conX	www.conx.co.uk	(0900) 777 0055
FreeUK	www.freeuk.net	(0900) 900 0900
Icom-Web	www.icom-web.com	(0800) 731 8419
Free-Online	www.free-online.net	(0870) 706 0504
Top 10 subscription ISPs		
Provider	*URL*	*Tel.*
I-Way Soho	www.i-way.co.uk	(020) 7734 5734
Intonet	www.intonet.co.uk	(020) 8941 9195
Primex	www.primex.co.uk	(01908) 643 597
Freedom to Surf	www.freedom2surf.net	(020) 8881 2111
U-Net	www.u-net.net	(01925) 484 444
Direct Connection	www.dircon.net	(0800) 072 0000
Frontier Internet Services	www.frontier-internet.ltd.uk	(0845) 601 1279
Claranet	www.clara.net	(0800) 358 2828
Newbury Internet	www.newbury.net	(01635) 569 123
Cablenet	www.cablenet.net	(0800) 195 8888

Which is best for you depends on how much use you intend to make of the service. Telephone charges normally come on top, although some providers throw this in as part of the monthly fee.

The advent of high-speed so-called 'broadband' services is imminent. These services, such as BT's ADSL product, promise to offer permanent web connections at much faster download speeds for an all-inclusive flat fee of around £40 per month, which could prove tempting for heavy users.

It is worth looking at an internet connection not just as a cost, but what getting connected can save you in other directions.

For example, the cost of electronic mail (e-mail) is negligible, with the connection time being a few seconds of local telephone time compared to perhaps 30 seconds or more per page for a fax, and 27p for a normal letter. E-mail can be used to send documents and files stored on your computer's hard drive, with the transmission time being just a few seconds and the costs just those of a local call, *irrespective of the destination*.

Using the web

Non-internet users and first-timers are often confused over the distinction between the internet and the world wide web. The two are often taken to be synonymous, whereas in fact the web is simply a part, albeit perhaps the most high profile one, of the 'net'.

The web is best seen as a passive information resource. Web 'pages' are designed and launched and can be visited or (in the jargon) 'hit' by any connected user simply by typing the site's unique address into their web browser.

The web is based around a concept known as 'hypertext'. Clicking on a highlighted area will transfer another set of data from the host computer to your own. This enables web pages to have complex links both to data and text embedded in their own system and also to other relevant sites operated by different organizations. They thereby allow the user to explore wherever the mood dictates.

As an example, a stock exchange site might have various pages highlighting new issues, trading volume and index statistics, biographies of exchange officials, articles of interest on relevant subjects, each accessed by clicking on an icon at the original 'home page'. But it will also have hypertext links to other exchanges, leading companies, other investment-related sites, regulators and so on. Each link is accessible through a simple point and click, and the transfer of data is normally accomplished within a few seconds.

There are already a large number of stock market related web pages available. The following sections of this chapter mainly deal with web pages related to different aspects of the investment process, and the information that can be gleaned from them.

Keeping track of new web pages that may be of interest can be something of a problem. One solution to this is the existence of so-called 'search engines' which, by working on search criteria carefully specified by the user, can quickly present a user with a list of web addresses that appear to be relevant to the subject matter being investigated. Some of these may turn out to be red herrings, but then again others may contain links to other sites that turn out to be of relevance.

The real beauty of the system is that a lot of the information is free of charge. One initial complaint about the web, that US content predominated in many areas, is becoming less valid as the system is gradually being filled out with content from other non-US sources. When you find a suitable page of information you might want to use again, the page can be saved with a 'bookmark' that allows easy revisiting in future.

As well as bookmarks, it is also possible to build up a list of broad jumping-off points that contain a large number of links to other sites related to the same subject. So-called 'portal' sites are designed to contain a lot of information and links related to a particular subject, and there are several excellent financial portals that can serve as a starting point for exploring the web.

Bookmarking sites like this means that a vast range of other sites are only a couple of mouse clicks away. Some of these portals are shown in Table 9.2.

So much for the basics. Now let's explore the types of resources that are available on the internet, what use they are to investors, and how they can be accessed.

Table 9.2   Search engines

Search engine	URL	Portals	URL
All the Web	www.alltheweb.com	ADVFN	www.advfn.com
AltaVista	www.altavista.com	interactiveinvestor	www.iii.co.uk
Ask Jeeves	www.askjeeves.co.uk	moneyextra	www.moneyextra.com
Deja	www.deja.com	hemscott.net	www.hemscott.net
Excite	excite.com	numa	www.numa.com
Google	www.google.com	uk-invest	www.ukinvest.com
GoTo	www.goto.com	EuropeanInvestor	www.europeaninvestor.com
Lycos	www.lycos.co.uk		
Northern Light	www.northernlight.com		
WebCrawler	wwwwebcrawler.com		

Resources for investors

Bulletin boards

One of the most interesting aspects of the 'net' is the ability it offers users to canvas the views of and make contact with a wide range of other individuals who also have 'net' connections.

Firstly, there are so-called newsgroups (sometimes called conferences) which offer the opportunity to request information, express opinions or contribute to a debate on virtually any topic.

Newsgroups are run by individual service providers, such as CIX, AOL and many others. They cover a variety of topics. There is also a whole raft of newsgroups run under the umbrella of Usenet, a US organization.

The newsgroup works as follows. The user logs on through his service provider to the newsgroups of his or her choice. Generally a user will read and compose a message to the groups selected while off-line, connecting only to post and retrieve new messages. In effect bulletin boards or newsgroups are simply a central point to which electronic mail can be posted for all other participants in the group to see. Users are then free to continue a discussion either by private e-mail, or in the public forum as they wish.

I have found newsgroups an interesting source of information, but it is worth restricting the number you log on to quite strictly. Some groups have more than 100 'posts' per day, which can take some reading. There are systems available which enable posts on particular topics or from particular contributors to be filtered out prior to the updates being downloaded, but even so the daily routine of ploughing through newsgroup messages can become a chore.

Newsgroups have allowed me to pick up some investment 'vibes' and investing ideas through keeping my eyes open when reading posts. Another good point is that though many newsgroups and bulletin boards are dedicated to share investing, there are also specialist ones around that cover other forms of investment.

These comments also apply with equal force to the more recent phenomenon of web-based bulletin boards, which have shown huge growth in usage in recent years. The difference between these and newsgroups is that they can, by definition, only be used while online.

Within the investment sphere there are both general and specialist bulletin boards. Many of the financial portals referred to earlier also have bulletin boards attached. While they can be a useful source of ideas, BBs that are open to all-comers tend to attract a lot of trite ill-informed and sometimes downright abusive comments, especially in relation to companies that are in the public eye or speculative favourites. It is worth exploring whether some of the paid-for BBs are worth joining (ADVFN is a good example –

www.advfn.com) simply to join a community that is more informed and where users who misbehave can be excluded more effectively.

One important point is that many portal sites with bulletin boards also have a portfolio monitoring facility. The best of these, like ADVFN and Interactive Investor (www.iii.co.uk), can not only provide up-to-date information on the value of your shares and other investments, but also direct links to both news and bulletin board comments on them, making them a very effective tool for keeping track of your investments.

Links to a range of these portal sites and search tools are available at www.linksitemoney.com.

Prices and data

One of the more interesting features of the internet and the web is the opportunity they offer private investors to access data that was once the preserve of the professional investor, and moreover they do so either free of charge or at relatively low cost. There are a number of web services that charge, but the charges are generally very modest.

Free sites are sometimes subsidized by advertising, since the connected community represents a target socio-economic group that advertisers find attractive. Registering for free services is sometimes used as a teaser to get the user hooked on the information being supplied, prior to charges being introduced at a later date or for an enhanced service.

One of the side effects of the growth of the web has been to open private investors' eyes to the information that is available in other markets (notably the USA) at relatively low cost, and therefore begin a process of exerting downward pressure on information charges in the domestic market concerned.

The cost of price data used to be a particular bone of contention in the UK, where the Stock Exchange exerted a rather baleful influence over data suppliers and their charges to end-users. More recently, the exchange has seen the light and made delayed data (usually 15 minutes old, and therefore effectively of little value to a professional user) available to private investors free of charge via any website that wishes to avail itself of the service.

Real-time prices are generally available for a relatively modest cost (as little as £5 a month) or in some rare cases free of charge. ADVFN, for example, offers free real-time prices and has recently launched a service offering detailed so-called 'level 2' prices (the type the professionals use) for private investors for £35 a month.

As discussed in the next section, many online broking services also allow their users access to delayed prices or even real time prices and price charts free of charge either when monitoring their investments or placing an order.

The web has also made it much easier for investors to access data to use in investment software packages. As we explored in the previous chapter, end-of-day price data is now widely available delivered via e-mail or the web to plug into investment software packages. Another option available to investors at some sites (Market Eye – www.marketeye.com – is an example) is the ability to download complete price histories for individual stocks free of charge in so-called ASCII or .csv format.

This means that it can be easily imported into a spreadsheet like Excel. Excel's chart-drawing facility can then be used to construct a basic chart without the need for any additional specialist software. This is a perfectly viable option for those who only use charts occasionally.

Many portal sites (UK-inVest – www.ukinvest.com – is the best example) also offer charting facilities that are on a par with those available in mid-range software products. The charts available at this site used Java programming to construct charts that offer a wide range of technical indicators and also the ability to switch the timescale the chart covers quickly and easily. Similar, though rather more basic, charts are available for a very wide range of stocks at the Yahoo Finance site (http://finance.yahoo.co.uk).

One highly positive aspect of all these developments is that they have opened up access to information that the professionals previously largely had to themselves. In so doing it has removed some of the mystique from the investment process. Without too much exaggeration, one can argue that it opens up the possibility of true shareholder democracy, where all shareholders and potential shareholders have simultaneous and equal (or at least nearly equal) access to relevant information about their investments and general market trends.

Recently, for example, the SEC in the United States ruled that companies had to open up their periodic briefings on trends in their businesses and their financial performance to all investors, and not just to a selected group of analysts and professional investors.

Online dealing

In the USA, investing is part of daily life for millions of people, even to the extent that many stockbrokers have a retail presence on high streets across America. In this environment too, the idea of clients dealing by PC or by some other automated means is commonplace – witness the recent phenomenon of so-called 'day-traders'.

One of the aspects of share investment in the UK that has arguably put off many potential private investors over the years has been the concern people have about being embarrassed talking to a broker. Will the broker have time to spend on my order? Will he be patronizing and snooty? Will he be too busy? Will I feel embarrassed betraying my ignorance about the ins and outs of the market? And so on.

In fairness to the private-client broking community, many of these worries are just old psychological hang-ups that may once have represented real problems. Now they no longer square much with reality, at least when it comes to dealing with execution-only brokers, who by and large are approachable and businesslike.

There are, however, those who find conversing with dealers a needless hassle, and who would be happy to do their share trading over a PC link rather than via a telephone conversation. I include myself in this group.

A considerable number of these services are now available to UK and European investors. There are now over 20 online dealing services operating in the UK and as the number of participants have increased, so commission charges have fallen rapidly with many brokers now offering flat fee dealing for as little as £10 a trade.

As explained in Chapter 5, the services offered fall into two parts. One is a wholly automated system available for a large number of leading shares and many smaller ones. These real-time systems allow you to log in directly to the market maker systems and place an order. Once confirmed, you are told the price available in the market and the cost of the deal and given 15 seconds to accept or reject the deal. If you accept, the deal is transacted instantaneously and a contract note e-mailed to you.

In the case of some smaller stocks and other types of investment, such as gilts and convertibles, that are not included in these real-time systems, the broker system will instead e-mail an order to a dealer for execution in the traditional manner at an indicative price, and the details of the transaction will be confirmed to you a little while later.

I have used both types of system extensively over the last few years and quite simply would not deal any other way. Several levels of security are built into systems like this. Initial login to the site is via a normal user id and password system, but placing an order requires an additional PIN number to be entered. The broking account is typically linked to a secure bank account, so that funds are credited and debited automatically as trades are done, but cannot be transferred to another account outside the system without written authorization.

Many brokers also provide basic information on shares and other forms of investment free of charge. This includes price charts, news, third-party research and in-house bulletins, as well as routine valuations online.

When using services like this investors must be prepared to accept that their investments are held in paperless form, either in the broker's own nominee account or via individual membership of CREST (the UK settlement organization). This is available to individual investors for a small annual fee and has the advantage of keeping the investor's name on the share register of the company, meaning that annual reports and other shareholder communications, as well as shareholder perks and the like, can continue to be received directly.

To recap, online brokers typically levy a charge to service an individual account, usually in the region of £50 a year. Some brokers make an extra charge for information services. In general these are worth avoiding, since there is so much free information available on the web for the DIY investor.

An important new trend for UK and European investors is flowing from the mergers between European stock exchanges and the increasingly close links between settlement organizations. As a result some brokers are now offering their clients the opportunity to deal in any European market or in the USA from the same account and have all the administration take place seamlessly behind the scenes.

A good example is an excellent service from the German broker Comdirect (www.comdirect.co.uk) which does exactly this, allowing the user to specify a currency in which the portfolio is valued and settled. This site also contains a wealth of information on a wide range of companies in leading markets around the world, displayed in a standardized form and including accounts data, price charts, news and many other items. See Figure 9.1.

Figure 9.1 Comdirect screengrab

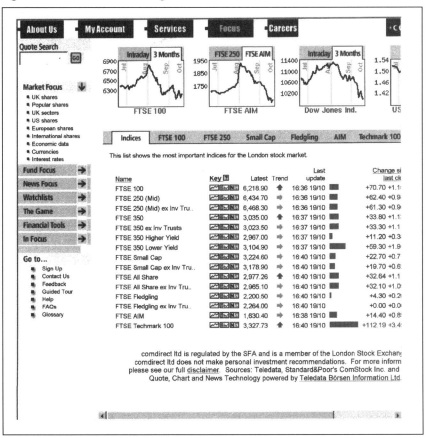

Services like this flow directly from the globalization of markets, but also from the increasing availability of company information. Investors may well be as familiar with Microsoft as they are with BT, or Volkswagen. If they like the look of a share, in whatever country it happens to reside, they can research it online and buy or sell it with ease.

Software

One of the advantages, and big cost-saving elements, of the internet and world wide web is the ability it offers to transfer software programs from a remote computer or website straight to your PC. There are several sites, almost all in the USA, where investment software is available and can be downloaded free of charge.

But remember the distinction between 'freeware' and 'shareware'. Freeware is totally free, but often has pretty limited functionality. Shareware is different. The programs are fully working versions that can be used perfectly well by the person downloading the software, but need to be registered to gain full user support, including manuals, access to later versions, and so on.

More recently, however, some software sites appear to be changing this policy. A number of software sites on the world wide web, for example, enable software to be downloaded, but only either in a demo version, in a version that self-destructs after a restricted number of uses, or in a version that is 'crippled' in some way so that the user is obliged to purchase the fully working version if he or she likes the look of the package.

The vast majority of software available for download is now accessed via special software websites such as Download.com and others. The system works in the following way. Browse the site using the categories provided or enter a search term to locate a particular type of software. Details of particular packages available can be viewed in more detail; the information usually provides a brief description of what the software does, how popular it has proved, ratings from users, and the size of the file and estimated time it will take to download.

Once located, clicking on the appropriate underlined and highlighted phrase or icon will initiate a download and prompt the user to specify a directory into which the downloaded software is to be placed.

It is a good idea to have already created an empty directory before contemplating a download. When the download is completed, clicking on the .exe file among those downloaded will normally initiate the setup sequence and create a new directory in which the program can reside. Once this is accomplished, the files in the 'download' directory can be deleted. Table 9.3 shows some of the commonly used download sites.

Table 9.3 Software download sites

Company	URL
CNET Download.com	www.download.com
Investor Software	www.investorsoftware.com
Tucows	www.tucows.com
Wall Street Directory	www.wsdinc.com
Winsite	www.winsite.com

Remember however that, as with most things in life, you get what you pay for. Many freely available or low cost programs have much more limited functionality than the commercial programs they seek to emulate. A big category in downloadable software, for example, is personal financial management programs, which seek to duplicate the functions provided by programs such as Microsoft Money and Quicken (see previous chapter). In many instances, though free, these programs are a pale imitation and may not be well suited for use by UK investors.

The other drawback is that much downloadable software originates in the USA, is designed specifically for use by Americans and compatible only with US data. Often some of the best programs are those that perform specific limited functions, such as calculating option prices, or simply ready reckoners for working out the fair value of a share.

However, the availability of software over the internet has had an effect in internationalizing the market for investment software. Like share price data sold by exchanges, software of this type used to be significantly cheaper in the USA, and this phenomenon has played its part in exerting downward pressure on the prices of software and data originating elsewhere.

Examples of some software programs available at Download.com are shown on the screenshot (Figure 9.2). Readers who are connected are encouraged to experiment in downloading them. It is an elementary precaution to check any downloaded program for viruses before installing it. Some other programs and spreadsheet add-ins are available at the software page at my website at www.linksitemoney.com.

Online publications and news

In Chapter 2, I highlighted the need for investors to be on the lookout for information in newspapers and other publications. At one time readers who followed this advice might, for example, have been shocked by the size of their regular weekly paper bill and concerned that this would make the cost of pursuing their investment activities prohibitive.

Figure 9.2 Download.com screengrab

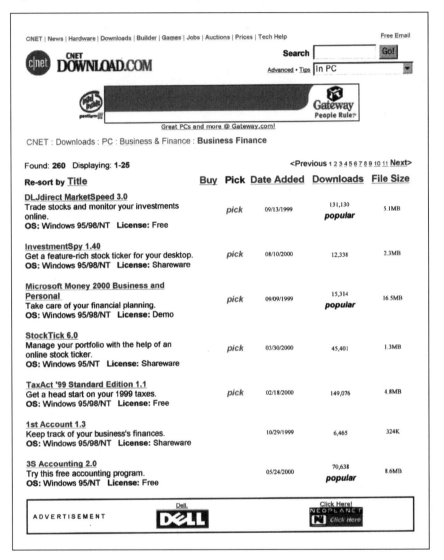

The internet has for some time offered a way around this. Newspapers are increasingly publishing online as an adjunct to their news stand product. Accessing these electronic papers can be a good way of making sure that the City pages of the leading quality papers can be read on a daily basis – at a fraction of the cost of buying the actual paper.

In the UK the *Daily Telegraph* has been the pioneer in this field with its site containing market reports and diary items as well as news stories and even cartoons. *The Times*, *Financial Times* and *The Economist* also have sites, as does the *Guardian*. All of these sites are searchable free of charge, making researching 'press clippings' on a particular company a relatively simple matter. A number of overseas publications, including the *Wall Street Journal* and various investment newsletters, also have web pages (see Table 9.4). More often than not these tend to be accessible in an unexpurgated version only by payment of a subscription.

In these instances, the reader needs to make a judgement about whether the cost of the subscription is worth the charge involved. The rules given earlier regarding the paramount need to feel that you get something tangible from a publication on a regular basis and that it is always keenly read on the date of issue should be the guiding principle here.

In the case of information on European investments, a wide range of Continental news organizations have websites, but few are available in English, so you need to have good linguistic skills to use them, or a means of translating the relevant items.

Table 9.4 Selected newspaper sites

Publication	URL
The Economist	www.economist.com
Financial Times	www.ft.com
Guardian	www.guardianunlimited.co.uk
New York Times	www.nytimes.com
Shares Magazine	www.sharesmagazine.com
Telegraph	www.telegraph.co.uk
The Times	www.the-times.co.uk
This is Money	www.thisismoney.com
Wall Street Journal	www.wsj.com

Exchanges

An increasing number of financial markets around the world have sites on the world wide web offering a variety of information about the exchange, trading statistics, share and option price data, and links to other sites of interest.

The London International Financial Futures and Options Exchange (LIFFE) also has a site (www.liffe.com) which contains a substantial body of information about the exchange and its products and prices of the various instruments traded, normally on a time-delayed basis.   ·

Investment exchanges in different territories are often a good source of information on the movement of local indices and leading stocks, providing a free source of information superior to that normally obtainable from newspapers or other sources. For investors who are interested in investing internationally, this is clearly a useful and valuable resource.

Table 9.5 gives examples of some of the exchanges displaying information of this type, and the addresses of their web pages.

Table 9.5   Selected exchange websites

Exchange	URL
Deutsche Boerse	www.exchange.de
EASDAQ	www.easdaq.com
Euronext	www.euronext.com
London Stock Exchange	www.londonstockex.co.uk
Madrid SE	www.bolsamadrid.es
Milan SE	www.borsaitalia.it
NASDAQ	www.nasdaq.com
New York Stock Exchange	www.nyse.com

Corporate information

One of the single most important developments in recent years has been the dramatic growth in investor relations websites of listed companies.

In the early days, the corporate sector in the UK was somewhat ambivalent about the development of the internet. An informal survey of the FTSE 100 I conducted in April 1995 revealed, for instance, that fewer than ten companies had an active internet presence at that time, while only a further dozen or so had any plans to develop one in anything other than the long term.

Now, however, all of the FTSE 100 and about 90 per cent of the Mid250 companies in the UK have corporate websites, while the same is true of other markets.

Corporate websites vary enormously in the help they offer investors. Some are designed clearly with the consumer, rather than the investor, in mind. While this is a legitimate position to take, there is no reason why the interests of both constituencies cannot be accommodated.

Online investors have specific needs. They require a speedy and efficient delivery mechanism for company information such as annual reports, results announcements, press releases, and other background information, perhaps a means of accessing a live share price on the company, and a mechanism by which an e-mail response can be easily generated from the company to a specific question of a financial or corporate nature.

It should be possible, for instance, for a private shareholder to e-mail a question about (say) a results announcement to a designated contact in the investor relations department of a large company and to receive a prompt official response. Yet comparatively few of the sites established by UK and European companies offer such a facility.

One of the big problems with corporate websites is that the companies which create them – supposedly as a vehicle for effective communication with the outside world – often have a different design agenda to the one that online investors might find useful.

As one commentator put it a couple of years ago, 'Corporations love graphics, and the bigger the better.' Websites can easily become corporate virility symbols. Rather than creating a simple and effective site that communicates its message efficiently, companies often get sidetracked into a competition to display more sophisticated graphics than their corporate rivals. The result is that sites become a triumph of style over substance.

My view of the ideal site is based around the following criteria:

■ Ease of navigation. For reasons previously outlined, low graphics content is basically considered good, high graphics content bad – unless the graphics really add something to your understanding of the company. The worst sites have heavy images which you have to download again each time a new page is viewed. A well laid-out site map with simple links is a plus point.

■ Whether an up to date annual report is available. This is pretty much a minimum requirement for a site to be useful. It is important too that the report is well laid-out on the site, with clear links to different aspects of its contents. Some reports require a PDF download and viewing via an Adobe Acrobat reader, but this is an acceptable way to display such information. It is important for investors to have access to the entire contents of a report and not just 'edited highlights'. Some of the more obscure parts of accounts are those that make the most interesting reading.

■ Whether press releases are available. The availability of company-issued news releases in full is also an important aspect for online investors. If they are available, you can then rely on the company site rather than keep voluminous files of news releases and press clippings. Company news releases should encompass both financially orientated releases and those related to trading, new product introductions, management changes, and so on. The more progressive sites have archived press releases categorized into different subject areas, which makes retrieving those of interest an easier task.

■ Whether there is any additional useful general information on the company. This could include product descriptions and prices, or separate sections on the site giving information about the company's main streams of activity, operating companies, or divisions. Some form of description of the company's evolution is sometimes given, and can be useful.

■ Whether there are any other special features available. Websites, particularly those of US companies, have developed hugely in this regard in the last couple of years, and among the items of interest that crop up frequently are: video and audio clips of analyst meetings and management presentations; downloadable PowerPoint presentations of the slide shows given at these meetings; downloadable fact books of financial and operating data; lists of the analysts and firms offering research coverage of the company and links to their websites; and the facility for those using the website to register for a service whereby future press releases from the company will be e-mailed as they become available.

■ Whether there is the facility for investors to e-mail queries on the company and its financial performance to the investor relations department or senior management at the company, and – more important – have the reasonable expectation of an intelligent response. Sites where a named investor relations contact's e-mail address is stated are more common in the case of US companies (but not unknown in European ones). It is bizarre how many otherwise highly sophisticated sites will include the name, address, telephone and fax numbers of an investor relations person, but not their e-mail address.

■ Whether there is an online share price and price chart. Share prices and price charts (often with a short delay) are now readily available from a variety of sources and arguably this reduces the need for them to be present at a corporate site. It also means, however, that there is little excuse for a company to omit such data from their websites.

■ Whether there are useful links available at the site. Companies sometimes fall down in not providing visitors to their site with an opportunity to explore in more depth by offering links to the websites of subsidiaries, industry organizations and other related sites. Some companies are particularly good on this score (drug companies, for instance, often provide exhaustive links to sites concerned with the medical profession and clinical research), but others are more isolationist.

I cover this subject in much more detail in my book, *The New Online Investor* (John Wiley, 2000), but Table 9.6 shows those I consider to be the best sites of this type as at the time of writing. I have scored the sites out of two on the basis of their ease of navigation and then added one point for each of the items mentioned above to get a score out a total of ten. The 'best sites' listed are those scoring ten.

Data on other types of investment

The internet's role in providing information on other types of investment should not be forgotten either. My book *Traded Options: A Private Investors' Guide*, (FT Prentice Hall, 2001) contains a detailed chapter on how the 'net' can be used to get information about traded options, including how to download options software. Options software was also covered in Chapter 8 of this book.

Investors in unit trusts and investment trusts have a number of very good sites to choose from, of which probably the best is Trustnet (www.trustnet.com) which itself is used as the source for the information on these investments at several other investment websites.

The data available at Trustnet includes details of performance and of different funds' portfolios, as well as management groups contact details. Some other websites and fund groups, including Interactive Investor, Fidelity and others, offer a means by which investors can buy unit trusts and other investments of this type online.

There are a number of good sites related to the bond market. Gilt prices can usually, though not always, be obtained through the usual market price display sites but web-based information on the bond market tends to be more qualitative – advising investors about the ins and outs of the market and the economic background that influences the market.

A good site for general information on the bond market and some government bond prices is the Bloomberg site at www.bloomberg.co.uk, which has several pages devoted to bonds, including a news page and page giving prices and statistics for a series of benchmark UK government bonds. The bonds included are by no means an exhaustive list, but probably the more actively traded ones.

Bond vocabulary is sometimes puzzling, but there are one or two points on the web that offer some guidance. These include general personal finance sites, some of which contain reasonable explanations about what bonds are, the variations available, and how they work.

Another good site is one set up by Kauders Investment Management, a specialist broker dealing in UK government bonds. The site, at www.gilt.co.uk, has a useful collection of essays and explanations about the rationale for bond investing and the mechanics of undertaking it.

Generally speaking, remember that using the web for investing is not necessarily just about shares. With a little diligence, it is perfectly feasible to research other investment choices.

Table 9.6 Best corporate websites

UK		US		Europe	
Company	URL	Company	URL	Company	URL
Billiton	www.billiton.com	ADC Telecomms.	www.adc.com	Adidas-Salomon	www.adidas.com
Cedar Group	www.cedargroup.co.uk	Atmel	www.atmel.com	Aegon	www.aegon.com
Centrica	www.centrica.co.uk	Broadvision	www.broadvision.com	Alcatel	www.alcatel.com
EMAP	www.emap.com	Coca-Cola	www.coca-cola.com	Credit suisse	www.credit-suisse.com
Kingfisher	www.kingfisher.co.uk	CMGI	www.cmgi.com	E.On	www.eon.com
National Power	www.nationalpower.com	Compuware	www.compuware.com	Nestlé	www.nestle.com
National Westminster Bank	www.natwestgroup.com	IBM	www.ibm.com	Nokia	www.nokia.com
Norwich Union	www.norwich-union.co.uk	Johnson & Johnson	www.johnsonandjohnson.com	Roche	www.roche.com
Scottish Power	www.scottishpower.plc.uk	Kodak	www.kodak.com	Royal Dutch Petroleum	www.shell.com
WPP Group	www.wpp.com	SBC	www.sbc.com	Zurich FS	www.zurich.com

To connect or not?

I believe strongly that the internet and online information sources are playing a central role in making the market more accessible to the needs of ordinary investors in a way that the privatization wave of the 1980s did not.

UK privatizations may have widened share ownership but they did not deepen it. They created many new shareholders, but most of these shareholders only held or hold a single share, and the success they may have achieved in this one instance has not yet been successfully broadened out into a wider interest in the market and a fostering of a regular investment habit. This is now changing, thanks to the web.

It should be stressed, however, that the availability of all this information does not eliminate the need for investors to make sound judgements about buying and selling shares, bonds, unit trusts or any other investments. Nor does it mean that all the work in selecting good investments in the first place will be done for you.

All the internet and other online sources can do is deliver information more efficiently. What uses the individual investor makes of this information is another matter entirely.

> I believe strongly that the internet and online information sources are playing a central role in making the market more accessible to the needs of ordinary investors in a way that the privatization wave of the 1980s did not.

IN BRIEF

■ Connecting to the internet offers investors a relatively cheap way of tapping into more investment information.

■ Internet newsgroups and bulletin boards are interactive forums in which a variety of topics are discussed. There are many of these, but some are of limited use.

■ The world wide web offers information on a variety of topics related to investment, and the ability to search for information on investment topics and companies.

■ There are a number of websites that offer the ability to download share price data either free or at low cost.

■ There are a number of web sites that offer the opportunity to download shareware or demo versions of investment software.

■ Various newspapers, newsletters and investment publications have internet sites. Using these can cut down on the costs of buying or subscribing to the conventional issues of the same publications.

■ Online trading is likely to continue to increase in importance in the future.

■ Corporate websites have grown dramatically in number in recent years and are a vital source of information for investors.

■ Extensive information is available on many other non-share forms of investment, including bonds, options, unit trusts and so on.

More advanced stuff – ratios and charts

In Chapter 3 we looked at how to calculate and interpret some basic financial ratios. This chapter and the next takes things a stage further, looking at some other, more complex ratios, other types of share price analysis, and techniques used for valuing shares.

Broadly speaking, these fall into several categories:

■ additional financial ratios that can be calculated from profit and loss accounts, cash flow and balance sheet numbers to help give a more in-depth picture of a company's financial position (this chapter)

■ additional ways of analyzing share prices and share price movements (this chapter)

■ using discounted cash flow techniques to value shares (next chapter)

■ using reinvested return on equity as a valuation yardstick (next chapter)

■ valuing asset-based and loss-making companies (next chapter)

■ sum of the parts analysis (next chapter)

These concepts may seem daunting, but they are essentially simple, and the mathematics behind them can easily be tamed using simple spreadsheet-based computer models or chart software. Since we have advocated the usefulness of getting connected to the internet in the previous chapter, for those who are online, examples of the spreadsheets used in this chapter and the next can be downloaded from the 'software' page at www.linksitemoney.com.

More financial ratios

In Chapter 3 we looked at how it was possible to examine company accounts and use the figures contained in them to calculate ratios that could reveal underlying strengths or weaknesses in performance.

To recap, the ratios we looked at were:

- gross margin – percentage of gross profit to sales
- operating margin – percentage of operating profit to sales
- pre-tax margin – percentage of pre-tax profit to sales
- interest cover – ratio of interest paid to pre-interest profit
- current ratio – ratio of current assets to current liabilities
- acid ratio – ratio of current assets less stocks to current liabilities
- gearing – percentage of net debt to net assets
- return on capital – percentage of pre-interest profit to capital employed
- return on equity – percentage of after-tax profit to average net assets.

These ratios remain the most important ones to calculate when first looking at a balance sheet and income statement, but there are some obvious omissions.

One gap that needs filling is to look at P&L account ratios that give a more detailed breakdown of a company's costs. A second is that none of the ratios mentioned previously are based on the company's cash flow statements, which can also be analyzed in a number of different ways. And a third is to look in more detail at working capital (stocks, debtors and creditors), and at how productively or otherwise the company's assets, both capital and labour, are used.

Calculating all these ratios might be considered time-consuming, but it can pay dividends in terms of the insight it can give you into the financial condition of a company in whose shares you might be contemplating committing a chunk of hard-earned surplus cash. Not spending a little time investigating a situation in greater depth is foolish.

In any case, as indicated previously, it is easy enough to program these ratios into a conventional computer spreadsheet and have them calculated automatically by inputting some of the basic numbers. Doing this cuts down the time involved, makes the whole process less daunting, and allows the investor to focus on what the numbers actually mean.

I have illustrated this approach using figures taken from the accounts of an actual company. The numbers are for illustration purposes only, and the company concerned is a pub group. The financial ratios shown in the tables were calculated taking numbers from the company's normal accounts and inputting them into a pre-programmed Excel spreadsheet. The template can be downloaded from the 'software' page at linksitemoney.com. It calculates the ratios mentioned in the earlier chapter and those additional ones mentioned below.

Profit ratios

In the profit and loss account, the additional ratios not previously mentioned primarily relate to cost items pulled out before arriving at operating profit. For instance, by law companies must disclose in their accounts staff costs and numbers, and various items relating to directors' pay and shareholdings.

Expressing total *staff costs as a percentage of sales* is the most convenient way of measuring this item. To get the full value from it, however, one needs to compare the trend in staff costs to sales over a period of years to judge whether or not the company has its wage bill under control. Similarly the total of staff costs and other operating charges (excluding depreciation), expressed as a percentage of sales, shows the extent to which the company has the costs (that are under its direct influence) under strict control.

Directors' pay can be a good indication of corporate management style. In almost every instance it should be taken as a positive factor if the directors have significant ongoing direct shareholdings in the business, ideally running into significant (say double figure) percentages of the share capital. Conversely large bonuses or ex gratia payments to directors and former directors, large share option grants and other devices for rewarding individuals are not necessarily a good sign.

Direct shareholdings are preferable to share option holdings because the latter may simply have been granted as part of a pay and perks package, and do not represent the actual investment or retention of hard earned personal cash in the business. A *sizeable stake held by management* in this way means that the management team is highly likely to act in a way that maximizes long-term shareholder value, since the board's own financial interests and those of the mass of shareholders coincide.

It should come as no surprise to anyone that management remuneration can be excessive. It is comparatively easy to work out whether management is giving value for money by taking the remuneration of the highest paid director (normally the chief executive) and/or the total for the board as a whole and expressing this as a percentage of either pre-tax profits or the market value of the company. Comparing a number of companies in the same sector in this way and relating it to their respective profit and share price performance gives some idea as to whether managements are over- or under-rewarding themselves.

This is subject to the proviso that, in proportionate terms, directors in small companies often appear to be paid more than those in larger ones, even though their salaries may be much more modest in absolute terms. But there is little excuse for a management team's pay to be substantially in excess of the average for companies of a similar size in the same industry.

The *tax charge* is simply the percentage that tax represents of pre-tax profits. This may be reduced by capital allowances if a company is investing heavily. Capital allowances allow a certain proportion of spending to be set off against tax. It is a good idea, if this is the case, to try and assess how likely the spending is to persist at this level. Good profits growth further up the P&L account can be eroded or even completely offset or reversed when it comes to earnings per share (a key driver of the share price) if the tax charge rises in the meantime.

The profit and loss account figures and the associated ratios for our illustrative pub group are shown in Table 10.1.

Table 10.1 Pubco – Profit and Loss Account items and related ratios

| | Year to 31 July | | | |
	1997	1998	1999	2000
Turnover	21,380	30,800	46,600	68,536
Cost of sales	7,773	10,784	16,835	37,616
Gross profit	13,607	20,016	29,765	30,920
Staff costs	4,226	5,791	8,372	12,562
Depreciation	523	908	1,422	2,397
Other operating charges	3,764	7,241	11,184	3,729
Operating profit	5,094	6,076	8,787	12,232
Non-operating items	–58	0	0	0
PBIT	5,152	6,076	8,787	12,232
Net interest paid	3,074	1,905	2,310	2,519
Pre-tax profit	2,078	4,171	6,477	9,713
Taxation	117	449	563	755
Profit after taxation	1,961	3,722	5,914	8,958
Minorities preference				
Attributable profit	1,961	3,722	5,914	8,958
Extraordinary items				
Dividends	350	1,546	2,234	2,927
Retained profit	1,611	2,176	3,680	6,031
Earnings per share	12.6	14.4	18.2	24.6
Dividend per share	2.38	5.4	6.6	8
Cover	5.29	2.67	2.76	3.08
Gross margin (%)	63.64	64.99	63.87	45.11
Operating margin (%)	23.83	19.73	18.86	17.85
Pre-tax margin (%)	9.72	13.54	13.9	14.17
Staff costs: sales (%)	19.77	18.8	17.97	18.33
Total op. charges:sales (%)	39.82	45.26	45.02	27.27
Tax charge (%)	5.64	10.76	8.69	7.77

It is important that the figures are entered precisely and that the subtotals calculated automatically by the worksheet are cross-checked to make sure they agree with the accounts. In this example 14 lines have to be entered, with the remaining 13 calculated automatically.

In fact this table illustrates some of the problems the diligent investor can come up against. In this case it can be seen that the figure for gross margin changes abruptly in 2000. This is not due to any underlying change in the business, but simply a change in the way the figures are presented in the accounts.

More pertinently perhaps, it can be seen from the operating margin line that this figure has dropped steadily over the four-year period but that, thanks to the company's ability to raise extra funds from its shareholders, and thereby limit its interest charges, its pre-tax margin has risen. Looking further down the table, staff costs have remained relatively stable as a percentage of sales, but the operating charges percentage has been distorted as explained above.

Most interestingly, the company's tax charge has been substantially below the 30 per cent plus norm, over the period. This is due to the heavy investment in fixed assets by the company, but the fact of a low tax charge always carries with it the possibility that at some future date it will rise and suppress growth in after-tax profit and earnings per share.

Cash flow ratios

Turning to the cash flow statement, this is often revealing enough in itself, without substantial further analysis. However, there are a number of ratios that can be calculated over and above a simple scan of the numbers and a look at the notes to the statement.

One of the main variables that can be picked out from the cash flow statement is the net amount a company has spent on new fixed assets. This can be compared with a number of other parameters.

First, with depreciation. As was explained in Chapter 3, this is the amount set aside to replace fixed assets. It is normally calculated by dividing the cost of the asset by their expected life. By comparing depreciation to spending on fixed assets, it is possible to gauge the extent to which a company is investing for growth rather than just replacing worn-out equipment.

In some instances this approach does not work. In the case of a company spending on plant and machinery, the likelihood is that this spending will be modestly in excess of the amount set aside to replace earlier acquisitions of equipment. In the case of companies with assets that depreciate slowly, such as freehold property, a growing company is likely to spend many times its depreciation charge each year.

Fixed asset spending can also be compared with sales and with capital employed to see how consistent the spending is over a period of years. Another way of looking at the figures generated in a cash flow statement is to compare broad groups of 'spending' figures with the total for operating cash flow.

Cash outflows for most companies fall into three broad categories: those going to providers of capital (such as interest and dividend payments); those going to the government (tax); and those going to suppliers of new fixed assets and vendors of businesses acquired. Leaving aside tax, the other categories can be respectively grouped together as the net cash outflow for finance (NCO (F)) and the net cash outflow for investment. (NCO (I)). Both of these aggregates can be compared with the overall operating cash inflow.

Normally the proportions of these ratios (represented in Table 10.2 by NCO (I):OCF and NCO (F):OCF) will move around a little over time. It is, though, important to remember that, taking several years together, if the ratios add up to more than 100 per cent it means that the company is consistently spending more cash than is coming in. The inevitable result of this is that some form of additional permanent financing, most likely a rights issue, will eventually be required.

In the case of the pub group used as an illustration, the numbers can be seen in the Table 10.2.

Here again, it is important that the figures are inputted precisely, and that the plus and minus signs are also recorded. Accounting conventions dictate that in published accounts a negative figure (that is a loss, outflow, or expense) is often represented by the figure concerned being bracketed.

Perhaps the most significant figure here is that fixed asset investment, as a percentage of sales has remained remarkably consistent. The figure immediately below reflects the company's orientation – typical for a pub group – towards investing in property. Pub property is normally assumed to depreciate very slowly. What the year 2000 ratio shows in this instance, for example (a figure of 1,569.46), is that the company last year spent on fixed assets a figure 15 times its provision for depreciation.

Fixed-asset investment as a percentage of net capital employed (NCE), again comparatively stable over the period, may be a better guide to the group's pattern of investment.

The bottom two ratios on the table show the grouped figures for spending allocated to providers of finance (NCO (F)), namely interest and dividends, and the similar figure for investment – namely spending on fixed assets, investments and acquisitions. These have been expressed as a percentage of operating cash flow. In each of the last three years, commitments in these two areas, taken together, have averaged well over double the figure for operating cash flow, painting a picture of the company as an overwhelmingly cash-hungry business – at least at its current stage of development.

This is actually the flip side of the low tax rate seen in the profit and loss account. If the company were to spend more within its means, then capital allowances to set against tax would be lower, and the tax charge would rise, depressing after-tax profits.

Table 10.2 Pubco – Cash Flow Statement and ratios

| | Year to 31 July | | | |
	1997	1998	1999	2000
Cash inflow from op.activity	7,142	7,713	11,028	19,762
Interest received	15	299	86	55
Interest paid	–3,472	–2.667	–2,370	–2,803
Dividends received	0	0	0	0
Dividends paid	–265	–865	–1,673	–2,601
Net cash outflow (finance)	–3,722	–3,233	–3,957	–5,349
Tax paid	–122	–266	–460	–655
Purchase of fixed assets	–11,700	–16,364	–23,217	–37,620
Purchase of investments				
Purchase of subsidiaries				
Sale of fixed assets	2,756	197	22	11
Net cash outflow (investing)	–8,944	–16,167	–23,195	–37,609
Net cash inflow pre-financing	–5,646	–11,953	–16,584	–23,851
Share issues	458	18,297	22,345	527
Loan repayments	5,899	–3,832	5,449	18,419
Change in cash/equivalents	711	2,512	11,210	–4,905
Net capital employed	48,222	66,937	100,614	127,093
Depreciation	523	908	1,422	2,397
Sales	21,380	30,800	46,600	68,536
Fixed asset inv:sales (%)	54.72	53.13	49.82	54.89
Fixed asset inv:dep'n (%)	2237.09	1802.2	1632.7	1569.46
Fixed asset inv: NCE (%)	24.26	24.45	23.08	29.6
NCO (I): NCE (%)	18.55	24.15	23.05	29.59
NCO (F): Op CF (%)	52.11	41.92	35.88	27.07
NCO (I): Op CF (%)	125.23	209.61	210.33	190.31

Balance sheet ratios

In the balance sheet, the more advanced ratios that can be calculated relate to the productivity of assets and employees and the efficiency of utilization of working capital.

Calculating the amount of *sales and profit produced per pound of assets employed* is a relatively simple concept. Comparing these figures over time should ideally yield a steady upward trend.

The same is true of the figures for *sales and profit per employee*. These are straightforward calculations that are intuitively easy to grasp.

Working capital ratios take a little more explanation. The concept behind these is that it is important that undue amounts of cash are not tied up in stocks, since this costs money to finance, and similarly that amounts owing to suppliers are paid in a controlled way and not unduly quickly, while debtors (amounts owed to the company) are collected as quickly as possible. It is also important that these amounts bear a reasonably consistent relationship to each other.

The normal way of looking at this is to express these 'current account' items as a proportion of the sales item they represent, and then present the ratio by calculating the number of days it represents. In a simple example, stock turning over four times per year would (by definition) turn over once every 90 days.

Reverting back for a moment to our fictitious company, Universal Widgets, to illustrate the point. If it has £100m of turnover, cost of sales of £80m, stocks of £33m, debtors of £20m and creditors of £15m, the way that the various working capital ratios would be calculated is as follows:

Stock days. £100m of sales divided by £33m of stocks is equivalent to stock turnover of three times per year and stock days of 365/3 or 122 days. It is something of a moot point whether stock days should be calculated on sales or on cost of sales.

Creditor days. Because creditors normally represent money owed to suppliers making up the total cost of the finished product – before profit margins are added on and the goods sold – creditor days are usually calculated on 'cost of sales' rather than the turnover figure. In this instance, creditor days would be creditors of £15m divided into cost of sales of £80m (i.e. collected 5.3 times annually), making creditor days equivalent to 365/5.3, or 69 days.

Debtor days. Here the same principle is applied except that, because debtors normally represent payments outstanding from customers for finished goods sold at the market price, the debtors figure is divided into sales. This gives, in this instance, £20m divided into £100m of sales, implying debtors collected on average five times per year, or every 73 days.

Looked at in a slightly different way, in this example the company is turning over its stock on average every 122 days, making its suppliers wait on

Table 10.3 Pubco – Summary of Balance Sheet items and ratios (£000s)

	Year ended 31 July			
	1997	1998	1999	2000
Tangible fixed assets	53,095	71,736	96,547	133,196
Investments	0	0	0	0
Stocks	302	485	604	885
Trade debtors	0	0	0	0
Other debtors	1,600	1,276	1,546	2,720
Cash	70	2,519	15,838	8,824
Total current assets	1,972	4280	17,988	12,429
Short-term borrowing	1,828	1,539	3,690	1,411
Trade creditors	3,322	4,209	4,670	8,343
Other creditors	1,695	3,331	5,561	8,778
Total current liabilities	6,845	9,079	13,921	18,532
Net current assets	–4,873	–4,799	4,067	–6,103
Net capital employed	48,222	66,937	100,614	127,093
Medium/LT borrowing	27,910	22,825	28,242	46,833
Other LT creditors	0	0	0	1,021
Provisions	0	0	0	0
Net assets	20,312	44,112	72,372	79,239
No. of employees	571	766	838	1,286
Sales	21,380	30,800	46,600	68,536
Cost of sales	7,773	10,784	16,835	37,616
PBIT	5,152	6,076	8,787	12,232
Pre-tax profit	2,078	4,171	6,477	9,713
Current ratio	0.29	0.47	1.29	0.67
Acid test ratio	0.24	0.42	1.25	0.62
Debt: capital employed (%)	61.67	36.4	31.74	37.96
Net debt: equity (%)	146.06	49.52	22.24	49.75
Interest cover (X)	1.68	3.19	3.8	4.86
Stock/cost of sales (days)	14	16	13	9
Track debtor days	0	0	0	0
Stock: total assets (%)	1	1	1	1
Trade creditor days	156	142	101	81
Sales: fixed assets (%)	40	43	48	51
Sales: total assets (%)	39	41	41	47
Sales/employee (£000)	37.44	40.21	55.61	53.29
PBT/employee (£000)	3.64	5.45	7.73	7.55
Return on capital (%)	10.68	9.08	8.73	9.62
Return on equity (%)	10.23	9.46	8.95	12.26

average 69 days before paying their bills and granting its customers an average 73 days credit.

The ideal might be to collect from customers rather more rapidly than suppliers are paid, but the real point about working out ratios like this is that the trend should be monitored for any significant changes. Problems could be indicated, for instance, if the rate of stock turnover falls (i.e. stocks are kept for longer), if debtors are collected more slowly (debtor days lengthen) or if creditors demand payment more quickly (creditor days shorten).

In calculating figures of this nature the norm is to take only short-term debtors and creditors, and also to work from so-called trade debtors and creditors, ignoring, for instance, National Insurance and social security payments, VAT and other debtors/creditors that represent statutory obligations and have unvarying payment periods.

As Table 10.3 shows, the nature of a particular business can have a major impact on these figures. In the case of the pub group, its customers naturally pay cash over the bar so debtor days are nil and creditors (brewers and other suppliers) are paid comparatively slowly, although the payment period has been falling. Stock turns over every couple of weeks, although here again this speed of turnover has apparently been distorted by the change in the basis of presenting cost of sales in the accounts.

It should be evident from these tables that using the balance sheet and profit and loss account and cash flow numbers in this way can give considerable insight into the financial characteristics of any business and accordingly into the likely worth of the company from an investment standpoint.

A section at the end of this chapter looks at how unscrupulous company directors can manipulate accounts, and what to watch out for. Thankfully accounting regulators are gradually tightening up on potential abuses, so examples of these are getting scarcer as time goes by.

The next chapter will look at several alternative methods of valuing shares, as distinct from the conventional PE and PEG approach described earlier. PEs and PEGs are all very well, but they have a number of drawbacks, one of which is that they only look at profits, which can be both misleading and manipulated. The other point is that many companies are not susceptible to profit-based analysis either because they are losing money or because they are more focused on building assets than earnings. Ways have to be found to value such companies that are not dependent on conventional earnings per share calculations.

As I have stressed at several points in this book, cash flow is generally at least as important as profitability when it comes to assessing the real worth of an investment. Along with sales figures, flows of cash are much more difficult for the accountants to fudge, and methods which use these figures to value shares are worthy of more attention than they sometimes get.

There are established techniques using cash flow numbers that can be used to pinpoint the true value of a company, or at least corroborate a calculation of its worth arrived at by other means.

Additional charting and share price analysis techniques

In Chapter 4 we covered a number of the most basic technical indicators that are to be found on many 'entry-level' and mid-priced technical analysis software packages. The ones described below are normally found only on the more expensive packages and provide additional insight into share price movements.

For reasons of limited space, only a handful of these indicators are mentioned below, simply to give a flavour of the variety of calculations that can be performed. They are split into those that relate to the market as a whole and those that are normally used with individual shares.

Readers are strongly advised to consult the manual that accompanies their technical analysis software package and more specialized literature on the subject if they intend to use these indicators for trading purposes.

Market-based indicators

In some technical analysis programs and indeed often in newspapers and TV commentaries on the stock market, mention is made of the advance/decline line. This is a widely-used measure of the overall condition of the market and is calculated by taking the difference between the numbers of rising stocks each day and the number falling. The daily surplus or deficit is then added to or subtracted from a cumulative total and drawn on the chart.

Like many technical indicators, it tells you something meaningful when there is divergence, i.e. when there is a difference between its movement and that of the market as a whole. If the market is strong, but the advance/decline line is falling, this means the continuing rise in the market is suspect. Likewise if the market falls but the advance/decline line is rising, the underlying tone of the market is better than the index movement is suggesting.

A variant of this concept is the breadth indicator. This takes the difference between advances and declines and divides it by the total number of issues traded. Study of past market peaks and troughs suggest a buying climax (i.e. the top of a bull market is reached) when advances represent more than 70 per cent of all issues traded.

Figure 10.1 Coppock indicator for the FTSE-100

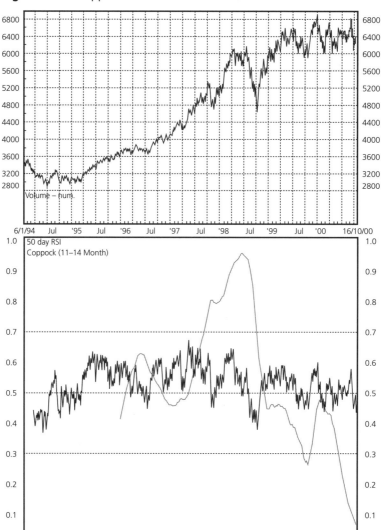

Another advance/decline indicator often used by technical analysts is the McClellan Oscillator. This plots the difference between the weighted 19-day moving average and a weighted 39-day moving average of advances less declines. Peaks and troughs are often reached before market turning points, typically when the oscillator is deep in overbought or oversold territory.

Lastly, many investors (including a number of private investors) swear by the Coppock indicator as a reliable measure of signalling the beginnings of bull markets. The indicator is normally calculated as a weighted 10-month moving total of a share price or index, and the calculations involve working out a monthly average for, say, the FTSE-100 index, and then calculating the percentage change over the same average 12 months previously. These percentages are then weighted in a 10-period moving average to create the chart. A buy signal is indicated when the chart rebounds from a low point. The indicator is held to be an unreliable generator of sell signals.

Figure 10.1 shows the current position of the Coppock indicator for the FTSE 100 index.

Share price-based indicators

There are also a number of other indicators that can be used to analyze the progress or otherwise of individual share prices. Many of these give the lie to the suggestion that technical analysis is simply about spotting abstruse patterns on share price charts. In fact, many technical indicators apply proven and well-respected statistical techniques.

It is possible, for instance, to perform regression analysis on a time-series of a particular share price. Once the so-called line of best fit is established, it is possible to calculate 'confidence limits' either side of the line. These are normally positioned either one or two standard deviations either side of the line itself. The standard deviation is, as its name suggests, the average amount by which the variable, in this case the share price, departs from the line of best fit.

Even if you don't find the theory that easy to grasp, using confidence limits is intuitively very easy. Take Figure 10.2.

It's fairly easy to see here that the confidence limits represent the extremes of normal share price movement, and that buying when the lower limit is breached and selling when the upper one is breached can, at least most of the time, be quite a profitable exercise especially if this technique is combined with the normal trading discipline of cutting losses.

The standard deviation is used in calculating a share's volatility. As explained above, this measures the amplitude of swings in a share price around its long-term trend line using standard statistical techniques. It is self-evident that volatility may vary over time, with shares having both quiet periods and those where activity is frenetic and movements in them significant. The chart of the volatility of a share price over successive periods of, say, 20 days or 90 days, can be graphed by many technical analysis programs and is particularly useful in the traded options market.

When buying traded options, for example, the idea is to purchase an option when the underlying share is at some sort of support or resistance level but also when volatility is low.

Figure 10.2 Confidence limits

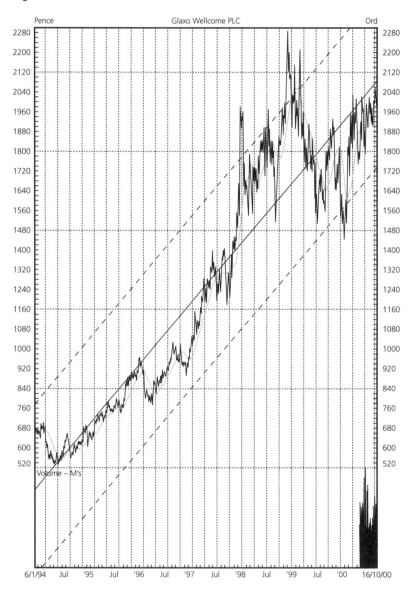

As an example, Figure 10.3 shows the moving total of the 20 day volatility of Glaxo.

As volatility increases so the price of the option should rise, and (with luck) if the volatility rises because of a sharp move in the appropriate direction, the option buyer will also make money as a result of the increased intrinsic value of the option. This subject was introduced briefly in Chapter 6. To reiterate, it is very important indeed to read up on the subject of option trading before any deals are contemplated.

Figure 10.3 Volatility

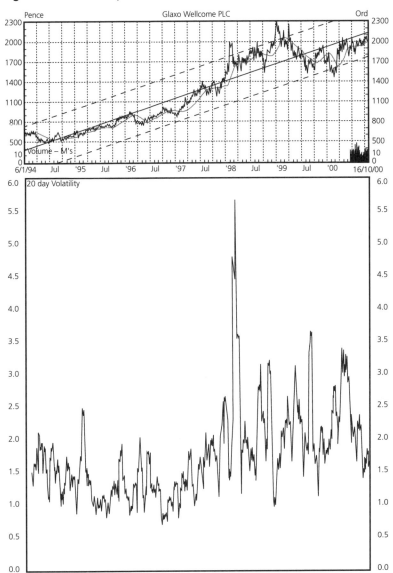

It is worth touching again at this point on a share's 'beta' factor. This is calculated by using statistical techniques to analyze the percentage changes in the price of a share over a particular period, relative to the changes in the underlying market over the same time period.

As explained briefly earlier, 'beta' encapsulates the percentage movement in the price of a share that can be expected for a given percentage movement in the market. Hence a stock with a beta of 1.2 could be expected to increase by 12 per cent if the market rose 10 per cent. A stock with a beta of 0.8 would rise 8 per cent if the market gained 10 per cent but conversely fall by less than the market. Hence, if you believe the theory, in general terms investors should seek out low beta stocks (or of course sell out altogether) if the market is expected to fall, and high beta stocks if they expect it to rise.

The 'alpha', that corresponds to the beta, is in simple terms the portion of the performance of the share price that can be attributed to non-market related factors, for example, to the management of a company or the quality of the portfolio manager in the case of a fund.

Trading volume indicators

I mentioned earlier that trends in the trading volume in a particular share can be a good guide to the movement in a share price. Upward or downward moves that occur on high volume are usually more significant than those that do not.

Several indicators have been developed that look at volume in more detail. An example is a technique called 'equivolume'. This attempts to draw a chart that combines the directional movement of a share with the volume of shares traded. Each day's trading is shown as a rectangle, with the vertical dimensions representing the day's trading range and the width of the bar proportional to the volume of shares traded.

Another method is called 'on-balance volume' (or OBV) and was devised by the US stockmarket guru Joe Granville. The idea behind this is that starting from zero, the current day's volume is plotted as either a plus or a minus depending on whether or not the shares closed higher or lower. If one day is followed by a second in which the shares rose, the volume is added to that seen in the first day. If there is a decline on the third day, the volume is deducted from the total of the previous two days, and so on.

As with other indicators, traders often watch for a divergence between the price chart and this indicator of volume. Another variant weights the volume of shares traded with the average share price for the day and aggregates the pluses and minuses arrived at over (normally) a 14-day period. The figures are then adjusted to arrive at an oscillator that fluctuates between zero and 100.

> Charts and fundamental analysis should be used together when assessing shares. Put simply, technical analysis can throw up interesting opportunities for further study, and also help with timing purchases and sales, but fundamental research is also vital in selecting portfolio constituents. Being painstaking over both aspects of the process narrows down the risks of losing money and increases the chance of making it.

The indicators described above, combined with those mentioned in Chapter 4, represent only a fraction of the various ways in which it is possible to analyze share price movements. There is an extensive library of material on charting and technical analysis, and the manuals of most chart packages also contain descriptions of how indicators are constructed.

I cannot stress too strongly my view that charts and fundamental analysis should be used together when assessing shares. Put simply, technical analysis can throw up interesting opportunities for further study, and also help with timing purchases and sales, but fundamental research is also vital in selecting portfolio constituents. Being painstaking over both aspects of the process narrows down the risks of losing money and increases the chance of making it.

It is also worth repeating the point made in the earlier chapters on computerized investing and online investing that the cost of data to use in investment software packages has come down sharply of late, and any serious investor can acquire software that gives access to many of these indicators for a relatively low monthly cost.

Postscript – interpreting 'creative' accounting

It is probably understandable (although it still shocks some investors) that company finance directors want to show their companies in the best light possible and that some seek to do this by choosing accounting policies that are designed to show a smooth upward trend in profits and to flatter the balance sheet.

Company year-ends are often chosen, for example, to be at the time when a company has the maximum amount of liquidity in its balance sheet. In the case of a seasonal business dependent on Christmas for example, the year-end might be 31 March, when all the cash from Christmas sales has been collected. For the remainder of the year, such a business may be a heavy cash user, and the balance sheet needs to be interpreted with this fact in mind.

However, creative accounting usually means something more than this.

The best book on this subject is *Accounting for Growth*, by Terry Smith, an analyst whose career at a leading broker was terminated abruptly because of his criticisms in this book of one of the company's corporate clients. The book is published by Century Business, priced £12.99 and, though now somewhat overtaken by events, is essential reading for all would-be investors.

Smith has since had the last laugh. The book was a best-seller, he joined a small firm which has recently been listed, making him a very wealthy man, and his former employers have since been absorbed into a large investment bank.

In the book, Smith highlighted a number of ways in which accounts can be camouflaged, many of which have since effectively been outlawed by regulators. It is worth highlighting some of the scope that remains to manipulate accounts.

Off-balance sheet finance

The use of off-balance sheet finance has also been considerably restricted as a result of recent changes to accounting guidelines.

This term is used where an expensive project, typically a development property or the financing of work-in-progress likely to take a long time to come to maturity, is placed in a joint venture company that is less than 50 per cent owned but where the true 'owner' has an option to reacquire the assets at some future date. This is done because it means the assets (or more importantly their related borrowings) need not be included in the group balance sheet.

As well as property companies financing major developments, scotch whisky companies in the past financed stocks in this way, by creating part-owned joint ventures with banks, which held their maturing stock for a period of time with loans backed against them. The increase in the value of the stocks as they matured more than covered the effect of rolling up interest payments in the joint venture.

Many examples of creative accounting like this are now well on the way to being eradicated in the UK, but others are alive and well. In particular, examples of adjusting depreciation policies, brand accounting, and capitalizing interest can all be commonly found.

Changing depreciation rates

In the case of depreciation policies, if assets are written off less conservatively than before (say, over five years rather than three) then profits will be boosted by the reduction in charge for depreciation. Applying a change of this type to an asset worth £100m previously depreciated over three years and now depreciated over five years would benefit profits to the tune of £13.3m. The old annual depreciation charge of £33.3m (£100m divided by three) is replaced by one of £20m (£100m divided by five).

This is actually less pernicious than it might sound, since the depreciation charge is itself a book entry and the change therefore has no effect on cash flows: it simply makes profits look better.

Capitalizing costs

Capitalizing costs (most commonly interest payments) is common in the property industry. Here interest accruing on financing long-term developments is not charged to the profit and loss account, but rolled up in the eventual value of the asset being created. If all goes well the charge is lost in the developer's profit margin. Short-term profits are boosted as a result, at the expense of some capital profit when the asset is eventually sold.

The problem with this approach arises when property values decline in the meantime, making the cost of the development, including this rolled-up interest, exceed its market value. This amounts to negative equity on a huge scale, and is normally likely to involve the developer in substantial write-offs.

It is also worth remembering that, while profits are benefited by this policy, in cash flow terms the interest still has to be paid to the lender at the appointed time.

These are only examples. There are plenty of other methods of obfuscation used by companies to beef up their results. The recent boom in internet companies has spawned several new examples of creativity. These range from treating services sold by way of barter as revenue when no cash has actually flowed into the company as a result, to presenting so-called pro forma results in addition to audited ones. This is usually accompanied by an explanation implying that the artificial constructs, which generally use some form of annualization to inflate revenue figures or disregard certain types of expense, are somehow more accurate than the more modest audited ones.

This is a new version of a dodge pursued by many companies over the years, i.e. recognizing the full amount of revenue on a contract as a sale, when only a proportion of the value would be received at the outset. This places a premium on companies continuing to increase their sales to avoid a disastrous dive in performance. Any faltering, and the whole scheme unravels.

The best advice investors can follow when confronted with something like this is to assume the worst. There are plenty of investment choices out there in the market without needing to buy those that have some kind of question mark over the robustness of their accounting policies. Company accounts should, within reason, be simple and transparent. If you come across companies that don't satisfy this test, avoid them.

This is one reason why I prefer, on the whole, to invest in smaller companies. Large companies are inherently more complex, and spotting those that are pulling a fast one is more difficult. With smaller companies, it is easier to distinguish between companies that are honest and those that are less so.

The next chapter looks at some of the more advanced techniques used to value shares, and how they work in practice.

IN BRIEF

■ There are a number of additional financial ratios that can be derived from company annual reports.

■ Profit and loss ratios break down the cost side of the equation in greater detail, cash flow ratios look in particular at levels of fixed asset spending, and balance sheet ratios look at sales and asset productivity and working capital.

■ Additional technical indicators include those relating to broad market advances and declines, to market momentum over time, to the volatility of individual shares, and to the analysis of trading volume.

■ Company accounts are frequently massaged to put a better gloss on the figures, though regulators have now outlawed the more flagrant examples.

■ Favourite creative accounting techniques include altering depreciation rates, bringing brands into the balance sheet, and capitalizing interest and other costs. As some loopholes are closed, new ones are opened up.

More advanced stuff – valuing shares

hapter 3 contained an explanation of the basics of valuing shares by comparing share prices and earnings (PERs), and price-earnings ratios and earnings growth (PEG factors). But there is more to valuing shares than this, and some of the other techniques that investors use can significantly add to the understanding of the true value of a business, or be used in situations where normal earnings-based measures break down.

This chapter looks at several such methods, under the following main headings:

- discounted cash flow (DCF)
- enterprise Value Analysis (EVA)
- reinvested return on equit.
- sum of the parts analysis
- valuation of internet companies (including incubators)
- assessing incubators.

Discounted cash flow

Discounted cash flow is a long-established technique originally developed for use by companies appraising capital investment projects.

In the investment world it is simply a means of valuing a share by adding up the current value of the future flows of cash expected to be generated by the company and comparing the total with the current value of the company in the market.

It works like this. Cash flow in each succeeding year is progressively adjusted downwards by a fixed percentage amount (i.e. discounted) to reflect the fact that uncertainty and the possibilities of future inflation mean that a fixed amount of cash expected to accrue at some point in the future is worth inherently less to an investor than the same amount expected to be received today.

So the current value to the investor of cash four years out is worth less than the same amount received in three years time, which is worth less than the same amount received in two years' time and so on.

If you find this concept hard to grasp, ask yourself whether you would place a higher value on £1,000 handed to you today, or £1,000 in a year's time. What would you think was worth more to you, £1,000 in a year's time, or £1,000 in five years' time? A rational individual would rather have cash now than cash in the future. Cash now can be invested to yield a greater amount in a year's time, two years' time and so on. By the same token, depending where interest rates stand, you forgo a calculable amount by waiting a year, or two years, for the same £1,000.

At the end of the process the discounted values of all the cash flows are added together and the total compared to the current market value of the company. Normally forecasts are made for a fixed number of years, and the years thereafter treated as a lump sum.

How to work out precisely what discount should be applied to future flows of cash can vary. Often the discount rate used is the so-called 'risk-free rate of return', that is to say the yield on an undated government bond. In some models this figure is adjusted to allow for differences in the levels of risk in different shares. The more volatile or risky a share, the higher the discount factor applied to its future cash flow. One way of doing this is to add a notional 'risk premium' to the risk-free rate and then multiply that by a share's 'beta factor' (which represents the amount by which statistically it has tended to move for a given percentage movement in the market). So, for example, if the risk-free rate of return is 5 per cent, the risk premium 3 per cent and the stock's beta is 1.2, the adjusted discount rate would be 8.6 per cent (5 per cent added to three times 1.2).

The higher discount rate will reduce the overall discounted cash flow value, other things being equal. In simple terms this means that a higher growth rate must be factored in to get back to square one.

Nowadays discounted cash flow models can be obtained that work as add-ins to Excel or other industry-standard spreadsheet programs. These normally entail simply plugging in basic historic P&L and cash flow data and making predictions as to cash flow growth on a year-by-year basis for, say, five years forward, and thereafter applying a constant growth rate out into the far distant future. Entering the appropriate discount factor will produce a per share value which can then be compared with the current share price.

Clearly this technique involves a considerable degree of subjectivity in assessing future rates of growth, but it has the merit that it is projecting forward from cash flow figures rather than, as analysts normally do, from a set of profit figures that, as the preceding section shows, need not be telling the whole story.

In addition, using market yields as the basis for discount factors has a greater degree of objectivity than projecting forward from assumptions about likely individual price earnings ratios and dividend yields. It is also useful in comparing valuations across companies in a relatively stable sector (brewing, food retailing, stores) where similar underlying growth rates can be reasonably confidently assumed.

The beauty of these models is that they can be constantly updated and the assumptions refined as and when, for example, new accounts are issued, bond yields and therefore discount factors change, and other new information comes to light.

There is also no doubt in my mind that companies contemplating acquisitions often use them to determine the appropriate level for a takeover bid.

Some years ago I produced a piece of research on the smaller companies in a particular sector, looking at their valuations on this basis, only to find less than a year later that two of the group of 15 had been on the receiving end of bids that equated almost exactly to their DCF valuation. Valuations done by this method – provided the assumptions made are realistic – should not be ignored.

Table 11.1 shows an example of this approach; the figures used being the actual accounts data from BT. Using a discount rate of 5.3 per cent, BT's valuation comes out at £11 per share, which at the time of writing was substantially more than the share price.

The spreadsheet used here is one based on the principles outlined in Robert Hagstrom's book, *The Warren Buffett Way* (Wiley, £17.95). The spreadsheet format has been devised by US investment guru Bob Costa. Unfortunately, Costa's website has been absorbed into a larger entity, but a copy of the spreadsheet is available on the 'software' page at www.linksitemoney.com.

To use this worksheet it is only necessary to fill in historic figures for as many years as are available. The figures that need to be entered are those in italics in the table, namely, the components of the free cash flow calculation, the operating cash flow figure, the figure for shareholders equity and for debt and the projected rates of increases in cash flow for the ten forward years and for the second stage phase of growth.

These figures can be tailored to take into account assumptions about the timing of growth or decline that are specific to the company, or that might be produced by the impact of the economic cycle. The total number of shares issued also needs to be entered, as does the appropriate discount rate and the current year-end date. The model calculates everything else.

Using DCF models is a good way of getting a handle on whether a particular share represents good value or not, although for obvious reasons it is not as good for use with shares that are particularly cyclical, for recovery situations, or for those that do not have a particularly predictable pattern of sales growth.

Table 11.1 Typical discounted cash flow model – figures for British Telecom

Historical	1992	1993	1994	1995	1996	1997	1998	1999	2000
Reported earnings	–	–	–	–	1,986	2,077	1,702	2,983	2,055
Depreciation					2,189	2,265	2,395	2,581	2,752
Other adjustments					906	725	6	(431)	(410)
less:									
Maintenance capital spending					1,000	1,200	1,400	(500)	1,600
Free cash flow	–	–	–	–	**4,081**	**3,867**	**2,703**	**5,633**	**2,797**
Earnings growth						-5.2%	-30.1%	108.4%	-50.3%
Operating cash flow					5,829	6,185	6,071	6,035	5,859
Shareholders equity					13,010	11,588	12,615	13,674	13,634
New equity					11,024	(3,499)	(675)	(1,924)	(2,095)
Debt					3,322	2,693	3,889	3,386	5,354
Total capital					16,332	14,281	16,504	17,060	18,988
Return on equity						29.7%	23.3%	44.7%	
Return on total capital						23.7%	18.9%	34.1%	16.4%

Projected	2001	2002	2003	2004	2005	2006	2007	2008	2009	2010
Prior year cash flow	2,797	2,517	2,266	2,266	2,492	2,791	3,210	3,691	4,060	4,263
Increase %	-10.0%	-10.0%	0.0%	10.0%	12.0%	15.0%	15.0%	10.0%	5.0%	1.0%
Cash flow	2,517	2,266	2,266	2,492	2,791	3,210	3,691	4,060	4,263	4,306
Discounted cash flow	2,391	2,043	1,940	2,027	2,156	2,355	2,571	2,686	2,679	2,569

Sum of discounted cash flows   23,417
10 year per share cash flow   £ 3.59

Residual value
Cash flow in year 10   4,306
Second stage growth rate   0.5%
Cash flow in year 11   4,328
Capitalization   4.8%
Company value at end of year 10   90,160
Present value of future cash flow   71,748
Shares (in millions)   6,514

Present value per share   **£11.01**
Assumes discount rate of 5.3%

Remember also that models like this tend to be very sensitive to the level of forecasts you make and particularly the discount rate you choose and whether or not you adjust it for risk. However, the technique clearly has more dimensions than straightforward PE or PEG factor analysis in that it can accommodate assessing shares with different expected levels of risk and return. Less volatile shares will get a 'head start' in the form of a lower risk adjusted discount rate. More volatile shares must produce better growth to offset their greater risk.

Using EVA

Another interesting and relatively new technique is Enterprise Value Analysis. This is more a tool used by company managements although some analysts also apply in-depth EVA analysis to companies.

Where it scores from the standpoint of the private investor is that its general principles can be used to provide a quick ready reckoner comparing companies in similar industries but in different countries. But it also uses figures which are cash flow and sales based, rather than profit numbers which are more subject to international differences in accounting policies.

It irons out differences in gearing ratios between companies in arriving at a comparative value, and also deals with the impact on the figure of partially owned subsidiaries and associates. The only adjustment that needs factoring in separately is if differing countries have wildly and consistently different corporate tax rates, since this will affect market valuations.

The techniques use four basic measures: sales, earnings before depreciation interest and tax, EBITDA (the preceding measure but also adding back depreciation and amortization), and 'free' operating cash flow. At its simplest, these are compared with the so-called 'enterprise value'. This is the company's market capitalization (i.e. its shares outstanding multiplied by the share price), plus debt, minus the value of any peripheral assets. If the company has net cash rather than debt, this is subtracted from market capitalization to arrive at EV.

Operating 'free' cash flow is normally defined as earnings before depreciation, interest and tax minus a 'maintenance' level of capital spending and (strictly speaking) a figure to represent the effect of inflation on net working capital. For most companies an educated guess needs to be made about the level of maintenance capital spending. It is also worth bearing in mind that there is a tendency, even among professional investors, to confuse EBITDA with cash flow, which is not strictly correct, since most definitions of free cash flow assume a minimum level of capital spending.

The attraction of using enterprise value as the numerator of the ratios that are calculated in this analysis is that it takes account of different levels of borrowing that companies may have, or the extent to which they have husbanded cash. A company with higher borrowings will have a higher enterprise value and therefore look less attractive when this is compared with sales, EBIT or EBITDA. Similarly a company with cash in the balance sheet will have a lower EV and hence look more attractive.

The question of what is and isn't an attractive investment proposition in enterprise value analysis is a moot point. I know of one prominent value investor who will not buy companies of any type that have EV greater than ten times EBIT. Certainly it is true that companies with EV/EBIT in single figures merit further scrutiny. Unless they can be expected to show radically different growth in the future, there is little justification for ostensibly similar companies in the same industry showing dramatically different EV/EBIT or EV/EBITDA. So if, say, you are contemplating buying shares in BT, it might be worth checking its EV/EBIT with that of Deutsche Telekom, for example.

EVA also allows some form of comparison to be made between companies that have high levels of interest payments relative to their trading profits and which therefore make losses at the pre-tax or net income after-tax level. This includes internet and other technology based companies, which are covered in a later section of this chapter.

Clearly there is more to EVA than this, but the important point for investors to remember is the concept of EV and its usefulness as the basis for ratios that represent easily understood relatively impartial international yardsticks. It is simply another tool in the investor's box of tricks.

Reinvested return on equity

Valuing companies using reinvested return on equity is an easy idea to grasp and is again susceptible to computerization via a simple spreadsheet.

Extracting a few figures from a company's report and accounts and making a small judgement here and there provides a useful guide as to whether a company's shares are good value or not.

The theory behind this form of valuation is comparatively simple.

A company's percentage return on equity is a key measure of its ability to continue to produce high returns in the future. If a company has a high return on equity, and retains a high proportion of it, that high return is therefore capable of being generated from a higher equity base, which in turn generates a still higher monetary return, which is added to the existing equity pot and the enlarged total put to work again, and so on.

The higher the return and the higher the percentage retained for reinvestment, the greater the intrinsic value of the company in the future, and the more the share price should rise.

Definitions are important here. Return on equity is after-tax profits expressed as a percentage of average shareholders' funds (including any accumulated goodwill). This is a more demanding definition than many use, but serves to separate the sheep from the goats in this sort of analysis.

The method used for this analysis can be reduced to a simple spreadsheet as shown in Table 11.2. This spreadsheet is available for download at the 'software' page at www.linksitemoney.com.

The items in italic are those that need to be calculated by the user. All other items are calculated automatically.

Calculate historic return on equity (ROE) by dividing after-tax profit by average shareholders funds and expressing the result as a percentage. The retention rate is calculated by subtracting dividends from after-tax profit and dividing by after-tax profits. The percentage retained is then multiplied by the ROE to produce the return on equity that is actually retained for reinvestment.

Table 11.2   Reinvested return on equity – how it works

Company		Universal Widgets	
Latest year-end		Dec 00	*
Historic shareholders' funds		105.00	*
Average shareholders' funds (£m)		100.00	*
Historic after-tax profit (£m)		25.00	*
Historic dividends ($m)		5.00	*
Historic ROE (%)		25.00	
Retention rate		0.80	
Reinvestment ROE (%)		20.00	
Shareholders ... (£m)	**Equity**	**Dividends**	
Year 1	126.00	6.30	
Year 2	151.20	7.56	
Year 3	181.44	9.07	
Year 4	217.73	10.89	
Year 5	261.27	13.06	
Total		**46.88**	
Year 5 PAT (£m)		**65.32**	
Benchmark yield (%)		5	*
Implied multiple		20.00	
Capitalized Year 5 PAT (£m)		1306.37	
Total return incl. divs (£m)		1353.25	
Current mkt cap. (£m)		500	*
% uplift/'margin of safety'		170.65	
Implied % compound return		22%	*

Figures marked with an asterisk are those required to be entered by the user. The rest are calculated automatically.

Historic shareholders' equity is then compounded at this rate for five years. Dividends are assumed to rise in proportion. The year five after-tax profit is then calculated either by grossing up the dividend in year five by the retention rate or by applying the historic ROE figure to the year five shareholders' equity figure. The result is the same either way.

Year five after-tax profit is then multiplied by a capitalization factor (discussed later), and the resulting figure added to accumulated dividends to arrive at a year five value for the company. This can then be compared with the current market capitalization to establish the percentage annual return required to get from one to the other, or, put another way, the long-term value implied by the current market price of the shares. The rate of return can be calculated either from compound interest tables or by using a financial calculator.

The choice of capitalization rate is clearly crucial in all this and it is here where opinions differ. The capitalization rate can be established from some form of benchmark yield (the capitalization rate would simply be the recip-rocal of the yield), or else it can be chosen on some other basis, perhaps the company's current earnings multiple, or a sector or market multiple.

If a yield-based yardstick is used, the obvious choices are the market rate of return (a yield on a benchmark gilt, for example), or a risk-adjusted rate of return calculated, for instance, by adjusting the yield for the beta factor of the stock.

It is of course possible to incorporate all of these options into the same table simply by copying the spreadsheet formulas and using slightly different assumptions (see Table 11.3).

The advantages of this approach are that it gives due weight to the importance of return on equity in generating value for shareholders, which many other methods of valuing shares don't. It also rewards those companies that retain a high proportion of their profits for reinvestment in the business.

Lastly it allows market-tested yields to be incorporated into the valuation, rather than some more randomly chosen variable.

There are also drawbacks to this approach. It works well only with those companies that have relatively straightforward balance sheets and a steadily growing business. Asset-based investments, or income orientated investments, do not fit well with this approach but can nonetheless be legitimate investment choices.

Companies that have come into being relatively recently, through takeovers or via the injection of an existing private company into a listed shell, are also not susceptible to this analysis because of the accounting distortions these processes introduce. This is not to say that they will be bad investments.

Table 11.3 Universal Widgets reinvested return on equity – different assumptions

Company	Original		50% payout		8% yield basis		50% payout and 8% yield basis
Latest year-end	Dec 00		Dec 00		Dec 00		Dec 00
Historic shareholders' funds (£m)	105.00		105.00		105.00		105.00
Average shareholders' funds (£m)	100.00		100.00		100.00		100.00
Historic after-tax profit ($m)	25.00		25.00		25.00		25.00
Historic dividends (£m)	5.00		12.50		5.00		12.50
Historic ROE (%)	25.00		25.00		25.00		25.00
Retention rate	0.80		0.50		0.80		0.50
Reinvestment ROE (%)	20.00		12.50		20.00		12.50
Shareholders ... (£m)	**Equity**	**Dividends**	**Equity**	**Dividends**	**Dividends**	**Equity**	**Dividends**
Year 1	126.00	6.30	118.13	14.77	6.30	126.00	14.77
Year 2	151.20	7.56	132.89	16.61	7.56	151.20	16.61
Year 3	181.44	9.07	149.50	18.69	9.07	181.44	18.69
Year 4	217.73	10.89	168.19	21.02	10.89	217.73	21.02
Year 5	261.27	13.06	189.21	23.65	13.06	261.27	23.65
Total		**46.88**		**94.74**	**46.88**		**94.74**
Year 5 PAT ($m)		**65.32**		**47.30**	**65.32**		**47.30**
Benchmark yield (%)		5.0		5.0	8.0		8.0
Implied multiple		20.00		20.00	12.50		12.50
Capitalized year 5 PAT (£m)		1306.37		946.07	816.48		591.29
Total return incl. divs (£m)		1353.25		1040.81	863.36		686.03
Current mkt cap. (£m)		500		500	500		500
% uplift/'margin of safety'		170.65		108.16	72.67		37.21
Implied % compound return		22.0%		15.8%	11.5%		6.5%

Figures in italics are those required to be entered by the user. The rest are calculated automatically.

Sum of the parts analysis

Another interesting way of valuing companies that have several discrete parts is to perform what is known as a 'sum of the parts' analysis. Essentially this consists of isolating the relevant figures for each division or subsidiary (sales, profits, assets, etc.) and then valuing each component separately to arrive, after deducting any central liabilities such as company borrowings, at a value for the whole group. This can then be compared to the market value of the shares.

In the past analysts have often used this approach, but it has sometimes tended to be viewed with scepticism by investors. The scepticism was generally along the lines that any value that was demonstrated to exist as a result of such an exercise would remain locked up. More recently, however, greater flexibility on the part of managements, and heightened corporate activity in the demerger area means that this can no longer be assumed to be the case, and performing analyses of this sort can be useful.

In some instances the companies concerned may have listed subsidiaries, allowing the value of the remaining businesses to be arrived at by deducting the market value and profit contribution represented by the listed company (Dixons and Freeserve is an obvious example). In the main, however, this approach relies heavily on assuming that each individual part being valued would sell on the multiple of earnings or EBIT appropriate for its sector.

An example makes it clearer how this approach can work.

Imagine that Universal Widgets has four subsidiaries: Widgets (its original engineering business); Widget Retail; Widget Telecom; and Widget Properties.

The sales, after-tax profits and assets of the four businesses are shown in Table 11.4. Assume also that Universal Widgets is currently capitalized in the market at £1,000m and has borrowings of £300m, putting the company on a multiple of 12 times earnings.

It is clear that these businesses need to be valued in different ways. The market rating is influenced by the perception that the group is largely an engineering company, and although engineering remains the largest single part of the business, the other businesses are significant in their own right and can be assessed separately.

A sum of the parts analysis would work something as follows. The engineering business should be valued roughly on the same multiple as the group as a whole. Retailing could be valued at, say, 15 times earnings, reflecting the higher rating on stores groups. Similarly the telecoms business should probably be valued on a revenue basis. Comparing this with other fledgling telecoms businesses might suggest a value of 1.5 times revenue, while the property business should be valued at a discount of, say, 25 per cent to net assets, reflecting the yardsticks normally used in the property sector.

As an aside, asset-based investments such as property companies and investment trusts represent a whole different subset of investments that tend to be valued in somewhat different ways. The key to them is net asset growth and typically those with rapid growth in this variable will stand at a premium to asset value, reflecting the anticipation of further growth. The norm, however, for slower moving companies is for the shares to stand at a modest discount to net asset value, the size of the discount increasing, the more seemingly moribund the company. This often gives rise to interesting valuation anomalies, especially if the investments concerned have been valued on an unduly conservative basis.

To return to the matter in hand, the effect of the simple 'sum of the parts' exercise can be seen in Table 11.4. This shows a sum of the parts of £1,800m and a net value, after deducting the group's central net borrowings, of £1,500m, 50 per cent more than the current market capitalization. An alternative way of looking at this is that the three non-engineering businesses are collectively valued at £1,200m, leaving the core business 'in for nothing'.

A spreadsheet template to allow you to do this exercise yourself is downloadable from the software page at www.linksitemoney.com.

It is important when doing calculations like this, however, to make sure that the component parts are valued on a reasonably conservative basis and that all central liabilities not otherwise accounted for are deducted from the total 'sum of the parts' to arrive at a true comparison. It is also important to recognize that there needs to be a reasonable chance of some form of demerger happening to release the value and eliminate what is commonly known as a 'holding company discount'.

These days, however, most managers are aware of the possibilities, as are potential bidders and corporate financiers. As markets become more global and get more efficient, anomalies like this should not persist.

Table 11.4 Universal Widgets – sum of the parts analysis

Subsidiary	Turnover	Net profits	Net assets	Valuation	Assumption
Widget Engineering	500	50	500	600	12 times profit
Widget Retail	500	20	200	300	15 times profit
Widget Telecom	500	5	100	750	1.5 times revenue
Widget Properties	50	10	200	150	75% of net assets
Total	**1,550**	**85**	**1,100**	**1,800**	

Valuing internet businesses

The roller-coaster movement in the stock market value of some internet stocks in the past year or so makes any objective analysis of this particular phenomenon difficult. In this section we look at how internet and other technology businesses should be viewed in general terms, and then how they can be valued on a reasonably objective basis.

Because they do not, on the whole, make profits, any analysis of internet companies is – much more so than for other businesses – heavily reliant on an assessment of the qualitative factors surrounding the business.

> Because they do not, on the whole, make profits, any analysis of internet companies is – much more so than for other businesses – heavily reliant on an assessment of the qualitative factors surrounding the business.

No one, apart from a few latter-day Luddites who have yet to 'get' the importance of the net, disputes that the rise in internet-related business is a huge opportunity for many companies. The real question is whether or not it will give rise to some form of profitless prosperity for the companies involved in it, or whether large, solidly valued companies will be the end result.

There is potential damage in store for those 'off-line' businesses whose traditional operating methods are threatened by the net (high street travel agents might be an example, or perhaps the music industry). The same is true for those who set themselves up as dot com businesses, but then fail to execute the basic strategy properly (by failing, say, to deliver the goods – literally and metaphorically – as promised). The hapless Boo.com was an example of this phenomenon.

Among the huge upsurge in net-related businesses in the past year, rather like the early years of the automobile, there will be many businesses that fail, or get swallowed up by larger rivals, or whose business models are simply not durable.

However, on balance, given the emergence of industry leaders such as Yahoo!, Amazon, AOL-Time Warner and others – all of which seem durable – it appears that many net-based companies, large and small, will eventually make profits. But in the meantime, how do you value them?

There are obviously big risks for investors, but they are risks that can to some degree be reduced through diversification by buying a spectrum of stocks of different sizes, in different areas, with different businesses, and different types of customer.

The problem then becomes one of determining whether or not the 'net' sector as a whole is fairly valued – with some stocks underrated and others well up with events – or whether the hype (and the subsequent crash) has resulted in all valuations first shooting ahead of reality only later leaving many stocks outrageously undervalued.

It goes without saying, of course, that net companies, with little in the way of tangible profitability to support their share prices, are potentially more volatile than the rest of the market.

The net presents a very different set of circumstances against which to analyze a business. It is not simply because of its potential for growth, though that is real enough.

User numbers outside of the USA in particular are set to rise sharply, driven by rising PC ownership, the still low penetration of internet access among existing PC owners, the likely cheapening of internet access costs, and the potential for cost-effective universal access (via high speed media such as ADSL and through interactive digital TV and mobile devices as well as the PC).

But there are other features, even more relevant to the ways businesses function. One is that a variety of products can be sold and delivered digitally (software, music, films and so on) in a highly cost-effective manner. The ease of gathering and processing customer information also offers new marketing opportunities.

Distance also becomes irrelevant: competition is both global and local. More important is the concept of marketing via network-enhanced word of mouth of the sort that propelled the growth of the Netscape browser in the early days of the web.

In this environment, establishing a pervasive presence quickly is vitally important in order to benefit from the beneficial effects of the network. This is often termed 'first mover' advantage.

The advantage that being first confers is often oversimplified. There is an advantage to being first mover, but the advantage goes to the first mover with the marketing muscle to establish a significant presence – rather than necessarily to the inventor of a concept. In this new environment the buyer is king: pricing is transparent and if you offer a superior service or product at the best price in the market, business will flow your way. If the market is big enough, second and third movers can flourish as well.

This does not mean there should not be a reality check when looking at net-based businesses. There are some broad qualitative principles worth considering before going on to look at how it might be possible to work out in practice whether a particular stock is fairly valued or otherwise by the market.

Quality of management is an essential for any successful business. Taking this as read, questions to be answered when looking at net businesses can be briefly enumerated as follows:

- Was the company first in its particular market?
- How big is that potential market; how much is the company having to spend to attract new customers?
- How much is it having to spend to retain existing customers, and how successful is it at doing that?
- What are the potential long-term operating margins of the business, and how long will they take to achieve?

In the case of many net companies, margins are some way down the road. This is usually because the businesses concerned are still putting the basics in place – building up their customer base, cementing loyalty, refining their business model, marketing heavily, and so on – all of which are necessary but costly. Many web-based businesses can choose when to begin making profits, but making profits now may not yet be in the best long-term interests of the business.

Because the net makes information gathering and product delivery so easy, margins (when they do materialize) may well be significantly higher than traditional businesses in the same industry once they do start to flow.

Measurement techniques

A range of new measuring techniques ('metrics', in the jargon) has been introduced to facilitate the assessment of internet stocks. In many cases these appear to have been developed simply to help justify what seem to be unduly high valuation measures on any traditional criteria. In the end, however, one must fall back on revenue and potential long-term profitability as the only sensible benchmark on which to base a valuation.

Hence, applying measures based on numbers of users of a particular site, or numbers of users, or 'subscribers' is only relevant to the extent that enables a better judgement to be made of the revenue earning potential of the business concerned – what it might mean for the advertising revenue generated by the site, for example, or its marketing reach. Ultimately revenue, and eventually profits and cash flow, are what matter.

Logical bases for valuing companies on a revenue basis do exist. In his book *What Works on Wall Street*, James O'Shaughnessy outlined his discovery that in the post-war stock market the best ratio for measuring superior long-term performance was the ratio of market value to revenue. Unfortunately for net stocks, he found that outperformers tended to be those whose price to sales ratio was less than one!

Other investors swear by ratios such as 'enterprise value' (market capitalization plus or minus net debt or cash) to EBITDA or EBIT. Here (as outlined earlier in this chapter) value investors would probably look for a ratio of less than ten on this measure, again out of court for most net companies.

Rationalizing these methods and attempting to distil them into an approach that works for high growth (but loss making) businesses in a rapidly changing market is the challenge.

The methods that can be used amount to searching for rational bench-marks and then applying them to the newer companies.

One way of responding to the challenge is to assume that the valuations placed on more mature businesses operating in roughly a similar area are rational, and compare those valuations to revenue growth and profitability. Hence one might arrive at the view that a certain level of revenue growth (or a forecast average) is typically priced at a certain multiple of revenue for these more mature businesses.

Observation of other technology businesses like Sage and Logica, for example, might lead one to the view that multiples of sales on these businesses should be no more than the average percentage growth in sales over (say) the past three years.

A conservative approach to this might be to deduct the risk-free rate of return for good measure in order to arrive at the appropriate multiple of revenue. In other words, a business growing at 7 per cent per annum in revenue terms should, if the risk free rate of return is 6 per cent, be valued at one times revenue, while a business growing at 16 per cent in revenue terms could be worth ten times revenue and so on.

Since the growth for much internet business is often out in the future, this method needs adapting slightly. The easiest method is to arrive at, say, average revenue growth from years three to five out in the future (or the average for the full five years), apply the appropriate multiple to arrive at a year five market value, and then compare this with the current market capital-ization to find out the compound annual return needed to move from the present value to the future one. In some ways this is a similar calculation to that performed in the reinvested return on equity method described earlier.

This is shown in Table 11.5.

A copy of this table is available for download at the 'software' page at www.linksitemoney.com.

This provides a dynamic (though still admittedly imperfect) way of assessing the value of internet stocks, basing their value on revenue growth, the risk-free rate of return, and the rate of return that might be judged appropriate for such speculative investments.

In my view, such is the risk with some of these businesses that some form of hurdle rate of return needs to be assumed at the outset, before even considering whether or not the stock is worth investing in. A return in excess of 30 per cent would need to be generated by this method to produce a cast-iron case that a company was cheap, bearing in mind the risks involved.

The other factor that must be looked at if at all possible is the rate at which the company is consuming cash. This is widely known as the company's 'cash burn' or 'burn rate'. This can be compared across companies by taking an average of monthly cash operating costs, less any profit made, and comparing this with the latest cash balances to give the number of months to zero cash. If need be this could be done by averaging the results from the company's latest six-monthly statement (arrived at by deduction for the second half of a full-year period).

The acceptable cut-off point between what is acceptable and what isn't varies with market circumstances and the ease with which companies are able to raise fresh capital, but those trading companies with less than 18 months' cash on present spending are – in the current climate – best avoided.

Valuing internet businesses is therefore rather less neat and tidy than for other types of investment. In short, one needs to look partly at the qualitative factors mentioned earlier that relate to management talent and the quality of the business idea, at likely revenue trends and at the company's chances of long-term survival within its present cash resources.

Of these, the least reliable are the revenue forecasts. Forecasts may be forthcoming from the company broker, friendly analysts, or the company's official documentation, but in many cases these are hedged around with disclaimers and should be treated with some scepticism.

Table 11.5 Example of an internet stock valuation model

Company	Widget.com	Price(£)		1.5
Base year to	Dec 00	Shs o/s m		12.73
	Revenue	£000s	% Op	£000s
Year to:	growth %	revenue	margin	EBIT
Base		100		0
Dec 01	600	700	0	0
Dec 01	100	1,400	0	0
Dec 03	50	2,100	0	0
Dec 04	35	2,835	20	567
Dec 05	25	3,544	25	886
Avge rev gr.	36.67	Current mkt cap. (£m)		19.1
Gilt yield	5.3	Mkt cap. Y5 (£m)		55.6
Multiplier	15.68	Impl comp rtn (%)		23.8
Cash chge Y1–5	−16.0	Y5 EV		42.8
Cash/(Debt) Y0	3.2	Y5 EV/EBIT		48.3
Cash/(Debt) Y5	−12.8			

Assessing incubators

Continuing the theme of the previous section, one is possibly on somewhat safer ground with so-called internet incubators or similar investment funds. These have proliferated in the past few years but as investments they offer a number of attractions. These can be listed as follows:

- management expertise in corporate finance
- thorough due diligence of potential investments
- management with inside knowledge of the investee companies
- a portfolio investing approach, and reduced risk through diversification
- observable historic data or returns generated by similar funds.

The method of valuing such businesses is comparatively easy. Take the company's latest published figure for net asset value. In most cases this is little more than cash balances and the book cost of unlisted investments and in some cases the market value of listed ones. Compare this figure with the market capitalization of the company.

The next assumption rests on treating companies like this essentially as private equity funds. That is to say they make their returns over a period of three to five years. Typically one or two huge successes out of a portfolio of maybe a dozen or more companies produce a solid return for the fund as a whole.

Statistics from the British Venture Capital Association show that funds investing in early stage technology businesses have variable rates of return, at best in the high 50s in percentage terms. That is to say that over a five-year period a fund's asset value might multiply in value by ten times from the starting point. The numbers are corroborated by figures from the European Venture Capital Association taken across a wider geographical spectrum.

Quite simply (and however unlikely at present), the closer a fund's market value is to this ten times original NAV figure, the more likely it is to be fully valued and the more susceptible to bad news, bearing in mind that problems with investee companies tend to come early on in a fund's life. An old venture capital adage is that 'lemons ripen before plums'.

It is, however, crucial that investors recognize that these rules are made to be broken, not all management teams in this area are created equal, and investments of this type need to be held for a lengthy period before they come to fruition. At the other extreme, many internet investment funds were valued, at the depths of the market depression about net investments, at less than the value of their cash resources. This ignored the fact that some investments could doubtless come good and, indeed, the fund could walk away from those that did not.

IN BRIEF

- Discounted cash flow modelling is a long-established method of valuing businesses, but needs to be used with care, as the results produced by such models are highly sensitive to the assumptions used.

- Enterprise value (EV) based ratios offer a useful way of comparing companies internationally, and are helpful in assessing those companies where interest costs and other charges produce negative pre-tax results and earnings.

- Reinvested return on equity is an excellent, and easily mastered, way of assessing certain types of company.

- Sum of the parts analysis is a technique used to identify value in conglomerates and other multi-line businesses.

- Valuing internet companies is a mixture of art and science, although it is somewhat easier to assess internet investment funds (or incubators) than trading companies.

Investing my money

On the principle that one thinks more of a restaurateur if he 'eats his own cooking', perhaps the best way of illustrating how investing works is to give examples from one's own personal experience. This should show not only the successes but also the failures and misjudgements to which all investors are prone.

By the time this book is published I should have completed 15 years of reasonably active stock market investing on my own account.

Although I began work in the stock market in 1970, prior to 1986 I either did not feel comfortable risking my relatively modest savings in the market, or else I felt the time was not ripe.

This in itself is an important point. Don't commit cash to the market that you can't afford to lose.

In 1986, the firm I then worked for was effectively taken over by an American bank, as many brokers were in the period before and after the City's 'Big Bang'. As part of this deal, I received cash in exchange for a proportion of the shares and share options I held in the firm and as a result had surplus capital that I was able to begin investing more actively.

I allocated £28,000 to begin my stock market trading career, but the lessons I have learnt in my dealings over the years are applicable whatever the amount you have available.

In the rest of this chapter, I have given a brief outline of my stock market deals since then. None of these details are exaggerated in any way, although I have omitted some of the more tedious ones to move the story along.

At this stage I should also mention some of the restrictions under which I worked in the City. As an analyst specializing in a particular sector, I was barred – by my firm's dealing rules – from trading in shares in the industry I analyzed and knew most about. As a financial journalist and consultant there have also been times when I have unearthed interesting opportunities, but been unable to deal for various professional reasons.

Many of the early deals I did were as the result of conversations with colleagues about companies in other industries that I thought looked interesting. There is no doubt that having this specialist advice to call upon informally helped considerably, although it is important to stress that at no time did I act on anything that could remotely be considered inside information.

Nevertheless, it must be recognized that those working in the market have often in the past had an innate knowedge and information advantage over the rest of the investment community. With the advent of the web, as explained earlier, this is now much less the case.

The other advantage a stock market employee has is favourable commission rates charged for staff dealing, although it is possible to make over much of this, especially in the light of the subsequent development of execution-only services for the small investor.

In broking, as a staff member my orders in the market took second place to those of clients, and like any other investor I also had to cope with the impact of the bid-offer spread.

I have divided the narrative into a number of distinct phases. In each case I will describe some of the deals I did and support this with some statistical information. At the end of the chapter I will try and demonstrate how you can informally measure your trading record against some of the more normal benchmarks, and draw some lessons from the resulting comparison.

Phase One: July 1986 to January 1988

For those who were not involved in the stock market at the time, it is almost impossible to describe the final phases of the 1981–87 bull market in shares in London. This was the era of the Unlisted Securities Market, dubbed the 'millionaire machine' by some in the City.

For much of the 1980s the bull market was a fairly sedate affair. In 1986, however, it began to assume the character of the 1920s. The events of 1986 and 1987 are probably the sort that only happen once or twice in a lifetime and one might count oneself as fortunate both to participate and to escape more or less intact. The 'internet madness' of early 2000 may come to be seen in the same light.

My first deal resulted in a loss of £500 or so. On the recommendation of a colleague I bought some shares in Commercial Union (now CGNU following its merger with Norwich Union). I made the mistake of both averaging down, buying 500 shares at 319p and then a further 500 at 307p. Averaging down sometimes works, but more often than not (and certainly most times I have tried it) it simply compounds the error. I eventually sold the 1,000 shares at 267p in November 1986 and resolved to be careful about the advice I took from then on.

In July and August 1986 I gradually invested most of the rest of my starting capital of £28,000. I picked a broad range of stocks, some of which are now no longer with us or which exist in a different form. The list included: textile group Illingworth Morris, at that time a management turnaround story; the acquisitive paper and packaging group Bunzl; the stores group Sears Holdings; Hanson (then called Hanson Trust); the motor distributor T Cowie (now called Arriva – quickly sold for a small profit, missing out on a much larger rise later on); SAC International, a small USM company involved in specialist engineering consultancy; and Mount Charlotte Hotels, subsequently taken over by the Australian entrepreneur Ron Brearley.

The years 1986 and 1987 were periods of intense corporate activity. The firm I worked for was involved in an advisory capacity in a number of the major bids occurring at that time. These included the Hanson bid for Imperial Group and the subsequent sale of the Courage brewing business to Elders IXL; the defence of The Distillers Company against the bid from Argyll Group and subsequent (and ultimately controversial) 'white knight' merger with Guinness – now called Diageo; and the Elders IXL bid for the food and brewing group then known as Allied-Lyons (now Allied Domecq).

There were also some other involvements, such as a steady flow of corporate work for Scottish & Newcastle, and work for corporate clients among the ranks of smaller brewing and distilling companies.

The result of all this activity was that for much of 1986 and the early part of 1987 I was so engrossed in my job that I was unable to pay much attention to my own financial affairs and the state of my investments. This had the fortunate result that I did not deal over-frequently, and hence was able to enjoy the fruits of the rise in the market over this period.

Readers will note from Table 12.1, showing the results of this first phase, that the annualized gain of 68 per cent recorded in this period was essentially the result of a simple 'buy and hold' strategy. I dealt in only 16 stocks over the 18-month period. It can also be seen that, although there were gains across the board, the lion's share of the increase (in fact £26,000 of a total net gain of around £30,000) came from just three of the stocks.

Note also that the period covered by the table includes that running up to and immediately after the October 1987 stock market crash.

My best success in this period came from a share known then as Control Securities (now called Ascot Holdings). This was at that time a small property company based in Wales, effectively little more than a listed shell. But it became the vehicle for the ambitous Ugandan Asian Virani family. Led by Nazmu Virani, who later served a prison sentence for his alleged involvement in the BCCI affair, the family injected some property interests into the business and turned the company into a glamour stock by means of frenetic property trading.

A colleague of mine had met Nazmu Virani shortly after this process began and became very excited about the prospects for the company. I decided to put some of my own money into the shares and bought a total of 15,000 shares at an average price of 19p a share, eventually selling the holding at 101p in September 1987.

I sold the bulk of my stock market investments in early September 1987 in order to buy a holiday home/investment property. I jokingly referred to it as my 'bear market bolt hole', without really realizing that this was precisely what it would become.

The timing of this move, I will readily admit, was part luck and part judgement. It was related both to the unease I and a number of colleagues felt about the market, and the excesses of the bull phase that had by then just about run its course.

In my personal life there had been some traumas too. I was becoming increasingly dissatisfied with life in the City in the post 'Big Bang' era, and at sharp odds with certain of my colleagues over the direction of the market and some other issues. There was some writing on the wall in both respects. I decided to take some evasive action.

My father had died very suddenly in February 1987 and a few months later it seemed a good idea to invest some of my stock market gains in a small holiday property close to where my mother lived, just south of the Lake District. Over the summer of 1987 we found a suitable property and agreed a price.

People are often astonished when I tell them that completion on this property deal was fixed for 13 October 1987 – six days before the 1987 market crash. The purchase price, £42,500, necessitated me selling a substantial proportion of my then stock market holdings in early September.

My unease over the course of the market was compounded by the chronic state of the settlement system at the time. As I attempted to wrest a cheque out of the system to send to my solicitor, trips to the 'back office' began to resemble nothing so much as a journey into a world peopled by characters out of a Kafka novel or a Breughel painting, with mountains of paper and a system that was clearly overloaded.

Something had to give. In the end, of course, it did. The ill-fated Taurus settlement system was abandoned and gave way to the launch of the CREST electronic settlement business successfully managed by a cadre of secondees from the Bank of England.

I was out of the country on a business trip to the USA when the 1987 hurricane and the stock market crash struck. My escape from the stock market was tainted by the fact that I still had some investments that had not been sold. Contrary to the views of colleagues who felt the setback was a temporary one, my own reading suggested that even if the stock market's leaders recovered, the smaller company sector (in which I had had some good gains) would take some time to get back to normal.

Two particular holdings caused me pain. They were Hawker Siddeley – an engineering company since taken over by BTR (now part of Invensys) –

Table 12.1 Phase One – 30 June 1986 to 31 December 1988

	Five best trades			Five worst trades		
Stock	Profit/loss	Held for (months)		Stock	Profit/loss	Held for (months)
Control Securities	12,182	7		Inoco	-1,622	3
Hanson	8,225	14		Hawker Siddeley	-1,581	3
SAC International	6,783	14		Control Securities	-835	22
Clyde Petroleum	2,963	4		TN	-644	2
Bunzl	2,239	12		CU	-520	3
Total gain in period	35,891			Total loss in period	-5,202	
Net investment income	-7,215			No. of stocks traded	16	
Annualized total return in period (%)	68%			Starting capital	£25,000	
No. of winning trades	11			No. of losing trades	5	
Average time held (months)	11			Average time held (months)	3	
FTSE-100 index at start of period	1649.8			Risk-free bond yield at start of period	8.80%	

and Inoco, then a small shell company being used as a vehicle by the 1960s and 1970s entrepreneur David Rowland.

As an aside, Rowland's son was one of the leading lights in the internet incubator Jellyworks, which enjoyed a brief stock market flowering at the time of the internet boom in late 1999 and early 2000.

I cut my losses in both companies after the crash, taking a loss amounting in total to about £3,000.

I still had some affection for Control Securities, having made so much money out of the shares in the recent past. I bought back 15,000 shares at a price of around 45p, but their performance was never quite the same again and I ended up selling this holding for a small loss two years later.

My temper was subsequently improved by a former colleague's inspired recommendation of Clyde Petroleum, a small oil exploration and production stock. I bought a total of 10,000 shares at an average price of about 110p, subsequently selling the shares in April 1988 at a price of 145p. Even in the depths of the psychological depression after the crash there was still money to be made, and recouping some of the earlier losses gave one some cause for optimism.

There was, of course, a reckoning from this phase of the market. Although I had gains that amounted to about £30,000 made from my starting capital of £28000, as a high-earning City individual at that time, I was subject to a hefty marginal tax rate. This had two consequences.

First there was a stored-up tax bill from the gain I had made exercising my share options and selling employee scheme shares, and also from my stock market gains. With better and earlier advice, the tax aspect of this might have been planned to better effect. That was my own fault, in a sense. The result was that I was faced with a later bill for £11,000 capital gains tax. Having said that, it pays not to let tax considerations drive investment.

On the plus side, my surplus funds had been invested in a high-interest-earning account and there was a total of some £4,800 in interest income, and dividends on the shares I had held over the period to offset (at least in my own mind) against this.

The 18-month period produced a gross gain of just in excess of 100 per cent on my starting capital of £28,000, swelling to about £35,800 on a total return basis after including gross dividend and interest income. I also had further capital to inject from the sale of my remaining shares in the business in the second half of 1987. This amounted to £32,000, structured as described in the next section. The effect was to bring the total available capital at the start of the second phase in my dealings to £60,000.

This set me up well for the next phase in my career, although gains have never been quite as easy to come by again, for reasons I will explain.

Phase Two: January 1988 to September 1992

In January 1988 I decided to leave the City and become a freelance writer. A severance package agreed with the firm I worked for took care of buying a car to replace the company one I had to give back, and also took care of the accumulated tax bill run up on exercising my share options.

The two payments almost exactly cancelled each other out and I was left with a clean sheet and the opportunity to sell my remaining shares, by then converted into tax-efficient floating rate notes, over a period of six years. With the high interest rates of the time, the quarterly interest payments produced more than enough to pay school fees and other essentials while my progress into the self-employed world began.

In calculating the figures in Table 12.2, I have assumed the capital injection came in October 1987, the date of the takeover, although in fact I kept most of it in the form of loan notes, cashing them in only gradually. The capital was gradually drawn down over a period of four or five years, and thereby produced a regular flow of lubrication for my stock market trading activities and other essential expenditure.

Phase Two began with a bang but as a whole was relatively inactive. It would be a mistake perhaps to describe this phase as an extended bear market, but certainly there were periods of it that were distinctly uncomfortable, notably the time aound the second anniversary of the crash and immediately prior to sterling's exit from ERM in September 1992.

I have to confess that I found it hard to adjust at first to no longer being at the centre of the market action. I found out quite quickly the degree to which private investors at that time were at a substantial disadvantage compared to City professionals.

So there are some examples in this phase of how taking one's eye off the ball, even for a few days, can result in big losses. The deals in this period are shown in Table 12.2.

For the whole of this period, I had staff dealing facilities, I moved my broking account to Charles Stanley, where a former colleague from a previous broking firm I had worked for handled my deals on a part advice, part execution-only basis. In the period of almost four years between January 1988 and September 1992, I did only 11 trades, as I was building up my own business. In the 1988–89 period there were two outstandingly successful deals and a number of less inspiring ones.

For a long spell in my broking career I had followed the tobacco sector and knew that BAT Industries had been a cheap stock for many years. I ended up paying £8,400 in all for a tidy holding. A few months later BAT was on the receiving end of a hostile bid and I sold out for a profit of £5,600. The profit would have been larger had I taken my broker's advice

Table 12.2 Phase Two – 1 January 1988 to 31 July 1992

Five best trades			Five worst trades		
Stock	Profit/loss	Held for (months)	Stock	Profit/loss	Held for (months)
BAT	5,649	19	BP	–1,486	2
Lloyds Bank	1,751	21	Aran Energy	–1,092	4
Hanson	1,424	8	Devenish	–970	9
Allied-Lyons	1,345	21	Slough Estates	764	16
Marks & Spencer	1,176	21	ICI	–202	7
Total gain in period	11,756		Total loss in period	–4,514	
Net investment income	6,268		No. of stocks traded	11	
Annualized total return in period (%)	4.90%		Starting capital	£60,000	
No. of winning trades	6		No. of losing trades	6	
Average time held (months)	18		Average time held (months)	5.5	
FTSE-100 index at start of period	1712.7		Risk-free bond yield at start of period	9.40%	

to sell at a profit of around £8,000. Yet again I also took a useful profit on Hanson shares, buying around 5,000 shares at 160p and selling at 200p. A similar small turn in Ladbroke added to the gains.

I learnt however to beware of stocks for which one had had a previous professional attachment. I had advised the JA Devenish pub group (long since taken over) in the later stages of my City career and thought highly of the management. But an attempt to capitalize on this experience ended in failure, proving that a detached view is essential to trade shares successfully.

The next burst of dealing in this phase was between 1990 and 1992. By October 1990 I felt that the market was set for another rise and picked a selection of early-cycle blue chips like Marks & Spencer, Allied-Lyons (now Allied Domecq), and Lloyds Bank (now LloydsTSB). A foray in the property sector via Slough Estates resulted in heavy losses, as did a later venture into BP ahead of the ERM débâcle. In the case of BP, had I only held my nerve and continued to hold the stock the profits would have been substantial. As it was I ended up with a £700 loss on Slough and a £1,500 drop on BP, the latter in the aftermath of a profit warning.

I sold the trio of blue chips in July 1992 with what in hindsight proved to be reasonable timing, not perhaps getting the best of prices, but missing the later downward spiral in August and early September.

The result of this phase was a total gain of just short of £12,000 offset by losses of about £4,500. Numerically gains and losses were more or less even, but the policy of cutting losses early and running profits once again proved its worth. (This is displayed to even better effect in the next phase.) My overall gains over this period were also boosted by substantial interest income from the loan notes and modest income from renting out the holiday property investment.

Phase Three: September 1992 to December 1995

I can freely admit that I missed the opportunity to buy into the market at the depths of the ERM crisis, although I remember graphically the point at which the market turned.

Part-way through the period I changed brokers, moving to the execution-only speciaist Fidelity Brokerage in early 1993, mainly in order to save on dealing charges. In the period between October 1992 and the end of 1995 I did 33 separate trades recording total gains of £16,500 and accumulated losses of £8,400. In this phase, the gains and losses were again numerically more or less equal, but the policy of cutting losses early, though it appears sometimes to result in missed opportunities, undoubtedly pays off as the years roll by.

There is another aspect to this, of course, which is not selling too early, something I am prone to do – as I have explained earlier in this book. The prime example of this occurred in this phase of trading, with a company called Whitegate Leisure. Its name was later changed to Northern Leisure and it has since merged with Luminar.

Whitegate was a company that had been set up by a former executive from First Leisure to develop interests in discotheques and bowling, but had expanded too fast in the run-up to the 1991 recession and experienced severe problems. It was a chance meeting with the management that brought this company to my attention, in the immediate aftermath of the ERM débâcle.

The company had an awful balance sheet, but interest rates were coming down and the signs were that the new management team had got a firm grip on the business. I bought 25,000 shares at 9p. Over a period of less than six months the shares rose to the 30s and I sold out in two stages for a total gain of more than £4,000 – more than doubling my money. The sting in the tail is that the shares went spiralling up from there and were eventually taken over by Luminar. Had I held on to the bitter end, I estimate my holding, bought for £2,500, would probably have been worth in excess of £70,000. See Table 12.3.

Other major successes during this period were in Eldridge Pope, a small West Country brewing group, where I also noticed a new management team moving in. This produced a gain of some £2,400. There was also another £700 turn in Ladbroke (now called Hilton Group, of course), a £600 gain in Invergordon Distillers on the widely rumoured and later consummated bid, and quick trades in Bulmer and Greenalls Group. Later on, I racked up a £1,500 gain in the Regent Inns pub group following its flotation, a £2,000 gain in the Yates Brothers pub group following its flotation and a near £1,000 gain in the Burn Stewart whisky company.

Interspersed with these successes, many of which arose as a result of the fact that this was an industry in the process of great change and one I had followed closely for almost 20 years, were an almost exactly equal number of small losses.

The worst catastrophes were: selling too early in Wace, the printing group that subsequently tripled from the price at which I sold at a small loss; a £700 loss in Simon Enginering; a £1,000 loss on Pentos, a company that looked attractive but which eventually went into receivership; a £1,200 loss in Harmony Property; an £800 loss in Dixons; and a similar-sized one in John Menzies as the high street boom failed to materialize. Again, had I held on to Dixons all might have been well. I sold at 45p: the shares are now 184p but have been as high as 400p at times in the recent past.

Over this period too, the property investment had been on permanent let and produced regular gross income of £4,000–5,000 a year to add to the stock market gains.

Table 12.3 Phase Three – September 1992 to December 1995

	Five best trades			Five worst trades	
Stock	Profit/loss	Held for (months)	Stock	Profit/loss	Held for (months)
Northern Leisure	4,101	8	Harmony Prop	−1,233	2
Eldridge Pope	2,432	10	Pentos	−1,022	2
Yates Brothers	2,115	6	Dixons	−831	4
Regent Inns	1,487	7	Menzies	−789	3
ACT	977	6	Wace	−716	1
Total gain in period	16,476		Total loss in period	−8,422	
Net investment income	3,714		No. of stocks traded	33	
Annualized total return in period (%)	6.03%		Starting capital	£60,000	
No. of winning trades	16		No. of losing trades	17	
Average time held (months)	7		Average time held (months)	2	
FTSE-100 index at start of period	2553		Risk-free bond yield at start of period	9%	

To complete this section on trading, this long-term property investment was sold in 1996 and produced proceeds in the region of £62,500, a gain of some £20,000, or just under a 50 per cent increase over the eight-year period of our ownership. This gain is made more respectable when the income component is taken into account.

Phase Four: December 1995 to June 1998

Phase Four was a transition phase, a time when there were a lot of things happening and several changes needed to reorganize my own and my family's personal finances: a major switch in my pension assets; my mother's death and dealing with her estate; the expense of children at university, and a consequent need for additional income; and so on.

In 1996 and for most of 1997 I was relatively inactive in the market, partly because, incorrectly as it subsequently turned out, I suspected it was unlikely to rise much further. Most of the personal account trading at this time was confined to a little dabbling in the options market, with little overall profit or loss.

I later came to the conclusion that I did not have the time to monitor options trades in the detail they demand when I lost over £1,000 on a FTSE index put (see next section), bought just before the market put on an upward spurt.

Elsewhere, with two children at that time going through university courses, my attentions were focused on investing for income, achieved through investment in high yield unit trusts and gilts. I have continued investing to the fullest extent possible in PEPs and ISAs since then, mainly (at least until very recently) in income- and bond-based investments.

I pursued this caution further, to the extent of switching the largest component of my personal pension fund away from a straight equity-linked fund into a smoothed with-profits fund, in effect locking in the gains that had been made over the previous ten years.

This highlights a point I referred to earlier – that any stock market investment you make needs to be considered as part of your wider net worth. Since this switch was made the day-by-day fluctuations in the value of the fund I previously held have been replaced by periodic bonus declarations, each one permanently 'locked in'.

The timing could probably have been better but in net terms I calculate I am only marginally worse off by having done this, while having considerably reduced the risk that a major market upset could decimate my pension fund.

The next catalyst for a change in trading style was my mother's death in September 1997. As an only child, the need to administer her modest estate, with the help of a local solicitor, took up a certain amount of time and again limited the degree to which I had time left over after work to devote to investing.

In the end my wife and I gave a significant portion of the proceeds of the estate to our children, and used the remainder to repay the mortgage on our house, with a little left over for investment purposes.

In the course of this period I also changed brokers, back to Charles Stanley – this time to their Xest online dealing service. This has a low flat-rate commission fee, ideal for someone dealing in the amounts I do.

This takes us to the beginning of the latest phase of dealing, dating from the final winding-up of my mother's estate.

Phase Five: June 1998 to date

The final phase begins with the portfolio consisting of, to cut a long and rather convoluted story short, a chunk of money held in a variety of tax-efficient bond-related investments (this was subsequently raised with the addition of regular ISAs), a low five-figure sum in for a private equity investment in a publishing venture with which I was associated at that time, and around £25,000 for more active share trading.

I deliberately made the amount designated for trading shares a relatively small proportion of the total because, having to a degree rethought my trading strategy, I wanted to make sure that any gains I made on equities did not suddenly overwhelm the bond part of the portfolio and lead to a loss of balance.

Table 12.4 shows some of the highlights.

Including significant investment income on univested cash and dividends from investments, the net gain on the £25,000 invested falls just short of £10,000, a 40 per cent uplift in just over two years (to the time of writing). In round terms the PEP and ISA investments have changed little in capital terms but have yielded around 7.5 per cent per annum, of which about half has been reinvested.

The EIS investment is coming to the end of its five-year tax 'lock-up' period, after which time it can be sold free of CGT: it remains to be seen whether or not an 'exit' opportunity presents itself, although the shares are probably currently worth somewhat in excess of their book cost.

In terms of trading listed stock market companies I have once again been guilty of ignoring my own advice regarding cutting losses promptly before they get too large. The largest loss, in eVestment (an internet incubator), happened quickly at around the time of the debacle in technology stocks. In buying the shares at 20p, I imagined I was close to the bottom, but the shares quickly halved from my purchase price. Averaging down to reduce the book cost to around 16p only compounded the error. eVestment (now EVC Christows) looks a very solid business for the long term, but enough was enough.

Table 12.4 Phase Five – 1 June 1998 to date

Five best trades		
Stock	Profit/loss	Held for (months)
Inter Link Foods	5,457	17
HACAS	4,625	18
GUS	2,114	9
Hansom	1,919	10
Belgo	1,283	7
Total gain in period	19,311	
Net investment income	1,356	
Annualized total return in period (%)	15%	
No. of winning trades	10	
Average time held (months)	8.5	

Five worst trades		
Stock	Profit/loss	Held for (months)
eVestment	–2,874	4
FTSE Index put	–1,344	4
Stylo	–1,234	5
Metroline	–960	3
VFG	–965	4
Total loss in period	10,739	
No. of stocks traded	23	
Starting capital	£25,000	
No. of losing trades	13	
Average time held (months)	3	

The loss on a 'footsie' index put option was a simple market misjudgement, again not helped by inattention and the fact that a chunk of the loss occurred when I was out of the country on business and unable to monitor the position properly. Like the other negative numbers in the table, none of these losses should have been allowed to get as large as they did.

On the plus side there have been several successes. In the case of three of these I have seen the shares more than double from the original purchase and taken the opportunity to take sufficient profits to reduce my book cost close to zero in each case, limiting my downside.

Inter Link Foods is a manufacturer of own label cakes run by extremely capable management with long experience elsewhere in the industry. I know the products and the management well and this is shaping up to be a very long-term holding. Similarly, I bought HACAS because its chosen area (social housing consultancy) seemed to be an area likely to boom with the advent of a Labour government.

A relatively quick turn in Belgo, bought immediately after the company returned to the market after metamorphosing from the former Luke Johnson shell company Lonsdale Holding, proved the right thing to do.

Although I could have got a higher selling price than I did on the shares (bought at 6p: sold at just under 10p), the shares subsequently dived to around 3p. The original rationale for the investment was personal experience of the chain of Belgian-style restaurants from which the group takes its name. I became disillusioned when the company took over a clutch of upmarket restaurants in exchange for shares, diluting the original concept and removing the tight focus that had been the hallmark of the group before that.

The other two big winning trades, both of which are still in the portfolio, are GUS and Hansom Group (not to be confused with Hanson). I bought GUS – partly on chart grounds – at close to the low point (at the high-water mark of the dot com boom) on the basis that GUS's logistics and credit checking business would be a beneficiary of any boom in internet trading, while the shares themselves might be susceptible to break-up. New non-family management at the group is now pursuing an e-commerce orien-tated strategy.

The second trade, in Hansom Group, was as a result of spotting that the company was advertising itself as a 'shell' in the pages of the *Financial Times*. Formerly a radio taxi business, a couple of well known shell operators had moved in and sold off all of the businesses for cash, leaving cash in the region of 10p a share, only marginally less than the then share price.

Management made it clear that the process would take some time and that any takeover would not be in the dot com area. The cash proved there was little downside risk. The shares have since doubled. I have now taken out my original stake, because sometimes a reverse into a shell does not produce the desired effect.

This means for three of the four substantial gainers in the portfolio currently, the shares are more or less in the books for nothing, and I can take a relaxed view of when to sell the remainder. The remaining trades over the period have been relatively modest in terms of the gains and losses – small gains in Great Portland Estates and BT, and small losses in Marks & Spencer, the whisky firm Glenmorangie, and Newcastle United.

Performance measurement

In assessing how my investment performance measured up to the indices and the professionals, I have tried to adopt a consistent method of measurement throughout.

Stock market net gains over a period of just under 15 years have amounted to £85,000 and losses to £39,000. Total investment income in the form of shares and deposit interest was £8,300.

There were a total of 79 stock market trades (i.e. matched buys and sells – 158 separate deals in all) of which 39 showed a gain and 40 were losses of varying size. Four substantially profitable trades remain open at the time of writing. But, and here is the most important message for the would-be stock market trader, the average gain over the period was some £2,125 and the average loss just under £975.

The total return on the early property investment (which was acquired partly out of the gains made in the 1986–87 period and did not represent an additional injection of capital) has been some £34,000 on an initial investment of £42,500. Taxed rental income, after allowing for letting expenses and maintenance, was in the region of £14,000 making the total return some 80 per cent, or a compound 7.8 per cent per annum over a period of just over eight years.

PEPs and ISAs have yielded around £4,400 in cash income, although this understates the true yield on the £50,000 currently invested, since some of the income has been automatically reinvested.

So total returns in both property and stock market trades over the period of about 14 years have amounted to some £132,000.

I am happy with this performance, although one is always conscious that had certain profitable trades been held for longer, or some losses been cut more quickly, the performance might have been improved. I will draw a veil over the current size of our investment portfolio, but it is currently divided as follows: 50 per cent in bond-related funds, 12 per cent in private equity, around 6 per cent in cash, and the remainder in UK equities, mainly smaller companies.

It is clear that my performance in the past few years has suffered from my being fairly risk averse and specifically from not investing in high technology shares to any degree although in part this has been due to my freedom to manoeuvre being limited by the topics I have written about professionally.

In addition, I have also channelled substantial surplus cash into a personal pension fund, the current total value of which is several times the value of the portfolio. Share investments, as is the case for many people (if they take the trouble to look), are overshadowed by the value of these and other assets.

Lessons for first-time investors

Regardless of its imperfections, I think this trading record demonstrates a number of important lessons for both first-time and experienced private investors. I have listed these below (in no particular order):

- It is obvious that company selection and trading discipline is as important an influence as the overall trend of the market over a long time span. Smaller companies will tend to do better in more buoyant markets, provided the right ones are picked, but even in dull markets there will be some good performers. But paying attention to the economic climate is important.

- The paramount need in the stock market is to cut losses early. I believe it can be demonstrated very graphically from the figures in the tables above just how important this is. One of my faults as a trader is that I occasionally, as it were, 'fall in love' with individual stocks, and become blind to their shortcomings in different phases of the market cycle.

- Equally one should stress that patience and the ability to resist the temptation to sell too early is vitally important. In my own case, I believe a little more patience might have produced better returns, but I am hamstrung by my personality and comparatively modest background. The novelty of being able to take a substantial profit of £1,000 or so, quickly made, often proves too tempting.

- What the tables also show is that diversification is good. In this case, apart from the initial bull market flurry in shares, I have held a mix of assets over the years including floating rate notes, investment property and its associated rental income, bond funds held in tax-efficient PEPs and ISAs, a private equity investment, and in the case of my pension contributions, in both professionally managed funds able to reinvest dividend income on a gross basis and in a life company with-profits fund.

- I believe that over this period my own efforts resulted in a marginal outperformance both over the professionally managed portion of the fund, and over the likely return during that period for a fund that tracked the index. Some of this may have been luck, and it would be a brave person who risked his or her nest egg on an ability to manage money better than the professionals.

■ Equally, taking control of one's own destiny, and above all maintaining reasonable liquidity does have its advantages. For the most part, it can be fun. Good performance can be achieved by following good disciplines.

■ Another clear lesson is that it pays both to be diligent in research, but also to use knowledge gained during the course of one's job to make judgements about particular investments. I do not mean by this the gaining of inside information, but simply keeping one's eyes open and investing where one's instincts lead, provided that at the same time proper risk control and loss-cutting principles are followed.

■ Part of the rigorous discipline of trading is also sticking to a strict trading unit. In my own case, I began investing in units of around £3,000 and have gradually raised this to around £5,000. I have attempted, frequently without success, to limit losses to between £600 and £700.

■ My experience gives me mixed feelings about using charts for selecting stocks to trade, except in the case of the options market where the gearing involved can produce big moves and where losses can be limited. In the case of equity investment, my experience has been that a chart may prove good at setting risk control parameters, and picking a buying range.

■ Precisely timing purchases and sales using charts has only worked well for me on three specific occasions. Using moving averages has been particularly poor, but using charts of volatility in the options market has worked up to a point. On the one occasion I used directors' dealings as a buy signal, the experiment was an abject failure.

Spending your gains

> Investment should be stimulating and fun. There is nothing wrong with spending your investment gains on other interests. The objective of investment is to produce gains that can provide you with more choices.

It does not take a mathematical genius to realize that, even though I have given money away to my children, paid off my mortgage and made other similar 'lifestyle' decisions, a chunk of the stock market gains have been spent on life in general.

Serious textbooks about investing may lecture you about the power of compounding your gains, but money spent on, for example, your children's education and first steps in the property market, and on travelling and other mind-broadening activities, is seldom wasted.

It is as well to keep this is mind, rather than to pursue investing as an activity purely as an end in itself. Spending the money is a pleasure, and even after the money has been spent, you can still keep score.

- The chapter summarizes the results of 15 years of trading as a private investor.

- The results demonstrate that it is possible for the small investor to beat the professionals, but that rigorous discipline needs to be observed.

- The income component and investment in alternative forms of investment (bonds, property etc.) should not be ignored.

- Sticking to a rigid trading 'unit' is important.

- Cutting losses early is highly beneficial.

- My own weakness as a trader is selling profitable investments too early. This is something to guard against.

- Above all, investment should be stimulating and fun. There is nothing wrong with spending your investment gains on other interests.

- The objective of investment is to produce gains that can provide you with more choices.

Index

accounting
  basic concepts 47–65
  creative 199–200
Accounting for Growth 199–200
acid test ratio 63–4
ADSL 40, 42, 165, 215
advance/decline line 193–4
ADVFN 167–8
agency broking 13
The Alchemy of Finance 38
alpha factor 198
Alternative Investment Market 136
Amazon 214
'The Analyst' (software package) 155
annual reports and accounts 47–8
AOL 167, 214
Association of Private Client Investment
  Managers (APCIMS) 99
attributable profit 50

Bacon, Geoff 158
balance sheets 59–61, 65
  ratios 61–4, 189–93
Bank of England 13
bar charts 74–5
Barings Bank 145
Barrons 37
bear markets 140
Beating the Street 38
beta factor 131–2, 137, 197–8, 204
BG (formerly British Gas) 22
Bloomberg 41, 179
blue chip companies, investing in 20, 119
bonds 2
  analyzing 66
  nature of 10
  reasons for buying 11
  websites 179
  see also gilts
Boo.com 214
BP 22
breadth indicator 193
British–American Tobacco 21
British Telecom 205, 206
British Venture Capital Association 219
broadband services 165
Buffett, Warren 4, 205
bull markets 140, 193, 194, 222
bulletin boards 167–8
burn rate 59, 218
Business Week 37

call options 23, 137, 139
candlestick charts 75–6
capitalization rates 210

capitalizing costs 200–1
cash, holding 122, 128
cash burn 218
cash flow 56–9, 65
  discounted (DCF) 203–7
  ratios 187–9
Charles Schwab 40
charts
  analysis 69, 88, 193–9
  interpretation 77–9
  software packages 79, 155–6
  types 74–7, 80–3
'chatter' 79, 80
CIX 167
Comdirect 171
commodity shares 22
companies
  annual reports and accounts 47–8
  balance sheet ratios 61–4, 189–93
  balance sheets 59–61, 65
  cash flow 56–9, 65, 187–9
  directors' pay 185
  discounted cash flow 203–7
  dividends 54–6, 64
  Enterprise Value Analysis 207–8
  performance 64–5
  price-earnings ratios 52–3, 64
  profit and loss account 48–50
  profit and loss ratios 51–2, 184–7
  reinvested return on equity 208–11
  sum of the parts analysis 212–13
  websites 176–9, 180
  working capital ratios 190
Company Guide 39, 152
Company REFs 39, 47, 48, 152
compounding 112–13
computer disks, downloading data by 154,
  160
computers, as aid to investment 145–61
confidence limits 194, 196
convertible bonds 23, 121–2
Coppock indicator 194, 195
corporate bonds 121
corporate websites 176–9, 180
corporation tax 50, 52
Corus 21
cost of sales 50
Costa, Bob 205
creative accounting 199–201
creditor days 190
CREST 100, 101, 102, 107, 170,
  224
current asset ratio 63–4
cutting losses 116–17
cyclical shares 21

Daily Mail 37
Daily Telegraph 174
data display services, downloading data by 154
day trading 17, 118, 169
DCF *see* discounted cash flow
debtor days 190
depreciation 48–9, 50, 187, 200
Diageo 20
directors-pay 185
discounted cash flow (DCF) 203–7
diversification 114–19, 127–40
dividend cover 55
dividend per share 50
dividends 54–6, 64
dot com companies 29, 59, 214
Download.com 172, 173, 174

E*Trade 40
earnings per share 50
East India Company 12
EBITDA 53, 207, 208, 216
The Economist 37, 174
EIS *see* Enterprise Investment Schemes
electronic trading *see* online trading
e-mail
    charges for using 165
    downloading data by 154–5, 160
Enterprise Investment Schemes (EIS) 136
enterprise value/earnings before interest and tax (EV/EBIT) 53–4, 208, 216
Enterprise Value Analysis (EVA) 207–8
equivolume 198
ERM *see* exchange rate mechanism
Estimate Directory 39, 48, 152
ETFs *see* exchange traded funds
European Venture Capital Association 219
EV/EBIT *see* enterprise value/earnings before interest and tax
EVA *see* Enterprise Value Analysis
Excel 146, 169
exchange rate mechanism (ERM) 29
exchange traded funds (ETFs) 24, 132
execution–only stockbrokers 14, 96–7, 104
e-xentric 21

Fidelity 179
Financial Services Act (1986) 92
Financial Times 37, 104, 134, 174
first mover advantage 215
fixed assets 58, 187–8
Foreign & Colonial Emerging Markets 22
free cash flow 59, 207
freeware 172
FT All Share index 77, 131
FTSE–100 index 73, 77, 131, 139, 176, 194
fund managers 15
fundamental analysis 45, 69, 199
    software packages 156–7

gearing 62, 139
The General Theory of Employment, Interest and Money 3, 4
gilts 2, 10, 12, 22, 120–1, 128–31
gold, as an investment 122–3
'golden cross' 81
goodwill 49–50

government bonds *see* gilts
Grail Systems 159
Granville, Joe 198
gross margin 51
gross profit 50
growth shares 20
Guardian 174

HACAS 21
Hagstrom, Robert 205
hedge funds 124
Hudson's Bay Company 12
hypertext 165

ICI 21
income gearing 62
income shares 21
Indexia 155, 158
indicators 80–8, 193–9
Individual Savings Accounts (ISAs) 55, 135–6
Inter Link Foods 21
Interactive Investor 168, 179
interest cover 52
internet
    as aid to investment 167–80
    connecting to 163–5, 181
    usage 215
    see also world wide web
internet businesses, valuing 214–19
internet incubators 219
Internet Service Providers (ISPs) 164
Intro (software package) 155
Invest (software package) 155
investment
    analysis 45–7
    anticipating trends 7–8
    author's personal experiences of 221–37
    checklist 34–5
    compounding 112–13
    computer–aided 145–61
    demystification of 91–2
    diversification 114–19, 127
    first-time 237–8
    fundamentals 4–6
    as a game 2–4
    the 'identikit' investor 36
    internet incubators 219
    internet resources 167–80
    level of 33–4
    measuring gains and losses 142
    psychology of 11–12, 28, 70–1
    purpose of 1
    realism in 31–2
    risk 112–13, 114–16
    software 155–61
    strategies 110–11, 113–19, 127–40
    successful, qualities needed for 30–1
    tax-efficient 135–6
    tools 36–42
    traps 28–30
    types of 18–25, 119–25
investment banks 93
investment trusts 22, 120, 133–4, 179
Investors' Business Daily 37
Investors' Chronicle 27, 37, 104, 144
Investors' Week 37
Ionic Information 157

ISAs *see* Individual Savings Accounts
ISPs *see* Internet Service Providers

java 169

Kauders Investment Management 179
Keynes, John Maynard 3–4, 5, 42, 46

Leeson, Nick 93
LIFFE *see* London International Financial
    Futures and Options Exchange
limit minders 40
limited liability 12
line charts 74
linksitemoney.com 168, 173, 183, 184, 205,
    209, 213, 217
liquidity 112
Logica 217
London Business School 131
London International Financial Futures and
    Options Exchange (LIFFE) 158, 175
Long Term Capital Management (LTCM) 29,
    145
LTCM *see* Long Term Capital Management
Lynch, Peter 30, 38

McClellan Oscillator 194
MACD *see* Moving Average Convergence and
    Divergence indicators
market-based indicators 193–4
market behaviour 114
Market Eye 154, 160, 169
market indices, trends 72–4
market making 13, 15–16
Market Wizards 38
Meisels indicator 84–5
Metastock (software package) 161
Microsoft Money (software package) 147,
    149, 173
minority interests 50
modems
    downloading data by 153
    speed of 163–4
momentum indicators 84–8
The Money Game 29, 38
money management, software tools 146–9
Moving Average Convergence and Divergence
    indicators (MACD) 81–2
moving averages 80–1
Murphy, John 155

naked writing 139–40
NCE *see* net capital employed
NCO *see* net cash outflow
net asset value (NAV) 64, 134, 219
net assets 61
    and value of shares 9
net capital employed (NCE) 188
net cash outflow (NCO) 188
Netscape 215
The New Market Wizards 38
The New Online Investor 178
newsgroups 167
newsletters, as aid to investment 38
newspapers
    as aid to investment 37–8
    online 174–5

Nikkei index 71–2
nominee service 101–2

OBOS *see* Overbought/Oversold indicators
OBV *see* on–balance volume
off-balance sheet finance 200
OHLCV *see* Open, High, Low, Close and
    Volume
Omega Research 159
on-balance volume (OBV) 198
One up on Wall Street 38
online trading 13–14, 94, 97, 98, 103,
    106–7, 169–72
Open, High, Low, Close and Volume (OHLCV)
    152, 153, 160
operating profit 50
Option Evaluator (software package) 158
Option Station (software package) 159
Option Trader (software package) 158–9
Optionbase (software package) 158
options 23, 104, 124–5, 136–40, 195–6
    software 157–9, 179
O'Shaughnessy, James 51, 216
Overbought/Oversold indicators (OBOS) 82–3

Pacific Media 21
PEG *see* price-earnings growth
penny shares 21
PEPs *see* Personal Equity Plans
PER *see* price-earnings ratios
Personal Equity Plans (PEPs) 135
point and figure charts 76–7
portals 166, 167, 169
Portfolio Evolution (software package) 157
portfolio strategies 109, 113–19, 127–40
portfolio structure 140–1
preference shares 23
price data
    downloading 151–4
    internet resources 168–9
price-earnings growth (PEG) 203, 207
price-earnings ratios (PER) 52–3, 64, 203,
    207
price relative charts 77
private client brokers 93, 94, 99
profit and loss account 48–50
profit and loss ratios 51–2, 184–7
profit before tax 50
profit margins 51
property, as an investment 123
proprietary trading 93
Psion 20
put options 23, 137, 139

quantitative fund managers (?quants?) 16
Quicken (software package) 147, 148, 173

Railtrack 22
Rate of Change (ROC) charts 85
real-time price displays 40
redemption yield (gilts) 128
reference material, as aid to investment 39
reinvested return on equity 208–11
Relative Strength Indicator (RSI) 85–6
retained profits 50
return on capital 62–3
return on equity (ROE) 62–3, 208–9

reversals 71
reverse yield gap 130
Rio Tinto 22
risk 112–13
    controlling 114–16, 127–40
risk-free rate of return 204
ROC see Rate of Change charts
ROE see return on equity
Rowland, David 226
RSI see Relative Strength Indicator
running yield (gilts) 128

Sage 20, 217
Sainsbury–s 20
sales ratios 51
Schwager, Jack 38
search engines 166
Sepal Software 158
Severn-Trent 22
SG Options (software package) 158
share-price-based indicators 194–8
shareholders
    funds 9, 61, 64
    limited liability 12
shares
    internet companies 216–18
    price movements 69–89, 193–9
    reasons for buying 11
    relationship of price to net asset value
        9
    trading online 14
    types 2, 20–2
    valuing 64–5, 203–20
    volatility 194–7
Shares 37, 145
Sharescope (software package) 157
shareware 172
Slater, Jim 119
smaller company shares 21, 119–20
Smith, Adam 29, 38
Smith, Terry 199–200
software
    as aid to investment 39–40, 155–61
    downloading from internet 172–3
Soros, George 38
Soros on Soros 38
Source Code Software 158
South Sea Bubble 12
spreadsheets 146, 169, 184
stochastic indicators 86–8
stock days 190
Stock Exchange (London), history of 13
stock exchanges
    interaction between 14
    websites 175–6
stock markets
    crashes 7, 224
    diversity 1–2
    importance of 24–5
stockbrokers
    charges 97–8
    choosing 99–105
    execution–only 14, 96–7, 104
    online 94, 97, 98, 103, 170–1
    placing an order with 106–7

private-client 93, 94, 99
    regulation 92
    reputation 92–3
    services 94–7, 100–3
    traditional 13
stockjobbers 13
stop-loss levels 116–17
sum of the parts analysis 212–13
Supercharts (software package) 159
Synergy Software 157

T+3 settlement 102, 107
tax charge 185–6
Techmark 100 index 132
technical analysis 46–7, 69, 71–2, 77, 88,
    193–9
Technical Analysis of the Financial Markets
    155
Techninvest 38
teletext 40, 153, 160
The Times 174
tracker funds 24, 123, 131–2
Traded Options: A Private Investors' Guide
    136, 179
Trader (software package) 155
Tradestation (software package) 159
trading volume indicators 198–9
Trendline 159
Trustnet 179
turnover 50

UK-inVest 169
Ultra Market Adviser (software package) 155,
    156
unit trusts 23, 123–4, 133, 179
Unlisted Securities Market 222
Updata 155
Usenet 167
utilities 21–2

venture capital 124
Virani, Nazmu 223

Wall Street Journal 175
Wall Street Journal Europe 37
The Warren Buffett Way 205
websites
    bonds 179
    companies 176–9, 180
    financial 41
    stock exchanges 175–6
Welles–Wilder Index 85
What Works on Wall Street 51, 216
Winstock 155
Wired Index Fund 132
working capital 57
    ratios 190
world wide web 165–6
    site design 177–8
    see also search engines

Yahoo! 214
Yahoo Finance 169

zero coupon bonds 122